D0746006

Wild Lilies: Poisonous Weeds

Wild Lilies: Poisonous Weeds
Dissident Voices from People's China

edited by Gregor Benton

'The wild lily is the most beautiful of the flowers in the hills and countryside around Yanan... although its bulbs are similar to those of other lilies, they are said to be slightly bitter to the taste and of greater medicinal value.' Wang Shiwei, *Wild Lily*, 1942

'Poisonous weeds are easier to uproot if they are allowed the chance to grow... They can be used as fertiliser.' *Renmin ribao* ('People's Daily'), 1 July 1957

Pluto  Press

This collection first published 1982 by Pluto Press Limited,
Unit 10 Spencer Court, 7 Chalcot Road, London NW1 8LH

ISBN 0 86104 374 X

Cover designed by Michael Mayhew
Cover picture: Camera Press

Typeset by Grassroots Typeset, London NW6
Printed in Great Britain by St Edmundsbury Press Limited,
Bury St Edmunds, Suffolk IP33 3TU

Dedicated to
supporters of the democratic movement in China
known to have been arrested

Chen Erjin *Yunnan Province*
Chen Honggang *Anyang, Henan Province*
Fu Shenqi *Shanghai*
Guo Shuzhang *Xinxiang, Henan Province*
He Qiu *Guangzhou*
Liu Er'an *Anyang, Henan Province*
Liu Liping *Changsha, Hunan Province*
Liu Qing *Beijing*
Lu Lin *Beijing*
Peng Guangzhong *Guizhou Province*
Qiao Zhonglin *Shanghai*
Qin Xiaochun *Guizhou Province*
Qin Yongmin *Wuhan*
Ren Wanding *Beijing*
Sun Feng *Qingdao, Shandong Province*
Tao Sen *Changsha, Hunan Province*
Wang Fuchen *Shanghai*
Wang Rongqing *Hangzhou, Zhejiang Province*
Wang Tanyuan *Tianjin*
Wang Xizhe *Guangzhou*
Wang Yifei *Guangzhou*
Wei Jingsheng *Beijing*
Wei Yuehua, Ms *Hangzhou, Zhejiang Province*
Xing Dakun *Qingdao*
Xu Shuiliang *Nanjing*

Xu Wenli *Beijing*
Xue Mingde *Chengdu, Sichuan Province*
Yang Guoliang *Beijing*
Yang Jing *Beijing*
Yang Xiaolei *Hangzhou, Zhejiang Province*
Yang Zaixing *Guiyang, Guizhou Province*
Ye Zongwu *Hangzhou, Zhejiang Province*
Yu Weimin *Nanjing*
Zhang Honglin *Anyang, Henan Province*
Zhang Jingsheng *Changsha, Hunan Province*
Zheng Yulin *Wenzhou, Zhejiang Province*
Zhong Yueqiu *Shaoguan, Guangdong Province*
Zhu Jianbin *Wuhan*

Contents

Acknowledgements

I am grateful to various people who helped me in producing this collection, in particular Rod Aya, Dirk Bergvelt, Ron Brown, Annelies Brugman, Chen Yunzhong, Walter Easey, Richard Kuper, Pierre Rousset, John Sexton, Wu XX and Henk Wubben; and those western authors who have generously given permission for their articles and translations to be reproduced. My main thanks go to my friends in the Chinese Democratic Movement Resource Centre and the Hong Kong Association for Solidarity with the Chinese Democratic Movement, who collect and publish the writings of democratic movement activists and work for the release of those arrested. These organisations have few helpers and little money, other than what they provide themselves, and urgently need donations from those who support their aims. Both publish bulletins, in both Chinese- and English-language edition. Subscriptions to these bulletins can be obtained from the addresses given on page xi.

List of organisations and addresses

The following is a list of organisations in different countries that work for the release of arrested members of the Chinese democratic movement:

Chinese Democratic Movement Resource Centre
  P.O. Box 89278
  Kowloon City Post Office
  Hong Kong

Hong Kong Association for Solidarity
with the Chinese Democracy Movement
  P.O. Box 60071
  Tsat Tsz Mui Post Office
  North Point
  Hong Kong

Socialist Committee to Defend the Democratic Movement
in China
  380 Edgware Road
  London W2, UK

Society for the Protection of East Asian Human Rights
  P.O. Box 1212
  New York 10025, USA

Comité international contre la répression
  61 rue Beaubourg
  75003 Paris, France

Comité Li Shuang
  35 rue Censier
  75005 Paris, France

Amnesty International, International Secretariat
  10 Southampton Street
  London WC2E 7HF, UK

Readers can write to the Government of the People's Republic of China requesting the unconditional release of the prisoners listed in the dedication to this volume, all of whom were detained for the peaceful exercise of their constitutional right to freedom of belief, expression and association. Protests and appeals can be addressed to the following officials at Beijing, People's Republic of China.

Zhao Ziyang, *Premier*

Wei Wenbo, *Minister of Justice*

Xi Zhongxun, *Director of Legislative Affairs Committee of the National People's Congress*

Jiang Hua, *President of the Supreme People's Court*

Huang Huoqing, *Chief Procurator of the Supreme People's Procuratorate*

A note on pronunciation

This book uses the Pinyin system of romanising Chinese, which has been adopted by the Chinese Government and is taught alongside characters in Chinese schools. Most letters in the Pinyin alphabet can be pronounced more or less as in English, but readers should note the following sounds:

c   is 'ts'
chi   is roughly like the 'ch' in 'chuff'
ci   is like the 'ts' in 'rats'
g   is always hard, as in 'go'
i   is 'ee' after all consonants except c, ch, s, z, and zh
q   is like 'ch'
si   is like the 's' in 'sud'
u   after j, q and x is like the French 'u'; otherwise it
        is like the English 'oo'
x   is something like the 'sh' in 'she'
zh   is roughly like the English 'j'

Here is a list of frequently recurring names in both their Pinyin spelling and the old commonly used equivalent:

Mao Zedong	Mao Tse-tung
Zhou Enlai	Chou En-lai
Jiang Qing	Chiang Ch'ing
Liu Shaoqi	Liu Shao-ch'i
Deng Xiaoping	Teng Hsiao-p'ing
Lu Xun	Lu Hsun
Beijing	Peking
Guangzhou	Canton
Tianjin	Tientsin
Guangdong	Kwangtung
Yanan	Yenan
Xinjiang	Sinkiang
Guomindang	Kuomintang

A note on the texts

The bulk of texts selected for this volume first appeared in China in 1978-81. They range from substantial analytical pieces like Wang Xizhe's or Wei Jingsheng's, through accounts of particular election campaigns or protest movements, statements of solidarity and interviews with leading lights of the democratic movement like Xu Wenli and Yang Jing, to Liu Qing's own account of prison life in China. I have also included a few texts dealing with historical antecedents of the democratic movement in the form of dissent within the Chinese Communist Party (CCP) before it had come to power — an introduction to and two articles by Wang Shiwei, and Wang Fanxi's appreciation of Chen Duxiu, founder of the CCP and, later, one of its leading dissidents. Finally a few articles by Westerners, who were in China before the suppression of the democratic movement, quote extensively from Chinese writings or discussions of the time and cast light on areas not otherwise covered in the main selection of dissident writings.

None of the translations of mainland Chinese writings printed here is complete, although some are more so than others. In an effort to make the texts more readable for a public not used to a Chinese Communist style of argument or writing, I have extensively cut or deleted from them. These cuts and deletions are mainly of repetitions, passages that I thought were excessively declamatory or rhetorical, redundant verbiage, long quotations from Marx or Mao, and explanatory detail that might help a Chinese reader but not a Western one. David Joravsky, justifying his editing of Roy A. Medvedev's *Let History Judge* (New York: Knopf, 1972, p. xix), said that the reason he changed Medvedev's style was because he saw him not as 'an exotic or antique source that must be translated verbatim to preserve its special flavour', but as a serious contemporary thinker whose work deserved the best English its editor could give. I approached these Chinese writings in the same spirit. I have done my best to streamline them, and I have mainly avoided terms and expressions that, although literal equivalents of the Chinese originals, read badly in English and would only subvert the substantive argument. (One example is *qunzhong*, 'the masses', which I have generally rendered by some more acceptable circumlocution.) Here and there I have inserted clarifying remarks (usually enclosed by square brackets) into the text to help readers not familiar with Chinese Communist history and terminology. I have normally marked editorial deletions by ellipses, except where they were made solely on grounds of style. In the case of three authors — Wang Xizhe, Yi Ming and Yu Guangyuan — I cut out some of the argument as well as the redundant verbiage, because my space was limited; but those parts of the argument of these writers that I kept are faithfully given. Most of the mainland Chinese writers represented in this volume are by now locked up, and therefore could have no part (even supposing they had wanted one) in the publication of this English version of their work. To them I apologise in advance for changing their work in ways to which, given the chance, they might well object. I refer specialist readers to the Chinese sources of these writings, which are normally given in the editorial prefaces.

Gregor Benton

The 'Four Greats' are 'great contending, blooming, big character-posters and debate' — Mao's four methods for carrying out 'struggle by reasoning'.

The 'Four Modernisations' were first introduced by Liu Shaoqi at the Eighth (1956) Party Congress and later by Mao in his 1957 speech on contradictions. They refer to industry, agriculture, science and technology, and national defence (but in Mao's version culture took the place of technology). They are now central to the programme of the current leadership.

Gregor Benton

China Spring: The Interrupted Rise of the Democratic Movement in People's China

In late 1978 an original dissident movement sprang up in the main cities of China under the slogan of democracy. For several months this movement had the protection of liberalisers like Deng Xiaoping in the party leadership and the strong approval of leading intellectuals and cultural figures in the media, the universities and the academies, so that it was able to win ground and widen its support. But it is now clear that, for the leaders around Deng at least, this movement was from the very start a disposable tool, and that once it had done its job of helping to winkle out the Maoist old guard and get the modernisation pro-gramme underway, it could be tossed aside and scrapped like similar ones before it. It is now four years since the streets of Beijing first rang to the shouts of youthful dissent and the first unofficial journals tumbled out of patched-up mimeographs. In those years the movement has suffered repeated blows, first to the head and later to the body. In early 1979 a few of its best leaders and organisers vanished into the camps and prisons where most of them still remain — bloodied but unbowed. Throughout 1979 and 1980 new arrests followed, until finally all the main leaders of the unofficial movement, and many of its active supporters, were rounded up in a nationwide swoop in April 1981.

But there are excellent reasons to think that this movement will sooner or later revive, and when it does so it will doubtless have learned from Deng's betrayal that it is far wiser to sink roots deep into the wider society than to depend on this or that faction at the top of the party. One reason is that the men and women of the democratic movement have long experience of political repression ever since their days as Red Guards in Mao's Cultural Revolution, and are therefore not likely to go down under this new wave of it. Another is that the movement has quickly differentiated in the course of its development, sprouting liberal and marxist wings each with a powerful and well-formed critique of present-day Chinese society. This dif-ferentiation has immeasurably strengthened the dissenters and overcome much of their earlier political and intellectual eclecticism, without — as Liu Qing's prison testimony shows — destroying an ounce of their solidarity. Finally, although the authorities have cast the net wide, reports smuggled out of China suggest that it caught mainly the big and medium fish, leaving most of the small fry still at large. It was therefore not wholly unexpected when news came out of China in the summer of 1981 that *Zeren* ('Duty'), the national organ of the Federation of Unofficial Journals, was still appearing clandestinely even after the final crushing of the open movement in April.

The Chinese democratic movement has many varied points of intellectual reference, ranging from Christ, Dada and Montesquieu's *l'Esprit des Lois* to Trotsky, Tito and the humanist writings of the young Marx. Wei Jingsheng, the movement's first prominent martyr, has argued forcefully for 'free enterprise' as the only economic system compatible with political democracy. Wang Xizhe, a veteran dissenter whose 1974 wall-poster (co-authored with three others) was in some ways the start of the unofficial movement in China, has searched out the elements for a powerful and original critique of bureaucracy from the marxist classics. Others are placed somewhere between these poles.

Background

The Cultural Revolution of 1966-68 was critical in two main ways for the emergence of the democratic current in Chinese politics in the late seventies. First, it plunged China into a terror that traumatised all social classes, not least the political elite — parts of which began to question their commitment to the methods of dictatorship. Second, it spawned the Red Guards, who swept China for a time and got an appetising taste of political independence.

The disaffected elite included a large group of top political leaders, managers, intellectuals, party cadres and others in the official world who had suffered persecution during the chaos of the Cultural Revolution, when the search for 'class enemies' grew ever more frenetic and the norms of political behaviour collapsed almost completely. Throughout the mid- and late seventies these people trickled back into office as the smashed administration was slowly restored. Many of them were far from being the hacks and stooges that their Maoist critics said they were. A good few had fought for the revolution in the thirties and forties, and even more had stubbornly — if surreptitiously — resisted Mao's excesses in the fifties and sixties, often at great personal cost to themselves and their families. Luckily for China, Mao was no Stalin; while he had few scruples about purging his rivals, he normally stopped short of killing them, on the grounds that once dead they could never be reformed. And thus many of those who returned to power after his death in 1976 were not career bureaucrats, like in Russia after Stalin, but experienced and independent-minded people, including a thick sprinkling of indomitable old revolutionaries. Naturally these 'returnees' were unlikely to question the ultimate foundations of their own power, but some of them were prepared to tolerate new thinking about the relationship between democracy and socialism, and for a while the fruits of this rethinking enlivened the pages even of China's main theoretical journals. It was from 'returnees' like Yu Guangyuan, whose essay on socialist lifestyles is reprinted below, that the strongest official pressure came for the democratisation — within limits — of China's political life and the strengthening of legal rights and guarantees.

The few hundred activists in the unofficial movement, which is the second and more enduring strand in China's democratic fabric, might have been eliminated much sooner had they not been connected to the hundreds of thousands who in varying degrees represented the democratic movement in the official world, and who were deeply questioning and doubting Maoist methods and values. These unofficial activists first entered politics as Mao's storm-troops in the faction fight of 1966-67, but they soon exceeded the limits that Mao's group had set for them. In analysing the Cultural Revolution it is therefore necessary to distinguish sharply between the anti-bureaucratic, egalitarian impulses that motivated its activists, and the efforts of party leaders to manipulate it from above. True, most Red Guards became bogged down under the influence of competing groups in the party leadership in an increasingly violent power struggle in which factional ties quickly overwhelmed political principle, but still a minority successfully resisted the meddling of party leaders and developed independent political positions.

After September 1967 the new ruling group around Mao, having managed to oust many of its rivals in the party-state, finally set about suppressing these troublesome 'little generals' and consolidating its position in the country. But it lacked a broad stable base either in society or in the party, and therefore had to resort more and more to dictatorial methods to keep itself in power. The betrayed Red Guards responded in various ways to this experience. Some retreated into cynicism, apathy or the assiduous cultivation of self-interest. Others gave themselves over to a melancholy romanticism of the sort best exemplified by the recently popular 'new wave literature' or 'literature of the wounded', with its recurrent themes of tragedy, betrayal and sacrifice. But a minority persisted with the political critique of bureaucracy that they had begun during the Cultural Revolution.

For them, as the essays of Wang Xizhe, Yi Ming and others show, the experience of the Cultural Revolution was by no means all bad, and given the chance they would doubtless distance themselves from some of the more extreme denunciations of it current in the West. The Cultural Revolution taught them the value of 'linking up to exchange revolutionary experience' — a lesson that they now put to excellent effect. It also taught them how to write, to edit and to mimeograph. But above all it taught them that 'to rebel is justified', and although the Maoist leaders at first tried to manipulate this rebellion to their own ends and eventually suppressed it altogether when it began to depart too radically from their circus-script, the lesson was not the sort that you could easily forget.

China's dissidents: a sketch

China's democratic movement is made up overwhelmingly of state-employed manual workers and technicians who identify almost without exception with the workers and peasants' cause. True, some are the offspring of influential party officials and army officers or of foreign-educated scientists and technologists, but even many of these people work in factories or workships. It is quite common in China for people to seek 'backdoor entry' to jobs in industry for their children. After all, factory work has high social status in China, and for a generation that went without formal education at a crucial time in their lives it is always better than the chief alternative: transfer to a village as part of the *xiafang* ('down to the countryside') programme. The result is that proportionately more young people, well informed through family connections about political struggles at the highest levels, work in urban industry in China than is the case in the Soviet Union or Eastern Europe; and it is largely from among these people that the leaders of the democratic movement are drawn. This is extremely important for understanding the nature of dissent in China, and the differences between it and dissent in the Soviet Union, which is mainly practised by intellectuals, many of them highly placed. In China even dissidents from well-off backgrounds distance themselves from their origins by wearing patched clothes of coarse peasant-style cloth, and all vehemently eschew the elitism common among their Soviet counterparts.

China's democratic movement activists were under no illusions about their strength in the winter of 1978-79, and were aware that they owed their freedom to publish and organise solely to the benign disposition of some party leaders. True, a mass movement — the Tiananmen demonstrations of April 1976 — had been the main factor behind the rapid collapse of the 'gang of four', and the democratic movement was directly descended from those events. But for the time being the broader social forces of April had withdrawn from active political roles and were ready to entrust the affairs of state to the new Deng government. Some saw the latter as a direct outcome and a guarantee of the 1976 political ferment. Although Deng had shown no enthusiasm for throwing the party open to criticism in 1957 and Mao had had no difficulty in turning the Red Guards against him and Liu Shaoqi as symbols of bureaucratic corruption in 1966, Deng had been both a main opponent and a main victim of the Cultural Revolution, and — so one hoped — had emerged wiser from the trauma. Others supported Deng because they were tired of struggling, or because the alternatives looked worse, or because they feared to rock the boat while it was changing course and all sorts of perils — especially economic ones — lay ahead. So the democratic movement was temporarily beached, and would have to make the best of it until a new rising of the tide.

But some of the movement's bolder supporters were not

content to bide their time and hold their tongues in the hope that they would continue to be tolerated. Instead they strove to break out of their isolation, and relentlessly exposed the gap between Deng's promise and his practice.

In 1979 sections of the movement tried to forge links to broader social bases, especially the returned *xiafang* youth and the *shangfang* petitioners. The conditions of the millions of young people sent out to the villages (*xiafang*) before and after the Cultural Revolution were often extremely harsh, and many believed that the procedures by which they had been chosen for rustication were arbitrary or discriminative. After the fall of the 'gang of four' the government took steps to improve the conditions of *xiafang* youth and allowed many to return home. The effect was to set in motion a huge influx of other young people into the big cities, where (like those described in Chen Ding's article on Xinjiang) they petitioned for relocation back to their homes. These *xiafang* youth were joined by crowds of peasants who had come to the cities to demand redress of wrongs done them by officials under the Mao regime. Together these two groups were known as the *shangfang* or 'up to petition' movement. In many cities they staged demonstrations and even riots. According to a Beijing wall-poster written by one Zhang Xifeng, an agricultural worker from Shanxi, at one time there were 10,000 such *shangfang* 'refugees' sleeping out on the streets of the capital, where they lived by begging, theft and prostitution. According to Zhang, these people were harassed, beaten and occasionally rounded up and interned by the city authorities. The authorities were in no position to put a quick end to the political and social grievances of the *shangfang* petitioners, even if they had had the will to do so. Their grievances were not only too many, but they originated mainly at the local level, to which the new 'liberal' norms had seldom sunk. The *shangfang* masses, largely unorganised and voiceless, were therefore an ideal target for the proselytising of the articulate but numerically weak democratic movement. When peasants wrote about their grievances on Democracy Wall, dissidents copied their statements and published them in their journals to give them a wider airing. Some activists organised and led demonstrations of poor peasants and other petitioners in front of the government buildings at Zhongnanhai.

Two other groups that played an important role in China's recent protest and dissent were the students and the cultural nonconformists.

Students were the main force in the Red Guard movement of the Cultural Revolution, but they played practically no independent political role in the decade after 1968. Students in the early seventies were educated according to the norms and standards of the Mao group, and after 1976 were poorly suited to the goals of the new pragmatic leaders, which stressed science and technology. Not surprisingly they showed no great enthusiasm for the programme of the new government, although there is little evidence that they opposed the changes after Mao's death. As for the classes of students recruited after 1976, most could be expected to identify closely with the new leaders' goals, in which they were destined to play a star role. It was therefore only natural that students at first took no great part in the struggles and debates that marked the rise of the democratic movement. But in late 1979 this calm on the campuses was suddenly shattered by strikes and militant demonstrations to protest against various grievances, and the ferment sometimes took overtly political forms. Gong Bo's report published below on the 1980 elections at Beijing University reveals a healthy scepticism towards formed authority and a widely held commitment to social reform.

Dissident poets, painters, writers and sculptors like the Xingxing group that Julien Blaine and Anna Gipouloux met in Beijing are inseparable from the unofficial political movement, and unofficial journals regularly carried their poems and stories and advertised their exhibitions. When Wei Jingsheng was gaoled in October 1979, several hundred poets met in public to declare their support for him. This strong link between cultural and political dissidence is natural in a system where art and literature are normally under tight political control. Despite the recent clampdown on unofficial art and the reimposition of a strong political censorship, many cultural leaders clearly approve of the experimentation in new literary and artistic forms, and have done their best to encourage and protect it.

Occasional calls for freer sexual relations were reported from Democracy Wall. In the past, PRC governments have advocated severe sexual repression, mainly on the grounds that sexual freedom in China would lead in practice to the greater exploitation of women. So it is not surprising that themes of sexual liberation should have been raised during the recent relaxation in China. Women too have taken the first steps towards independent organisation, just as they have in the Soviet Union in recent years. During the Cultural Revolution women were told that they 'held up half the sky' and urged to better their position in society. But now repressive notions of traditional 'femininity' are being revived; and the rapid growth of urban unemployment will no doubt affect women first, in China as elsewhere. In the meantime, Chinese women are scandalously under-represented at all levels of political life, especially the top ones. Now that Western trends are being eagerly followed by young people in China's big cities, it surely will not be long before some form of feminism catches on there.

The repression of the movement

The strategic goal of the post-Mao leaders is to create the conditions — political, cultural, social and economic — for modernising China before the century is up. For Deng, this means streamlining the administration, releasing the energies of the managers and the technocrats, and throwing out the old class shibboleths, which he sees as an unnecessary source of social tension and an artificial constraint on talent. Since Deng's return to office hundreds of thousands of officials have gone back to their posts at all levels of the party-state, and large numbers of purged thinkers, writers, teachers and artists have been rehabilitated (some posthumously). The cases of millions of common citizens denounced or persecuted over the last thirty years have been put under review, and the 'class enemy' label has been removed from all but a handful of 'unreformed' landlords, capitalists, rich peasants and others. Many of these rehabilitated 'rightists' are scientists and intellectuals whose skills and knowledge can now be mobilised for the good of China. As for the legal system, new procedures have been introduced to replace the old ad hoc methods that caused such widespread dissatisfaction under the 'gang of four'.

But the new government quickly made clear the limits beyond

which this liberalisation would not go. If a measure of democracy was indispensable for 'emancipating the mind' and thus for promoting scientific progress, this democracy should not go so far as to challenge the party's monopoly on political power. If legal guarantees were necessary to protect common citizens against the arbitrary exercise of official power, the judiciary should still bow where necessary to the political authorities. For the present leaders have hard-won positions and material interests to defend and little knowledge or experience of democratic organisation even during the revolution. When they saw the unofficial movement begin to go too far, they therefore took steps to curb it, and then to crush it.

But for a while, at least, the ferment around Democracy Wall was extremely useful to Deng Xiaoping and his supporters in the government, whose programme still faced opposition from Maoists who had survived the fall of the 'gang of four' and from the centrists around Hua Guofeng. Deng Xiaoping, having spent the Cultural Revolution 'in the cowshed', could hardly be blamed for its crises, and for the time being he enjoyed great prestige among ordinary citizens. He was perhaps the only remaining leader who, like Mao in his time, could risk whipping up mass movements on the streets in order to influence decisions in the Politburo. By conjuring up the spectre of popular discontent he could frighten into submission his opponents in the leadership, who were too compromised with the Maoist past to feel comfortable about protest rallies and calls for human rights, democratic reform and the bringing to book of those responsible for the 'decade of catastrophe'. And so he finally won out in the policy debate. Meanwhile, the movement that he had earlier encouraged was threatening to get out of hand. Sections of it were taking their criticism of Mao to unacceptable lengths, and raising questions about the whole system of party rule in China. At the same time disorder was breaking out on the streets of the capital, at a time when China's generals were fighting a difficult war against the Vietnamese.

On 16 March 1979 Deng Xiaoping made a speech setting narrower limits to the political ferment on the streets of China's cities. When Wei Jingsheng and others protested, they were seized by the police, and Wei was later gaoled for fifteen years. In

November further arrests followed at Democracy Wall, and shortly afterwards the Wall was moved from Xidan to a less central place and was then closed down altogether. In February 1980 the Four Great Freedoms — including the freedom to put up wall-posters — were excised from the Constitution, and subsequently it was forbidden to sell unofficial journals in public.

These measures hit the democratic movement hard. Most unofficial journals stopped appearing, although a few continued to go out by post, thus getting round the ban on public sales. What ties there were between groups in different parts of China were loose, and it was not easy for them to mount a coordinated response to the crackdown. That is not to say that there were no local protests. Mu Changqing, a leader of the Nameless Association, committed suicide in protest against Deng's speech announcing the repression, thus giving the movement its first martyr; and in Guangzhou City, Wang Xizhe and his friends caused a stir by standing up at a public meeting of the Communist Youth League and criticising the suppression of the Four Greats. These were acts of individual heroism; they gave the movement moral stature. What the movement needed next was the quieter heroism of the collective: hard organisation. And it almost came within their grasp. In January 1980 three unofficial journals in Guangzhou launched the first national appeal for freedom of the press, and others throughout China soon followed suit. In May representatives of various groups issued a joint protest against the arrest of Liu Qing; and on 29 August dissidents from Guangzhou, Wuhan, Changsha and Shaoguan got together to discuss setting up a committee to defend Liu Qing. Two days later He Qiu and three others implicated in this action were arrested and held by the police for several days. But despite this pressure from the authorities the moves towards greater cooperation went ahead, and a month later 21 unofficial groups finally joined together in a national Federation, and appointed He Qiu to edit the all-China unofficial journal *Zeren*. The birth of this new Federation — it still lives underground in China, although its present strength is not known — was a major achievement that, given time, would have greatly strengthened the movement by providing a vehicle for the practical expression of solidarity across provinces, and by quickening the flow of information and ideas.

At the same time, the movement took steps to strengthen its external ties. In some areas — what bolder challenge to the 'Party of the Proletariat'? — its constituent groups began to win friends among disaffected factory workers. True, China's dissidents were themselves mostly workers, but few of the factory rank-and-file had up to then actively identified with their positions, although many may have passively sympathised with them. Now all this began to change. Here and there the movement began to break out of its isolation and to find new allies outside the fickle elite. In Shanghai Fu Shenqi, editor of *Renminzhi sheng* ('Voice of the People'), stood for election in an engineering works after the government had announced — rashly, and not for long — that candidates need no longer have party approval to be nominated. Fu headed the factory poll at the first count, despite strong party pressure on the electors to vote for the two official candidates. In Changsha too a dissident student (married to an American woman) collected large amounts of money from local factory workers to finance his election campaign in the face of official harassment. In Wuhan oppositionists even managed to lead a strike. And in Beijing Xu Wenli, editor of *Siwu luntan* ('April Fifth Forum'), wrote an Open Letter to Lech Walesa praising him as a 'shining example for working classes in socialist countries the world over'. Even in the vast countryside pin-pricks of democratic agitation began to appear.

It would be foolish to exaggerate the victories that the democratic movement won among the workers. But the possibility of eventually making ties with large numbers of them was certainly there, in which case its role in Chinese politics would have been immeasurably strengthened and the government would have found it far harder to suppress when the time arrived. China is a desperately poor country, and Deng's policies are aimed at greatly widening the range of inequalities in it. These are the ingredients for acute social tension. The democratic movement, which inherited from the Maoists a principled aversion to privilege and inequality, would have been strategically placed to intervene in social conflicts in the factories and on the farms, and to win broader support for its political programme.

But this possibility did not escape the notice of the party leadership.

In late 1980 the trial began in Beijing of the 'gang of four' (led by Mao's widow Jiang Qing) and the 'Lin Biao clique' crushed after allegedly trying to overthrow Mao in 1971. Jiang Qing, found guilty of persecuting Communist leaders and conspiring to subvert the nation, was given a suspended death sentence, as was her fellow-Maoist Zhang Chunqiao; the other defendants in the case were sent to prison for long periods. Although the link between this trial and the final crackdown on the democratic movement may not be immediately obvious, there was such a link and it is important not to overlook it.

First, this trial, repeatedly postponed, signalled a resolution of the power struggle and a temporary stabilisation of the leadership. This had important consequences for the protest movement. As long as cleavages continued at the top of the party, the movement had some slight space in which to work. But as soon as the dominant faction had succeeded — for how long remains to be seen — in imposing its will on the refractory remnants of the Maoist old guard and overcoming the last obstacle to a (limited) criticism of Mao, the game was up.

Second, the trial signalled the definitive and unabashed return to 'class justice' and thus paved the way for extra-legal measures against political deviants. Officially, this trial was billed as a chief symbol of the return to 'socialist legality' under Deng; and compared with Stalin's show-trials and with the increasingly violent way in which faction-fights were resolved in Mao's old age, there can be little doubt that in principle it was a move for the better. But by any normal standards of justice it was a contemptible fraud. Whatever Jiang Qing's crimes, she did nothing that her accusers would not also have done in the fight for power, and in that sense her only real crime was to be defeated. In any case, the verdict against her was clearly reached before the trial, and the trial itself was heavily censored and attended by a raucous and squalid campaign of sexist smears and innuendos. Judges and prosecutors sat together, distinguished only by the colour of their tunics. The defence lawyers based their cases entirely on evidence compiled by the prosecution. They objected to none of the prosecutors' questions, cross-examined no prosecution

tion witnesses and called no witnesses of their own. (See the account of Ma Rongqie, Jiang Qing's defence lawyer, reported in *International Herald Tribune*, 8 January 1982.) Shortly after Jiang's sentencing, Amnesty International said that it was 'concerned that the standards applied at the trial of the ten former officials might have an adverse effect for the conduct of other political trials in the People's Republic'. Amnesty's concern found little echo in the political world, either on the right (which was busy ganging up with Deng against the Russians) or on the left, which seemed largely indifferent to Jiang's fate. Unfortunately Amnesty — which has long experience of such things — was right. It was widely said in China before Jiang's trial that through it Deng wanted to convince sceptical Chinese that the courts 'attack tigers as well as flies'. But if seditious tigers get only the semblance of a trial, should it surprise us when the flies are sent to gaol with no hearing at all?

And so, on and around 10 April 1981, 25 leading oppositionists and an unknown number of lesser ones were arrested in a nationwide crackdown on the democratic movement. As far as is known, these people were not put on public trial and were not formally charged with any crime. At the same time the police questioned many activists not yet arrested, searched their houses and confiscated books, paper and printing equipment.

Prospects for the future

Is this the end of the road for China's democratic movement? Will it now go the same way as the Hundred Flowers of 1957, which sank almost without trace under the waves of party intolerance? A comparison with past unofficial movements sheds useful light on the strengths and weaknesses of China's present dissidents. The course of past criticism movements — the main ones were in 1942, 1957 and 1966-68 — was drearily, if tragically, predictable: the party leaders urge the people to speak out; sooner or later the critics overstep the limits; the party leaders reassert control by repressing the critics; the themes of criticism lie dormant until the next sponsored round of 'blossoming and contending'. Or so it was until the Cultural Revolution. But here the first big difference between present and earlier forms of dissent becomes apparent. For whereas the clampdowns in 1942 and

1957 were more or less complete, so that the next generation of contenders was forced to start out with a blank sheet, the effects of a political earthquake like the Cultural Revolution could not so easily be wiped away just because some bureaucrat wanted it so. The Cultural Revolution was a mass movement of unprecedented proportions and it will still be some time before its shockwaves die down completely. And thus the democratic movement started out not with a blank sheet but with a considerable body of theory and experience.

As for the Hundred Flowers campaign of 1957, there are many parallels between it and the recent movement, and these parallels are even officially recognised. The repressing of the Hundred Flowers has been widely described in China's press as the beginning of the 'left' tendency and China's troubles, and victims of the 1957 clampdown have not only been rehabilitated in their tens of thousands but are today saying many of the same things they said before their arrest nearly twenty-five years ago. But the differences are even more striking. In 1957 all sections of the party were united behind their historic leader, Mao. The party had stabilised its rule and had radically restructured the Chinese economy. But Mao's Great Leap Forward of 1959, which plunged China's economy into deep crisis, destroyed much of his support in the party hierarchy. Today the combined effects of time's tooth and repeated power struggles have led to the shedding of many old leaders, and China's economy and society are emerging only with the greatest difficulty from a period of debilitating chaos. In 1957 Mao launched the Hundred Flowers by deliberate choice, to curb bureaucratic conservatism in the party and forestall 'a Hungarian-style incident'. The forces he mobilised were students and older intellectuals newly emerged from the furnace of thought reform. But the democratic movement developed largely independently, over a long period of intellectual ferment and experimentation. It is made up mainly of young workers hardened by years of personal privation and political struggle. It shares some notions with the students of 1957, but on the whole its programmes have greater theoretical depth and articulation than those of 1957.

A comparison with the Cultural Revolution is also instructive. In 1966 the party leadership was badly split. The students and youth who formed the mass base of the Cultural Revolution were politically raw and easy prey for manipulation from above. The rival factions in the party hierarchy vied with one another to recruit a following from among the Red Guards, who lost sight of the substantive issues and became hopelessly embroiled in factionalism and violence. But although some of today's dissidents were at one time open to pressure from Deng Xiaoping, most were all along independent of him and followed their own lights, with no more than a token nod in Deng's direction every now and then. Today's dissidents succeeded in avoiding a gross personalisation of their politics despite the stridently personal official campaign against the 'gang of four', and argued that one should look not at the shortcomings of this or that individual leader, but at the social system that underlies them.

The two great planks on which the present leaders were hoisted into power are modernisation and democracy. It is unthinkable that they would risk alienating their support by backtracking entirely on their promises of reform. The 'antifascist' mood among the Chinese people, particularly the intellectuals and the workers, is too strong, the memory of the 'lawlessness' of the Cultural Revolution is too fresh in people's minds, and the new leaders' authority is immeasurably weaker than was Mao's in 1957, when he cracked down violently on the 'rightists' exposed during the Hundred Flowers. And so the prospect of a Chinese spring remains.

Yet, as the events of recent months show only too clearly, the party leaders will not tolerate the bolder forms of independent politics advocated by the democratic movement, or open up the system to the fresh gusts of mass-based dissent. Their goal is the creation of a comparatively well-ordered society in which 'democracy' is carefully modulated to reinforce and stabilise the regime. The recent sponsored revival of the handful of docile 'democratic parties' that have supported the government uncritically since 1949 was entirely compatible with that project. The further growth of a non-conformist democratic movement was not. And so the movement was repressed. But by arresting its main leaders and driving its supporters underground, the authorities are running the risk that in the long run they will strengthen its coherence and force it to deepen its roots in the working class and peasantry.

Wang Xizhe

Mao Zedong and the Cultural Revolution

Wang Xizhe was a student in Guangzhou City when the Cultural Revolution began in 1966. Like millions of other Chinese youth, he joined in denouncing the authorities and 'making revolution'. In 1968 the Maoist leaders decided to put an end to the Cultural Revolution, which was by then getting out of hand. Wang, along with many other of Mao's 'little generals', was arrested in late 1968. A year later he was freed and sent to work in the countryside, but he was allowed back to the city when his parents pointed out that he was their only son. Through his parents, he found a factory job.

In November 1974 Wang and three others, Li Zhengtian, Chen Yiyang and Guo Hongzhi put up a 67-page wall-poster in Guangzhou. This poster, signed Li Yi Zhe after three of its authors, advocated socialist democracy and made veiled attacks on the Maoist leaders. In late 1974 Wang, Li and Chen were sent to work 'under supervision' in the countryside, and put under intense criticism. It was not until March 1977, several months *after* the fall of the 'gang of four', that they were formally tried and sent to labour camps. With supreme irony they were charged with being followers of the 'gang', as well as with having links with Taiwan and with the Hongkong Trotskyists. Under the 'gang' they had been labelled merely as 'reactionaries'; now they were charged as 'counter-revolutionaries'.

In 1978 China's unofficial press began a campaign for Li Yi Zhe's release and Amnesty International adopted them as Prisoners of Conscience, but it was not until 1979 that the three were finally freed and rehabilitated.

After their release they joined the newly born democratic movement. Wang Xizhe wrote an impressive manifesto called 'The struggle for the class dictatorship of the proletariat' in the Guangzhou unofficial journal *Renminzhi sheng* ('Voice of the People'), which he described as a refinement of the 1974 Li Yi Zhe poster. This manifesto is a sustained and theoretically original critique of post-capitalist society. It argues that when the proletariat takes power in a backward country, it can either close its doors to the outside world and retreat into a regime of 'feudal socialism', or it can enter the world system and become a 'big cooperative factory' — 'a bourgeois state without a bourgeoisie' — producing for the capitalist world market. But because the workers are uneducated, not they but the vanguard — the Communists — will administer this cooperative. In future either the workers' cultural level will rise so that they can take over administrative tasks; or the vanguard will become 'alienated into something opposed to the proletariat', i.e. a dictatorship of 'Communist bureaucrats'. There is still the social basis for such a dictatorship in China: the 'gang' were not the cause but the symptom of social conditions. (For a translation of Wang's article see *New Left Review*, no. 121, June-July 1980.)

The essay translated here analyses Mao's role in the Chinese Revolution. Wang's view — expressed at a time when it was still dangerous to say anything critical about Mao — is that Mao was not a Marxist revolutionary but a peasant leader, and that this was both his strength and his weakness. Like peasant leaders throughout Chinese history, Mao's aim was to become emperor. Although he boldly incited movements against the bureaucracy, his real aim was to remove his rivals and become sole ruler. On many points Wang's positions coincide with those of party reformers like Deng Xiaoping, and this has led some observers to suggest that he was not really a dissident at all. But this is to misunderstand Wang's tactics. His support for Deng was never un-critical, and the extended logic of his position was not Deng's. His criticisms of the system go much further than Deng's, and his aim is clearly to push reforms to the limit. Wang's article throws important light on the way in which the Cultural Revolution influenced Chinese youth. China's present rulers, and many foreign observers too, now argue that the Cultural Revolution was irredeemably bad. But Wang's article suggests that it taught some youth to think independently, and thus paved the way for the democratic opposition.

In May 1980, when the dissident Liu Qing was arrested, Wang published an open letter in which he said:

> A precise legal system and trials that conform rigorously to the law: that is the best lesson China could learn from the last thirty years... The people expect no miracles. They expect no one to produce democracy and a legal system out of a hat. They are content to ad-vance one step at a time, but they will tolerate no turning back.

On 20 April 1981 Wang Xizhe was arrested at his place of work, at the same time as a score of others were arrested in cities throughout China. Hongkong students who went to Guangzhou to appeal for Wang's release reported that he had not been charged and 'is not allowed to meet any family members or friends'.

The text published here has been greatly abridged. Deletions have not been indicated; a complete translation by Anthony Kwok is available from Plough Publications, Hongkong 1981.

The struggle for and against reform in China

My friend Jin Jun of the Democratic Youth group wrote me a letter saying: 'Mao's greatness lies in the fact that he spared nothing in criticising the state he had set up. He disrupted order in a society in which he, as Chairman, was supposed to maintain it. He disrupted the party that called him Chairman.'

But why did Mao disrupt the state and the party? Was he dissatisfied with their growing Stalinisation? Not at all. He was suspicious of the forces for change that were springing up irrepressibly in them, and thought that they were not autocratic and authoritarian enough. He wanted to set up a new state and party that would be a Mao dynasty disguised as a dictatorship of the proletariat.

After the victory of the revolution in 1949, the party set up a new-democratic order that was to be long-lasting and stable. Since China was economically and culturally backward, socialism could not yet be brought in. Instead, production would be organised through state capitalism, within which were the germs of socialism. Individual and corporate capital and the communal economy of the villages were to be preserved and developed, for economic laws are natural laws, not to be circumvented.

Mao Zedong, however, disagreed. He would be even greater than the legendary three kings and five emperors. He would make miracles to prove that Marx's view of development through stages was that of a mere academic. And so he began to issue commands to the country's economy.

Mao Zedong, this peasant from Hunan, declared his great principles of agro-socialism. He said that despite primitive tools and peasant ignorance, socialism could still be built by mobilising human labour and changing the forms of ownership. He believed that the poor peasants, because of their misery, are a vast reservoir of resources with which to build socialism. Marx and Lenin thought differently. For Lenin, even workers in big industry would never come to socialism without an outside agency. But Mao said that poor peasants are instinctively socialist, and that the party's task is simply to mobilise them and nothing more. Now if the peasants are instinctively enthusiastic about socialism, then anyone who is not so is probably a reactionary. And if the party's task is to mobilise existing potential, then any party member who does not do so can only be a right-opportunist and a capitalist-roader. Furthermore, since agro-socialism develops not naturally but through human agency, the power of decision must be concentrated in the party, and more specifically in the

Great Leader, Mao. And so the theory of agro-socialism turns out in practice to be the theory of Maoist authoritarianism.

From the very start leaders like Liu Shaoqi opposed the authoritarian trend, and called for the democratisation of Chinese politics. Their struggle more or less coincided with Khrushchev's denunciation of Stalin and his calls for party democracy and a collective leadership. This was good news for Liu Shaoqi's group, which in September 1956 succeeded in getting the references to Mao Zedong Thought deleted from the party rules, and in winning other reforms that marked the first stage in the party's democratisation.

The Twentieth Congress of the Soviet Communist Party created waves of anti-Stalinism throughout Eastern Europe, and in Hungary Soviet tanks, with Mao's strong support, quelled a people's rising. The events in Hungary caused a great ferment in China, where students and intellectuals began to call for democratic reform. Faced with pressure from both inside and outside the party, Mao decided to hit back. His strategy was to lure his 'rightist' opponents into the open by telling them to speak freely, and then to destroy them.

Who were these so-called rightists? True, some were reactionaries, but most were simply people who were unhappy with the bureaucratisation of the party, the collusion of state and party, party control of appointments, and the bureaucratic ways of petty officials. They were opposed to Russia's chauvinist foreign policy. They wanted more freedom in thinking, academic study and politics. For Mao, all these demands were subversive, although as a revolutionary he had fought for the same demands ever since graduating from Hunan Normal School.

The purge of the 'rightists' outside the party was at the same time a warning to the 'rightists' inside it. From now on these 'rightists' would be wise not to oppose Mao's speeding up of the revolution. Having acquiesced in the concentration of power in Mao's hands, they could hardly oppose the Great Leap Forward. Soon the personality cult was revived, and Mao started out on his agro-socialist experiment.

Irrigation is central to the Asiatic mode of production. In China, Mao hoped to abolish droughts and floods overnight as proof of the miraculous power of agro-socialism. He wanted to mobilise the bare hands of millions of peasants through a huge administrative network, and to nationalise without compensation the innumerable drops of capital scattered throughout China's countless villages. Mao's administrative 'new creation' was the People's Commune. Marx and Engels could never quite bring themselves to construct for posterity a model of how communism would be, but Mao not only projected such a utopia but even put it into action. In the commune political and social life were to become fused, as were industry, agriculture, commerce, education and defence. Mao even told the peasants (and announced through a resolution of the Central Committee) that China would finish building Communism in eight to ten years, and catch up Britain in steel production in one to two years by mobilising 90 million peasants to run small village furnaces.

Mao Zedong obviously believed that the national economy could be directed in the same way as an army. But putting the economy under military rule requires a commander. The obvious choice for such a commander was Mao, who now began his assault on the idea of collective leadership. He said:

> It is interesting that some people are opposed to the cult of the individual. Well, there are two forms. One is correct, such as that of Marx, Engels, Lenin and Stalin. These we must forever and ever revere. We can't do otherwise; the truth is in their hands... A squad should revere its squad leader. The question at issue is not whether there should be glorification of the individual, but whether what is being upheld is the truth. If it is, then the individual should be revered. If it is not, then even collective leadership will not help. Better that I become a dictator than let you become one.[1]

The ground won by the party democrats in the fight for collective leadership was soon lost. This was not so much because of Mao's influence as because Mao's agro-socialism is a product of the Chinese Communist Party's basic constituency: the peasants. China's peasants have never even seen modern industry, let alone worked in it. Scientific socialism therefore means nothing to them. For them, Communism is a heavenly kingdom of peace where all are equal. If Mao can bring such a kingdom into being, then Mao shall reign over it.

But the party democrats did not simply sneak from the battle-field. Mao's Great Leap Forward led to widespread famine and chaos, and as a result Mao was severely challenged in the leader-ship by Peng Dehuai and Zhang Wentian. Peng courageously argued that 'it is abnormal and dangerous to build up personal rather than collective authority'. At this Mao, who could tolerate anything but a challenge to his own authority, flew into a rage against Peng, venting all the anger and frustration he felt as a result of the failure of the Great Leap Forward. He declared Peng an opportunist and a reactionary, stripped him of the right to speak, and subjected him to hysterical and unscrupulous criticism. At the same time, he had Peng replaced as head of the armed forces by the Maoist Lin Biao.

Nevertheless, the economic collapse in 1960-61 forced him to retreat from his Great Leap Forward and to grudgingly agree to new economic policies. Liu Shaoqi described the crisis of 1960-61 as 'due 30 per cent to natural disasters and 70 per cent to human error'. These mistakes, he said, were caused by the pride and conceit of some comrades and by the weakening of democratic centralism. Thus Liu lined up with Peng and Zhang Wentian. For the time being Mao had no choice but to accept the situation, and he even made a now famous speech praising democratic centralism and admitting that his own authority was limited by the Central Committee and the Politburo. But he was put under scarcely any pressure. The Chinese, unlike the French or the British, are traditionally forbearing with their rulers.

Before long Mao was back on the attack. After the crisis of 1959-61 consumer goods were scarce, especially in the villages. Some officials were taking advantage of their office to embezzle collective property, and while Liu Shaoqi's new liberal agricultural policy did revive the village economy somewhat, it also led to hoarding and other illegal activities. With time these problems, which can be explained as the lingering after-effects of Mao's leftism, could have been resolved, but Mao was deter-mined to exploit them to show that his opponents in power were on the capitalist road, and that he was the one who had always followed socialism.

His strategy was to begin by attacking Khrushchevism. In

Chinese eyes Khrushchev's policy towards China was unpardonable. But if Khrushchev was wrong and bad, then so must be destalinisation and democratic reform, and anyone who favoured these must be a Chinese Khrushchev. The obvious candidate for this label was, of course, Liu Shaoqi, who had reformed the village economy, carried out Libermanist experiments, loosened the controls imposed in 1957 on intellectuals, and even tried to rehabilitate Peng Dehuai (just as Khrushchev had tried to rehabilitate Bukharin).

Mao began his counter-attack with plots and intrigues. By 1963 no one trusted him any longer, so he introduced his wife Jiang Qing into literary circles, and in less than two years she had gathered around her a large coterie of writers ready to support Mao. In September 1965 Mao tried to get the party's backing for a criticism of two plays by Wu Han that he saw as veiled defences of his disgraced critic Peng Dehuai. But Peng Zhen, representing the Central Committee, courageously resisted Mao's demand, so Mao had no choice but to move to Shanghai, where Jiang Qing and Yao Wenyuan drafted their own pro-Mao critique of Wu Han's work. Soon Peng Zhen was brought down, and the way was opened for a general assault on the reform group in the party.

So to answer my friend Jin Jun, the reason Mao 'spared nothing in criticising the state he himself had set up' was not because he was great, but because he was reactionary. He wanted a more autocratic and centralised party-state, but the democratic reformers thwarted him. He could no longer ride the party like a horse. That is why he set out to destroy it and to found a Mao Zedong fascist party.

The Cultural Revolution and Mao's victory

People throughout China rejoiced at the fall of the Gang of Four in October 1976, but some young democrats both at home and abroad said that this was a defeat for the left and a victory for the bureaucrats. They believed that Mao, who never knew when to put a stop to the revolution, had come in his old age to the same conclusions as Trotsky and Tito: that China was bureaucratic not just in parts, but to the core; and that society must be mobilised to crush the bureaucratic institutions, even though it was against Mao's personal interests to do so. But, they conclude, Mao failed because he depended on the wrong people and because the bureaucratic institutions were too strong.

However, this view is wrong. Mao may now and then have said things against bureaucracy, but he saw nothing wrong in principle with a system whereby several hundred thousand ruled several hundred milion. All he wanted was that the cadres should be disciplined to prevent them from oppressing the people.

Of course, there's nothing new here. Throughout history rulers of bureaucratic systems have always tried to discipline their middle and lower ranks. Otherwise they would risk a complete breakdown of the whole system.

Marx wanted the workers to crush bureaucracy and replace it by democracy, and the Bolsheviks followed him in this. But Stalin and Mao simply replaced the old bureaucratic system with a new one — the Communist bureaucratic system. True, this new system was the inevitable product of the turmoil of the October Revolution. But whereas for Lenin it was a bitter fruit, for Stalin and Mao it was a delicious one.

Why, then, did Mao repeatedly summon the Red Guards to disrupt what he called the bureaucratic stratum, and why did he declare the Paris Commune to be a model? The answer is, because he wanted to be in sole control of the party. He knew that conflict between local officials and the people was inevitable, especially after his own extremist policies had plunged the country into poverty and chaos. His aim was to wipe out his opponents in the party. But to do that, he needed support. How could he get such support? By painting his opponents as the scoundrels and bureaucrats who were responsible for all the suffering, and by calling on the people to overthrow them and to put Mao Zedong, the true Marxist, in power forever. By late 1966, he had succeeded in his main aim: amid the bluster and confusion, it really did seem as if Mao was on the side of the people against the bureaucrats.

But in a deserted back-street of Beijing a bespectacled young man of slight build was coolly jotting down his thoughts:

3 August 1966. Took part in purge session against Song Yuxi organised by a factory unit. Song stayed rather cool.

During the session, it rained. Most people managed to find umbrellas or some other shelter. Song had to stand there in the rain. If I had had an umbrella, I would have let him share it... Did I sympathise with him? Not at all. He had been living well enough, and he was always good at finding fault with others. All these years he had served only himself, and for that I hated him. But I could never endorse the stupid charges the crowd made against him: 'Why did you censor the eight principles?' 'Why didn't you let us study Mao's works?' 'Why didn't you let Mao's works be printed?' This was ridiculous. It was as if being against Mao was a heinous crime.

The man who made these notes was Yu Luoke, who was executed as a 'poisonous weed' in March 1970 at the age of 27. Yu's comments mirror three kinds of conflict: that between cadres and the people; that between cadres and Mao Zedong; and that between the people and Mao Zedong. The people purged the cadres as bureaucrats. But bureaucratisation was the fault not of individual cadres but of Mao's autocratic system, which did not allow people to control their own fate. This the people could not see; they criticised the cadres because the cadres opposed Mao. In the second half of 1966, therefore, the people's instinctive struggle against bureaucracy became a weapon in Mao's fight for even greater autocracy. The people threw up the spears when the battle cry rang out, but were pierced by them as they fell back to the ground.

Now things were going well for Mao, he called a plenum of the Central Committee where he vanquished Liu Shaoqi and Deng Xiaoping and appointed Lin Biao as his successor, under the watchful eye of Maoist 'teachers and students of the revolution' and backed by the 38th Army, which was stationed outside the city. But Mao won by only one vote, so the crisis was not yet over. In order to wipe out the opposition from top to bottom, the people would have to be mobilised. Accordingly, Mao dressed up in soldier's uniform and went to Tiananmen Square, where he summoned millions of Red Guards to 'rebel' against all those who opposed him or who were suspected of opposing him.

At first Mao encouraged people to believe that the aim of

the Cultural Revolution was to destroy bureaucracy and re-place it with a democratic system based on the Paris Commune. But when the Shanghai 'rebels' set up the Shanghai Commune on 23 February 1967, Zhang Chunqiao told them on Mao's behalf:

If everything were changed into a commune what would happen to the party? Where would we put the party? On the commune committee are both party members and non-party members. What would we do with the Party Committee? To change the system throughout the country would require a change in the political system and in the country's name. Some people might not recognise it, and that would cause a lot of trouble. In any case, such a change would be of no practical significance.[2]

A few months later, talking with foreign visitors about the Cultural Revolution, Mao was quoted as saying:

Some people say elections are very good and democratic. To me, the word 'election' is quite civilised, but I don't think there can be real elections. I was elected as a people's representative for the Beijing area, but who in Beijing really understands me? Zhou Enlai became premier because he was appointed by the Central Committee.

For Mao, democracy was just a means to an end. As soon as he alone represented the people, his democracy would become theirs, and his wishes would become theirs. If you were against him, you were against the people. This is the sum total of his political philosophy.

The Cultural Revolution and Mao's defeat

On 13 September 1971 Lin Biao, Mao's 'close comrade-in-arms' and heir apparent, died in a plane crash over Mongolia after a failed coup attempt. This event rocked China. No one could imagine Lin Biao without Mao's Little Red Book gripped firmly in his hands. What in heaven's name was going on?

For many years Lin Biao had fitted nicely into Mao's political scheme. Mao wanted to turn China into a military camp in which industry, farming, trade, schooling and the army would be merged. Moreover, it was very important during the chaos of the Cultural Revolution that there should be a strong army in the background. And so Lin Biao's power grew formidably in those years.

When an impostor finally wins out, his first big problem is how to remove his cronies from the scene. After Mao's victory in the Cultural Revolution and at the 1969 Ninth Congress, the question of what to do with Lin Biao became pressing. But once Mao's interests clashed with those of Lin and the rising class of military bureaucrats, Lin's worship of Mao stopped, and the battle started.

But unlike Mao's struggle with Peng Dehuai in 1959, this was a battle not between good and evil, but between rival intriguers, without any obvious principles at stake. As a result, people's eyes were opened, and all kinds of repressed social currents flooded to the surface.

To boost his flagging credibility, Mao published a letter of July 1966 to Jiang Qing in which he had expressed some doubts about Lin Biao, but it had little impact. Some suspected it was forged. Others wondered why Mao had chosen Lin as his successor if had had doubts about him. But Mao's letter heartened those cadres purged during the Cultural Revolution, who now reasoned that since Mao had taken so long to discover that Lin Biao was a scoundrel, he might also eventually come to see that they were not scoundrels, and rehabilitate them.

By 1972 the campaign to criticise the extreme 'left' had become so strong that it turned into a spontaneous mass movement. The implications of this movement were all too clear. It expressed the forces of reform that were resurfacing within the party, as well as the Chinese people's new awareness of their interests and their willingness to defend them. Mao would never again be able to deceive millions of people into joining a crusade against his political opponents.

Towards the end of 1972, Mao's counter-attack against this movement started. A series of articles in the official press insisted that Lin Biao was not a leftist but a rightist, and that to criticise him as a leftist was a veiled way of criticising the Cultural Revolution. Why did Mao organise this hasty counter-attack? The answer may be found in the new relationship between the classes in China after the Lin Biao affair. Lin's downfall had not only raised the question of how to evaluate the Cultural Revolution, but had also left behind a power vacuum.

Who would fill this vacuum? The only survivors of the victorious Maoist bloc were the Cultural Revolution Group of Jiang Qing and her associates. These people had made their fortunes instantaneously. They were ambitious and greedy for more power. They wanted to perpetuate the social as well as the political relations consolidated at the Ninth Congress in 1969.

The other main contenders were the group defeated in the Cultural Revolution, including both the democratic reformers and those opportunist bureaucrats who were brought down in the general turmoil. These people were able to breathe more easily now that the pressure was lifted somewhat. With Liu Shaoqi dead, they now looked to Zhou Enlai as the only person capable of uniting the party and saving them from oblivion. Within a short time a large number of veteran leaders, including Deng Xiaoping, were rehabilitated under Zhou Enlai's auspices. Thus a new power centre gradually formed around Zhou, even though he may not have wanted this to happen.

As for the people, they had long had enough of Maoist oppression and deceit and looked back wistfully to the early sixties, when the new economic policies were in force. They were angered by an education system that produced only 'ignorant fools'. Among them support for the veteran cadres grew ever stronger, and Zhou Enlai became the symbolic focus of this support.

With endless patience Zhou Enlai tolerated a series of veiled insults and challenges to him from the Cultural Revolution Group, who were determined to bring him down. In 1974, the Movement to Criticise Lin Biao and Confucius got underway. There is no evidence that the criticism of Confucius was originally meant to topple Zhou Enlai, even though it was clearly aimed at stemming the anti-leftist tide in China. Although Mao's old rivals were gathered around Zhou, Mao knew Zhou as a man without personal ambition, and needed him as a symbol of justice in the regime. It is the same with autocratic regimes everywhere: if the emperor himself is not a symbol of justice, then some good minister must be one, so that the oppressed people have somewhere to look in their suffering; otherwise, there is bound to be trouble.

But the Cultural Revolution Group were determined to turn the movement into a new Cultural Revolution. Unfortunately for them, however, the world had changed since 1966, and the people turned a deaf ear to their calls to overthrow Zhou Enlai. Moreover, a famous wall-poster went up on the streets of Guangzhou titled *On Socialist Democracy and the Legal System*. This poster symbolised the rejection of Mao Zedong by those who had grown up in the Cultural Revolution. It argued that to criticise Lin Biao was not enough, and predicted a mass movement that would overthrow the entire system of which Lin Biao was a mere symptom.

It was at about this time that Deng Xiaoping, a resolute opponent of the Cultural Revolution Group, returned to political office. In January 1975 Zhou Enlai proposed launching the Four Modernisations. This proposal was widely supported in China. Millions of school-leavers were without work and wages had been frozen for many years, so that social tensions were rising. Moreover, rapid economic development in other countries was putting pressure on China to accelerate the rate of growth of her own economy.

As chief executive of the modernisation plan, Deng Xiaoping began to propose measures for its implementation. But shortly after Zhou Enlai's death in January 1976, Deng suddenly disappeared from the political scene again, not to reappear until after Mao's death several months later. After 1949 most Chinese had boundless confidence in Mao. They believed he could make the sun shine and the rain fall. Even his failures they were prepared to blame on his opponents. But the Lin Biao affair changed all this. When Mao tried to dismiss Deng Xiaoping after more than ten years of 'anti-revisionist' struggle, the people turned in a trice to the 'revisionists', and took to the streets to demonstrate against Mao.

The Tiananmen Square incident of April 1976, one of the greatest revolutionary mass movements in Chinese history, was a plebiscite in which the people, in the absence of proper democratic procedures, cast their votes in the form of wreaths, poems and speeches. But Mao Zedong was always contemptuous of elections, so he was determined to suppress the movement.

His clubs and bayonets easily scattered the tens of thousands of unarmed demonstrators. But his victory was short-lived. He died on the day of the Mid-Autumn Festival, when Chinese are traditionally reunited with the families. Some people say that this symbolises the fact that Mao will never be reunited with the Chinese people.

Mao's merits and demerits

Mao himself said that during his life he had accomplished two things of note: driving out Chiang Kai-shek, and launching the Cultural Revolution. We have already looked at the Cultural Revolution; and everyone agrees that Mao chased out Chiang Kai-shek. So does that mean that Mao's achievement was 50 per cent good and 50 per cent bad? No, that is too simple a view. Let us recall some of the milestones in Mao's struggle against Chiang.

In the autumn of 1927 the first Chinese revolution was in shreds as a result of Stalin's defeatist line. All Stalin could think of was to put the blame on Chen Duxiu. As for Trotsky, he came up with the impractical call for a Constituent Assembly. This was out of the question in a country where the landlord class had just put down a revolution of the workers and peasants. Besides, the people would never have welcomed it. Obviously Trotsky's strategy was modelled on the experience of the 1905 Revolution in Russia. Luckily the Chinese revolution did not adopt this strategy of retreat, or it would have plunged into a disaster from which it would never have recovered even to this day.

Mao Zedong was the only one to come up with the right strategy. He showed great courage in those difficult times. He called on Communists still wanting to continue the struggle to go out into the villages. He formulated a strategy that combined land reform with the use of revolutionary war to generate a revolutionary crisis. And so he saved the revolution from disaster. During the war against Japan and the ensuing civil war against Chiang Kai-shek, Mao once again resisted Stalin's orders and went ahead with strengthening and expanding the revolutionary army, right up to final victory.

Without doubt, Mao was a national hero. His outstanding achievement was that he firmly resisted Stalin's attempts to tailor the Chinese revolution to suit Soviet foreign policy. But one must not forget that the revolution he led was a peasant uprising. True, Mao overthrew a landlord regime, but this was something peasants too can do. Zhu Yuanzhang overthrew the Yuan dynasty and founded the Ming. Li Zicheng led a huge uprising against the Ming. And the Taipings almost overthrew the Qing. As for Mao's Jinggangshan (Chingkangshan) stronghold, it had many predecessors in the history of Chinese banditry, of which the most notorious was the Liangshanbo. Mao Zedong, as someone who got his learning in China, stood head and shoulders above most Communist dogmatists in that he was more interested in the road to Liangshanbo than the road to St Petersburg.

As a peasant leader Mao was unsurpassed, and it is not surprising, considering his peasant outlook, that he later became an emperor. But as a marxist and a workers' leader he had few achievements. Marxists must search for ways of freeing the proletariat, of realising popular democracy, and of making the people prosperous. But Mao achieved none of these — on the contrary, he raised obstacles in the way of achieving them.

The launching of a mass movement to purge the democratic reformers from the party in 1966 had two main outcomes. On the one hand, it led to Mao's personal dictatorship. On the other hand, it taught masses of young people to see themselves as equal rather than inferior to government officials. It taught them self-confidence through confrontation. And this is precisely the first step to democratic reform. Some even learned to analyse discrete problems of Chinese society in terms of the system as a whole. It was as if the Cultural Revolution had succeeded in moulding a new generation that dared to think independently about questions of national import and to shoulder the responsibility for bettering society.

Some young comrades of the democratic group see this as a positive outcome of the Cultural Revolution, and treasure it. But they are wrong. Mao's aim was to found a dynasty, and he had no wish for a 'thinking generation'. The aim of his Cultural Revolution was to destroy several hundred million brains. When he had routed his opponents in the party and installed new loyalists in their place, did he let the Red Guards say what they thought about the new regime or express their doubts and criticisms? Ask the young democrats in Shanghai! They can vividly recall how the Shanghai Red Revolutionary Association was immediately suppressed when it criticised the Maoist Zhang Chunqiao. Need I remind you that those who were suppressed in Tiananmen Square in April 1976 were precisely the 'thinking generation'?

The emergence of a 'thinking generation' in China was merely a by-product of the Cultural Revolution. But all reactions have revolutionary by-products, just as all revolutions have reactionary ones. Of all the European nations, the Italians are the most politicised and have the biggest political parties. Scholars say that this is because the mass movements launched by the fascists got people used to political participation. Should we thank Mussolini for that?

Carry socialist democratic reforms through to a conclusion!

The victory of October 1976 was won by a united front of all those forces opposed to the Gang of Four. But after the victory splits were inevitable. The first split came over the question of reform: here the group around Wang Dongxing, which was opposed to the Gang of Four but not to Mao, came out against Deng Xiaoping and the reformers. The second split, which has not yet happened, will be over how far reform should go.

Right now Deng Xiaoping is in the same position as was Khrushchev in 1965. Unless he exonerates the millions of Chinese who suffered under Mao, social tensions will persist. Unless he breaks completely with the Stalin-Mao economic system, opens wide to the outside world and carries out reforms, the national economy will stagnate. Unless he stresses socialist legality and civil rights, intellectuals and young people in particular will trust socialism even less. Unless he improves the relations with sister parties that were strained by Mao's dogmatism, China will lack access to the theory and experience she needs to guide and defend her reforms.

But none of these things can happen unless thinking is liberated, and thinking can only be liberated if we drop the Mao cult and point out that Mao was fallible. This the dogmatists around Wang Dongxing were not willing to accept, so battle was joined between them and the party pragmatists.

At the same time the dogmatists were being criticised even more severely from outside the party. The extra-party democratic movement of 1978-79 was in every way a continuation of the Tiananmen movement of April 1976; many of its leaders had actively participated in the Tiananmen demonstrations. The democratic movement developed in the struggle to reverse the verdict on the Tiananmen incident (which the Maoists had labelled counter-revolutionary). Their chief opponents in the party were precisely the dogmatists around Wang Dongxing, who supported the suppression of the Tiananmen movement because Mao had ordered that suppression. Not surprisingly, these dogmatists were scathingly criticised by the young people of Beijing, and under blows from both inside and outside the party they were soon defeated.

The criticisms of the party reformers and of the extra-party democratic movement were so well coordinated that both the dogmatists and many Western observers believed (groundlessly, as it happens) that this was a Maoist-style operation launched simultaneously from inside and outside the party. But whatever the similarities, the young people's struggle could no longer be directed by the Central Committee, unlike in 1966. Since April 1976, young people have learned to work for policy changes that are in line with their own interests.

Deng Xiaoping welcomed the democratic movement and even told Western reporters that 'the Chinese people need freedom, freedom!' and that 'we do not have the right to stop people putting up wall-posters'.

But some members of the democratic movement soon extended their criticism of the party dogmatists to the bureaucratic system as a whole, which is the ultimate source of dogmatism and Maoist autocracy. In the nineteenth century there were no professional revolutionaries in Communist movements, and revolutionaries earned their living like everyone else. This was in line with the Social Democratic policy of carrying on struggles within the confines of the law. At the beginning of this century Lenin, as part of his preparation for armed struggle, set up a vanguard party staffed by full-time revolutionaries. And he was right to do so, since the revolution could never succeed without people who were prepared to devote their whole time and energy to it. But every thesis has its antithesis. After the victory of the revolution, the question arose of what to do with the professional revolutionaries. Lenin died before he could answer this question adequately. But it is well known that Lenin wanted elections along the lines of the Paris Commune, so that no one would be allowed to occupy a post permanently, however great his or her contribution to the revolution. If this principle is not followed, there is nothing to distinguish a Communist revolution from a peasant one. Unfortunately, under Stalin's influence the group of professional revolutionaries became life-long bureaucrats, first in Russia and then in China, thus ensuring the reproduction of a new generation of bureaucrats.

However, two kinds of Communists must be distinguished. First, there are those who dislike bureaucracy and who dislike belonging to the bureaucratic system. They see bureaucracy as something contrary to the socialist convictions to which they commit their lives. They fight ceaselessly against the growth of bureaucracy and autocracy in the party. These are the party's democratic reformers. Then there are those who, having tasted victory and won high office, gradually began to search for ways of securing the system from which they benefit. To be fair, most of them started out as sincere revolutionaries. But now the general welfare of the people is secondary to them, and they lack firm principles. In the party struggle, they bend before the strongest wind. These are the opportunist bureaucrats.

The opportunist bureaucrats were purged along with the democratic reformers during the upheavals of the Cultural Revolution. They had not much liking for Mao and the Red Guards, and they were jealous of upstarts like Jiang Qing. When they regained their former positions after the fall of the Gang of Four, they were in a hurry to make up for their losses over the previous ten years. So when they saw the young people of the extra-party democratic movement daring to criticise the bureaucracy, they became angry and worried, and wanted to close the movement down.

In the democratic movement too there were some disturbing developments. Some young people misunderstood the reasons for the disasters of recent years, and put the blame on marxism.

Moved by the misery around them, they demanded that the party immediately realise their wishes, or they would overthrow it. The many social problems inherited from the Mao era are fertile soil for adventurism. The democratic youth movement that had spread throughout China was in danger of being closed down as a result of a few subversive incidents to which the people were opposed.

In these circumstances, Deng Xiaoping decided to put out a warning. He ordered a severe sentence on the dissident leader Wei Jingsheng. Some people criticise Deng for sentencing Wei Jingsheng simply for having spoken up. I disagree. Deng's main problem was how to keep the situation under control after a long period of repression. Both history and common sense show that social upheavals that are too radical often alienate the people.

But in another sense Deng Xiaoping was undoubtedly in the wrong. With undisguised contempt, he refused to distinguish between the different sorts of democratic activists. He forgot that in the darkest night most of them had openly come out in his support and had even shed their blood for him. In banning wall-posters he said that 'the Four Freedoms never did any good'. This remark broke many hearts. Will today's youth, remembering the Four Freedoms that Mao gave them, support a revival of the Gang of Four? Perhaps Deng Xiaoping did not give sufficient thought to whether or not he had the support of the 'thinking generation'. Some day, when he sees his reforms jeopardised by the opportunist bureaucrats in the party, he may have reason to regret that.

If the aim of the dogmatists is to 'protect the Cultural Revolution', then the aim of the opportunist bureaucrats is to go back to the days before the Cultural Revolution. They don't want reforms, they only want safe jobs. Before the Cultural Revolution they had just that, and were under no threat whatsoever.

But China can no longer afford a policy of stagnation and seclusion. China must throw open its doors to the outside world if it is to become developed. If China is still propelled by the engine of bureaucracy, it is bound to capsize in the waves of world competition. The bureaucratic machine is in bad repair. It is wasteful and inefficient, and the officials who run it are alarmingly ignorant and incapable of coping with the immensely expensive foreign technology that they have been importing over the last three years. The national economy is in grave crisis. Khrushchev's political career was cut short by the wheels of the bureaucratic machine. Khrushchev did try to change things here and there, but he never touched the basic machinery of the bureaucracy. It seems as if all reforms in Eastern countries are doomed to fall at this second hurdle.

Should we retreat to a policy of isolation? The opportunist bureaucrats would like to do precisely that. But the people want to go forward, to dissolve the bureaucratic system completely and to achieve the Four Modernisations. Retreat would mean the failure of modernisation and the defeat of the party reformers; which is precisely what the dogmatists want.

The Central Committee, now led by the reformers, has already taken the first step towards overhauling the bureaucratic system. It has scrapped jobs-for-life, and it has permitted elections and workers' councils. It has investigated the Baoshan Iron and Steel Works [which was assigned a construction site in the middle of quicksands] and even put those responsible for the Bohai II disaster [a notorious accident where 72 people died] up before the courts. All these measures have unsettled the opportunist bureaucrats, who are preparing for the worst and grabbing what they can while they can. Their active interference in the elections is further proof of their hatred for democracy. But by doing these things they are simply stoking up even more resentment among the people, and thus hastening their own downfall.

But the opportunists are bound to unite in defence of their power. When the pragmatists defeated the dogmatists, the opportunists stood by with folded arms, since that struggle did not touch their vital interests. Even if ninety-nine of Mao's hundred principles were discarded it would matter to them not one jot. But now their privileges are threatened, they too rally to the great banner of Mao Zedong.

The party reformers should understand that if they duck an open and scientific discussion of events and experience since the CPSU's Twentieth Congress, especially the failure of Khrushchev's reforms, then some day they will be attacked as Chinese Khrushchevs by the joint armies of dogmatism and opportunism. This struggle has not yet come, but it will come. 'The wind will not subside just because the tree is tired.' Human will cannot avert class struggle. But when the struggle comes, the party reformers, the young democrats and the Chinese people will once again join hands.

Postscript

Dear Comrade Jin Jun,

A year ago I received your letter headed 'The Precious Thoughts of the Older Mao Zedong'. This essay is a belated reply to it. I first thought of writing such an essay in 1969, when the Cultural Revolution was being wound up and peace was returning. So many of my comrades had died that I felt I owed it to them to elucidate the causes and consequences of the Cultural Revolution. Surely they could not have died for nothing? With this essay I repay my debt to them.

The writings of Yang Xiguang, leader of Hunan's Shengwulian group in the Cultural Revolution, gave me valuable insights. Yang was the precursor of the 'thinking generation'. But I never quite agreed with his social and political analysis. He thought that Zhou Enlai represented the conservative bureaucrats and that Mao and Lin Biao were radical revolutionaries. But if so, then why did people hate Lin Biao and look back fondly to when the 'capitalist roaders' were in power? I asked this very question in discussions with friends, and for doing so I was subsequently charged and persecuted.

I was accused among other things of 'opposing Mao Zedong Thought', like everyone else who fell foul of the political authorities in those days. But actually I was then quite loyal to Mao and always tried to see him in the best light. In 1973, when I wrote *On Socialist Democracy and the Legal System*, my attitude to Mao was like yours is now. But events revealed Mao's true nature. In the face of mounting evidence, I resolved to thoroughly reassess my past positions.

My present views on Mao are shared by only a minority of people, even in unofficial circles. Perhaps I will be severely criticised or even suffer another disaster as a result, but that is a risk I am prepared to take. Deliberate vagueness would be the more discreet course, but it is not the style of a marxist.

Some people may say that I am too optimistic about the party reformers, and that Deng Xiaoping, Mao and the Gang of Four are all equally bureaucrats and therefore equally incapable of initiating a thorough reform. But my optimism stems from my belief that the CCP is not just a petty-bourgeois or a peasant party, but that it is imbued with a revolutionary ideology, marxism. We have already seen what an enormous influence ideology or tradition can have on a society, a nation or a political community. Even though being determines consciousness, being can never be reduced to mere economics.

The party reformers know that China's present economic system is irrational and inefficient, and that it is bound to disintegrate under the impact of international capital. Moreover, the reformers have been oppressed for twenty years. They have lived close to the people, and know their sufferings. Therefore they are more determined than Communist reformers in other countries to make a thorough reform, and have an exceptionally wide basis of support. In today's China, is there any organised political force outside the Communist party that could carry out thorough reform? I don't think so.

I am criticised for viewing the Cultural Revolution through the eyes of a sentimental petty bourgeois, and for not understanding that it was the product of acute social contradictions. But today millions of former Red Guards are convinced that the Cultural Revolution was a fraud perpetrated by Mao rather than a genuine rising against oppression. Was beating up school teachers 'the product of acute social contradictions'? Is that why students criticised officials for not letting them read Mao, or for protecting intellectuals? Was it because of 'acute social contradictions' that fanatical Red Guards burned books (but not Mao's of course) and destroyed historical relics? Wherever the student movement won control strict censorship was enforced, on the pretext that the press was 'spreading rumours' and 'not propagating Mao Thought'. But whenever the workers organised, they turned out to be 'die-hard conservatives' in opposition to the students, and refused stubbornly to respond to the manipulations of a handful of malicious bureaucrats.

If the Cultural Revolution really was the product of acute

social contradictions and if Mao really was on the side of those oppressed by the bureaucrats, then why did Mao's support not grow as the movement quickened? In 1966 the Red Guards and some workers supported Mao. In 1974, at the time of the Movement to Criticise Lin Biao and Confucius, the former Red Guards and the workers were indifferent to Mao's appeal. When they finally did rebel, in 1976, it was against Mao, not for him.

In fact there were two Cultural Revolutions: Mao's, and the people's; and only the people's Cultural Revolution can be rightfully described as the product of acute social contradictions. The people's Cultural Revolution had its roots in the early sixties, when the party reformers began to relax the controls introduced by Mao's extremist regime in the late fifties, and when there was what people today describe as a golden age. This liberal interlude greatly hampered Mao's efforts to Stalinise the bureaucracy. The people's Cultural Revolution finally erupted in April 1976. It is continuing even today, and no one person could declare an end to it.

Nowadays many young theoreticians are writing letter after letter to convince me that Mao was a great Marxist. They claim that it is precisely because Mao saw so much wrong with Stalin that he began the Cultural Revolution. Clearly their minds are full of cobwebs. They should gather facts dispassionately and talk less carelessly.

With best wishes,
Xizhe

Notes

1. 'Talks at the Chengdu Conference', in *Mao Zedong sixiang wansui*. English translation in Stuart R. Schram, ed., *Mao Tse-tung Unrehearsed, Talks and Letters, 1956-71*, Harmondsworth: Penguin, 1974. (There are important and rather misleading omissions in Wang's quotation of Mao's remarks.)
2. 'Direction on the Great Cultural Revolution in Shanghai', in *Miscellany of Mao Tse-tung Thought*, p. 454.

Yi Ming

China: A History That Must Be Told...

Yi Ming's article is interesting for its analysis of the roots of the party's degeneration and the causes of its gradual alienation from the Chinese people. Like Wang Xizhe, Yi Ming thinks that it is wrong to reduce the Cultural Revolution to a political ploy by the Mao group, and that in some ways the Cultural Revolution was a genuine mass movement. He also makes the important point that there was as much continuity as there was change between Mao's regime and that of the 'revisionist' Liu Shaoqi, who is today revered as all-wise but who was a hate-figure for the Red Guards of the Cultural Revolution. It is not known who Yi Ming is, or what has been his fate.

This article, here abridged, was first published in *Renminzhi sheng* ('Voice of the People'), 8 July 1979.

The Cultural Revolution is dead, but it has left a deep mark on our people. Millions of China's sons and daughters died during that immense mobilisation and we must analyse its causes and look for its deeper source rather than content ourselves with blaming individuals...

During the war years enemy pressure forced us to correct mistakes quickly and to replace the leaders responsible for them. But after 1949 there was no longer anyone to pressure us, so that over the years a left opportunist line developed and spread. More than once it damaged the party's gains, and finally it led to the catastrophe of the Cultural Revolution... Immediately after liberation there were two different points of view in the party. One current, represented by Liu Shaoqi and Bo Yibo, favoured the consolidation of new democracy and based itself on Lenin's theory of state capitalism... Its supporters thought that in an economically backward country like China the proletariat in power could and should let capitalism develop within the limits of law in order to gradually build up the bases for socialism. The other current, which was utopian socialist, advocated peasant egalitarianism. Its supporters saw that the economy was being progressively rehabilitated and that a section of the peasantry was beginning to enrich itself and regain pre-war living standards. They argued that the classes were polarising, the workers and peasants' alliance was in danger, and the rich peasant line was winning out...

The struggle between these two groups ended in compromise. The party decided that there would be a fifteen-year period of transition during which China would be industrialised and there would be a socialist transformation of capitalist agriculture, handicrafts and trade. But this line was quickly pushed aside by the ultra-leftists... In 1955, 500 million peasants were collectivised. Ration coupons were introduced, and the number of coupons required grew daily... Before the lower-stage agricultural cooperatives had had time to stabilise, they were transformed into higher-stage ones: by 1957 tasks that were supposed to take fifteen years to accomplish were done in less than four... Although class struggle largely died out after the main socialist transformations and collectivisation had been carried out, the left opportunists began for their own purposes to falsify the doctrine of 'class struggle'. They made no effort to use democratic methods in the ideological field, and refused to use discussion as a means of advancing marxism and overcoming differences. Instead, they... resorted to repression, pinning the 'rightist' label on oppositionists and sending them off for labour reform. Thus they not only struck at the elite (millions of intellectuals) but helped create a favourable climate for the Great Leap Forward. After this, no one dared speak the truth inside or outside the party.

After liberation we threw away the chance to establish relations with the Western countries, and leant towards the Soviet Union instead. This was not intelligent, but at least with Soviet aid we achieved the economic goals set by the first Five-Year Plan. Under Zhou Enlai and Chen Yun the economy grew at an annual rate of 10.9 per cent (18 per cent in industry, 4.5 per cent in agriculture) between 1953 and 1957. But then came the Soviet condemnation of Stalin's mistakes, and our confidence in 'big brother' disappeared. The traditional idea of 'greater China' began to flower again.

As a result, strictly Chinese inventions like the Great Leap Forward and the People's Communes began to mushroom on all sides, and party journals began to fantasise about one *mou* of land producing ten thousand *jin* of rice, or about reaching Communism after one year's hard struggle... Of course, not everyone had gone mad; some simply kept quiet because they were interested in saving their skins. Only Peng Dehuai dared speak the truth, but he was got out of the way...

As a result of the left line food output fell from 250 million tons in 1958 to 150 million in 1959. In 1960 it fell by another 12.6 per cent and by 1962 it was a further 2.4 per cent down. In 1961 industrial production fell by 38 per cent and in 1962 by a further 16.6 per cent. Twenty million workers lost their jobs and were sent back to the villages. More than one hundred million people suffered malnutrition.

Faced with this crisis, the ultra-leftists were forced for a time to withdraw. For a few months, it seemed that democracy was re-established and that cultural life was freer. Under 'rightist' direction the economy began to revive... But in the second half of 1962 the leftists returned to the attack... and at the Ninth Congress in 1969 they got their political programme accepted. They had finally established their feudal overlordship. They had reached the pinnacle of their power, and were thus in position for their downfall.

Reading Comrade Mao's letter to Jiang Qing [criticising Lin Biao] and his conversation with Edgar Snow, it is easy to see that he disliked the cult of the personality. He knew that it was not materialist and that it was against party principles. But he still considered it an effective weapon in the factional struggle. History has shown that Lin Biao and the Gang of Four took advantage of this to pursue their own ends.

It is not possible to advance history by relying on people's superstitions and backwardness. Nor is it possible to consolidate the party's gains if you damage democracy within it. Our party is made up mainly of peasants and petty bourgeois. It lacks the democratic life (from the bottom to the top) of the Bolsheviks, and its regime is even further removed from that of the original marxist organisations in the West. To lead the revolution it had to fuse marxism with traditional Chinese culture. But since feudal society has no democratic or humanist traditions, this aspect of marxism was neglected...

The democracy of the Yanan period is a model in our party's history, but even it was not entirely healthy. Some educated youth with more definite ideas about democracy were shocked and discouraged when they went to Yanan from the White areas and found veteran cadres enjoying the pleasures of the dance floor and chasing the women students. [See Wang Shiwei's article below, pp179-86.] When they voiced their discontent they were denounced as spies and counter-revolutionaries. These people were the forerunners of millions of others since denounced on the same charges.

It was the rule in old China that 'the winner is king and the loser is a bandit'. This attitude stayed deeply rooted in the party. After some of Mao's views were proved to be correct, he was widely flattered as the people's 'saviour'. Even Comrade Liu Shaoqi flattered him. When he drew up the Constitution and the party statutes, he included references to named leaders.

Khrushchev's revelation of Stalin's mistakes deeply shocked our party. Shortly after it Comrade Deng Xiaoping made a report in the leadership's name in which he stressed the need to combat the personality cult, and at the Eighth Congress individual leaders' name were removed from the party statutes. But after the Sino-Soviet split these changes were reversed, on the principle that 'what our enemy defends, we must denounce'... Narrow nationalism distorted the thinking of some comrades, and the anti-marxists took advantage of this. After 1960 Lin Biao wore the title of Chairman Mao's 'star pupil' on his chest in order to peddle his voluntarist schemes and promote the idea of 'absolute authority'. According to the information available, there was very little resistance before the Cultural Revolution to the excesses of 'Lin Biao thought', except for some disapproving comments by Deng Xiaoping, Lu Dingyi and Luo Ruiqing.

For a long time, many older comrades did not understand the need for democracy in the party. They made no effort or sacrifice to achieve it (except for Peng Dehuai, who was far-sighted). They thought that the personality cult could protect the party, and thus they helped prepare public opinion for Lin Biao's counter-revolution. They woke up when disaster struck, but by then it was too late...

Today there is a tendency to make a sharp distinction between eleven years after liberation [i.e. the end of the Great Leap Forward] and seventeen years after [when the Cultural Revolution began]. According to this view, seventeen years after was heaven, and eleven years after was hell. But this view is ahistorical, and deliberately tries to cover up the link between the two periods.

No one could create the Cultural Revolution on their own, and that goes both for the glorious Mao Zedong and for the Gang of Four. History is always written by the people, whether it is the April Fifth Movement of 1976 or the Cultural Revolution. Clearly, without the support or passive acquiescence of the majority of youth and citizens, the Gang of Four and Lin Biao would never have been able to take on the party as a whole.

In the twenty eight years between [the CCP's foundation in] 1921 and [its taking power in] 1949, the Chinese people got to know it as a firm, honest and courageous fighting force that represented hope for the future... They therefore willingly gave it their support. These qualities of the party were forged in prisons and on the battle-field. After 1949 the party became a fount of honours and social rank, and some members became degenerate as a result of flattery. But the Three Anti's campaign of 1951-52 rooted out much of this corruption, and saved the party's honour.

By 1957 the party had been in power for eight years and it was becoming increasingly difficult to combat bureacracy and corruption simply through ideological re-education. So the party appealed to the people to rectify it from the outside. This measure was very popular, but it was soon rescinded. Those who had responded to the party's appeal for criticism were labelled 'rightists' and sent for labour reform. So the cadres, far from improving their behaviour, grew even more arrogant. Now they could say: 'Anyone who dares touch me is against the party.'

The main targets of the 'anti-rightist' campaign were the intellectuals and most workers and peasants were not yet affected, but nevertheless the tie between the party and the people disappeared, and people deliberately avoided the party. Between 1958 and 1962 the party's honour was fatally damaged as cadres became more and more corrupt, violent, dishonest and deceitful. Now it was the workers and peasants' turn to suffer... They continued to support the party, even though their confidence in it was shaken... But the leadership took no measures to resolve these problems, and instead simply tried to pin the blame on the rank and file. Successive political mobilisations only widened the gap between the cadres and the people, and between the party and the people.

At the same time the party launched the anti-revisionist movement internationally, even though the people were not familiar with the situation in the Soviet Union.

In China the cadres, worn out by the 'two-line struggle', felt their revolutionary determination faltering. They were getting older, and they were no longer concerned with the interests of the people, but were concerned only with their own privileges.

The younger generation, which was not fully informed, was blaming the bureaucrats for the disasters of the previous few years. Young people put all their hope in 'absolute authorities'... They wanted to destroy the bureaucratic caste so that they could develop their knowledge and intelligence. So they tried to carry the fight against 'revisionism' from the international to the domestic sphere...

In 1966 people felt a certain distaste, even contempt, for the 'seventeen years', especially the last nine of them. The people dreamed of something better, although they did not yet know what. And so Lin Biao, Chen Boda, Kang Sheng and Jiang Qing, taking advantage of the prestige of the Great Helmsman, could offer the Cultural Revolution as a panacea. History knows many similar episodes. The French king linked with the citizens in order to weaken the aristocrats who were threatening his throne. The Cultural Revolution Group relied on the Red Guards to destroy the structures of the party.

During the Cultural Revolution the people educated themselves. They learned through experience that the new authorities were a hundred times harsher than the old, that 'eleven years are not as good as seventeen', and that the revival of feudalism is a much more real danger in China than the rebirth of capitalism.

Combating corrupt officials will not solve society's problems. Superstition and anarchy are no match for the bureaucracy and the privileged class. Only democracy and a socialist legal system can bring the Four Modernisations to China and ensure it a brilliant future. We must draw deep inspiration from the experience of the last thirty years, firmly follow the path of marxism, and advance boldly under the correct leadership of the Chinese Communist Party.

Wei Jingsheng

Democracy or a New Dictatorship

Wei Jingsheng, who is in his early thirties, worked as an electrician at Beijing Zoo while continuing his studies at Beijing University. He was born in Anhui Province in Central China. He was editor of *Tansuo* ('Explorations') and author of a famous article titled 'Democracy, the Fifth Modernisation'. As a result of his writings, and the persecution they brought him, he became China's best-known dissident both at home and abroad. But he was hardly typical of the democratic movement. He was the most right-wing of its better-known activists, and few other dissidents shared his view that the main source of socialist totalitarianism and of China's 'poisoning' is the philosophy of Marx.

In mid-March 1979 the Chinese authorities began criticising people who were advocating an 'individualistic' philosophy and announced restrictions on the democratic movement. In Beijing the municipal authorities decided to ban posters and publications 'opposed to socialism and to party leadership'. Wei Jingsheng was arrested on 29 March, a day before these restrictions were announced. Six months later he was tried and sentenced to fifteen years' imprisonment after a show-trial from which his friends and family were excluded. Wei's publishing activities were described as 'counter-revolutionary'. He was also charged with giving 'military secrets' to a foreigner, but the information he was said to have given was common knowledge at the time, according to foreign sources. Wei is now being held in Beijing Prison No. 1. He is said to be confined to his cell at all times and not to be allowed visits even from his family.

This article was first published in a special issue of 'Explorations' in March 1979. This translation by John Scott and Pamela Barnsley first appeared in slightly different form in *Harpers and Queen* (March 1980). The article was cited by the prosecution at Wei's trial as an 'incitement to overthrow the dictatorship of the proletariat' and as an example of 'counter-revolutionary agitation and propaganda'.

Everyone in China knows that the Chinese social system is not democratic and that this lack of democracy has severely stunted every aspect of the country's social development over the past 30 years. In the face of this hard fact there are two choices before the Chinese people. Either to reform the social system if they want to develop their society and seek a swift increase in prosperity and economic resources; or, if they are content with a continuation of the Mao Zedong brand of proletarian dictatorship, then they cannot even talk of democracy, nor will they be able to realise the modernisation of their lives and resources...

Where is China heading and in what sort of society do the people hope to live and work?

The answer can be seen in the mood of the majority. It is this mood that brought about the present democratic movement. With the denial of Mao Zedong's style of dictatorship as its very prerequisite, the aim of this movement is to reform the social system and thereby enable the Chinese people to increase production and develop their lives to the full in a democratic social environment. This aim is not just the aim of a few isolated individuals but represents a whole trend in the development of Chinese society... Those who doubt this need only recall the April Fifth Movement in 1976, for those who were judged by the court in the minds of the people then, even when they were some of the most powerful in the country, have not escaped its ultimate verdict.

But are there people who remain unafraid of such a judgment? Of course there are — and more than a few of them. Several of those at the top who are drunk with wielding power often forget such niceties as the people's judgment, and others out of personal ambition and despotic inclinations abuse people's credulity. For example, the speech that Vice-Premier Deng Xiaoping made to leading cadres of the Central Committee on 16 March (1979) was an attempt to take advantage of the people's past confidence in him to oppose the democratic movement itself. He levelled all sorts of charges at the democratic movement and tried to lay on it the blame for the failure of China's production and economy when it was Hua and Deng's political system that was at fault. Thus the people are made scapegoats for the failure of their leaders' policies. Does Deng Xiaoping really deserve the people's trust? No political leaders have a right to expect the people's unconditional trust. If they carry out policies beneficial to the people along the road to peace and prosperity, then we should trust them. Our trust in them is for their policies and the means to apply these policies. Should they carry out policies harmful to the people's interests, the path they are treading is a dictator's path and should be opposed. The people are as much opposed to this path as they are to measures harmful to their interests and to policies undermining their legitimate rights. According to the principles of democracy, any authority must give way to opposition from the people.

But Deng Xiaoping does not give way. When the people are demanding a widespread inquiry into the reasons for China's backwardness over the last 30 years and into Mao Zedong's crimes, Deng is the first to declare: 'With no Mao Zedong there would be no New China.' In his speech he even flattered Mao Zedong's ghost when he called him 'the banner of the Chinese people' and claimed that Mao's weaknesses and mistakes were so insignificant as to be unworthy of mention.

Is he afraid that an investigation into Mao's mistakes would lead to an investigation into Mao's collaborators? Or is Deng simply preparing to continue the Mao Zedong brand of dictatorial socialist government? If the former, then Deng has nothing to fear, since the tolerance of the Chinese people is great enough to forgive him his past mistakes provided that he now leads the country towards democracy and prosperity. But if the latter, we will never forgive him, even if recently he has been the best of the leaders. If his aim is to continue the Mao Zedong style of dictatorship, his course of action can only lead to economic ruin and the abuse of the people's interests. Anyone forgiving such a criminal would be indirectly guilty of crimes against the people.

Does Deng Xiaoping want democracy? No, he does not. He is unwilling to comprehend the misery of the common people. He is unwilling to allow the people to regain those powers usurped by ambitious careerists. He describes the struggle for democratic rights — a movement launched spontaneously by the people — as the actions of troublemakers who must be repressed. To resort to such measures to deal with people who criticise mistaken policies and demand social development shows that the government is very afraid of this popular movement.

We cannot help asking Mr Deng what his idea of democracy is. If the people have no right to express their opinions and criticisms, then how can one talk of democracy? If his idea of democracy is one that does not allow others to criticise those in power, then how is such a democracy different from Mao Zedong's tyranny concealed behind the slogan 'The Democracy of the Dictatorship of the Proletariat'?

The people want to appeal against injustice, want to vent their grievances and want democracy, so they hold meetings. The people oppose famine and dictatorship, so they demonstrate. This shows that without democracy their very livelihood lacks any safeguard. Is it possible, when the people are so much at the mercy of others, that such a situation can be called 'normal public order'? If 'normal public order' gives dictators the right to wreak havoc with the people's interests, then does it benefit the careerists or the people to safeguard such an order? Is the answer not painfully obvious? We consider that normal public order is not total uniformity; particularly in politics, where there must be a great diversity of opinion. When there are no divergent opinions, no discussion and no publications, then it is clear that there is a dictatorship. Total uniformity must surely be called 'abnormal order'. When social phenomena are interpreted as the occasion for criminal elements to make trouble and are used as an excuse to do away with the people's right to express their opinions, this is the time-honoured practice of fascist dictators both new and old. Remember the Tiananmen Square incident, when the Gang of Four used the fact that certain people had burnt cars as an excuse to crush the popular revolutionary movement. Above all the people should be forever wary of placing unqualified trust in any one ruler.

The people should ensure that Deng Xiaoping does not degenerate into a dictator. After he was reinstated in 1975, it seemed he was unwilling to follow Mao Zedong's dictatorial system and would instead care for the interests of the people. So the people eagerly looked up to him in the hope that he would realise their aspirations. They were even ready to shed their blood for him — as the Tiananmen Square incident showed. But was such support vested in his person alone? Certainly not. If he now wants to discard his mask and take steps to suppress the democratic movement then he certainly does not merit the people's trust and support. From his behaviour it is clear that he is neither concerned with democracy nor does he any longer protect the people's interests. By deceiving the people to win their confidence he is following the path to dictatorship.

It has been demonstrated countless times throughout China's history that once the confidence of the people has been gained by deception, the dictators work without restraint — for as the ancients said: 'He who can win the people's minds, can win the empire.' Once masters of the nation, their private interests inevitably conflict with those of the people, and they must use repression against those who are struggling for the interests of the people themselves. So the crux of the matter is not who becomes master of the nation, but rather that the people must maintain firm control over their own nation, for this is the very essence of democracy. People entrusted with government positions must be controlled by and responsible to the people. According to the Constitution, organisations and individuals in the administration must be elected by the people, empowered and controlled by an elected government under the supervision of the people and responsible to the people: only then is there a legality for executive powers.

We would like to ask the high officials who instigate the arrest of individuals — is the power you exercise legal? We would like to ask Chairman Hua and Vice-Chairman Deng — is your occupation of the highest offices of state legal? We would like to know why it is the Vice-Chairman and the Vice-Premier and not the courts or organisations representing the people who announce who is to be arrested. Is this legal? According to Chinese law, is a 'bad element' a criminal per se? And on whose judgement is such a criterion made? If these simple questions are not clearly answered there is no point in talking about rule by law in China.

History shows that there must be a limit to the amount of trust conferred upon any individual. Anyone seeking the unconditional trust of the people is a person of unbridled ambition. The important problem is to select the right sort of person to put one's trust in, and even more important is how such a person is to be supervised in carrying out the will of the majority... We can only trust those representatives who are supervised by us and responsible to us. Such representatives should be chosen by us and not thrust upon us...

Only a genuine general election can create a government and leaders ready to serve the interests of the electorate. If the government and its leaders are truly subject to the people's mandate and supervision those two afflictions that leadership is prone to — personal ambition and megalomania — can be avoided. No one should blame leaders for being prone to power fever. Nor should we blame the people for not daring to strike a blow in their own interests. This may happen because we are without a social system in which a wise people supervises and counterbalances equally wise and worthy officials.

Furthering reforms within the social system and moving Chinese politics towards democracy are prerequisites for solving the social and economic problems that confront China today. Only through elections can the leadership gain the people's voluntary cooperation and bring their initiative into play. Only when the people enjoy complete freedom and expression can they help their leaders to analyse and solve problems. Cooperation, together with policies formulated and carried out by the people, are necessary for the highest degree of working efficiency and the achievement of ideal results.

This is the only road along which China can make progress. Under present-day conditions, it is an extremely difficult path.

Interview with Xu Wenli

Xu Wenli, the son of a doctor, is married and in his early thirties. After leaving the army in 1963, he became a maintenance electrician in a Beijing factory. In 1979 he and Liu Qing founded *Siwu luntan* ('April Fifth Forum') whose title commemorates the demonstrations of 5 April 1976 in Beijing's Tiananmen Square. 'April Fifth Forum' became the most influential and widely published unofficial journal in North China. In November 1979 Liu Qing was arrested (see below, pp. 135-56) but Xu continued to publish the journal until the spring of 1980, despite the government ban. Sources in Hongkong say that Xu appealed to the authorities about Liu Qing on 10 January 1981. Liu Qing himself had been arrested for questioning the arrest of another dissident, Wei Jingsheng. Xu Wenli was arrested at midnight on 10 April 1981.

This interview, here excerpted, is by Alain Jacob of *Le Monde*. It was first published on 6 February 1980.

Xu Wenli lives with his family in two small rooms, where he received us. Visitors of all ages knocked at the door during the interview, some asking for the latest issue of the journal and others to take part in the conversation or listen to it.

Xu Wenli vigorously rejects the charges levelled at the democratic movement because of its contacts with foreigners. 'We are all patriots', he said. 'Many had the chance to emigrate but didn't, because they want to devote themselves to building the country.' Xu Wenli is shocked at the suggestion of 'manipulation by foreign agents', which he regards as a sign of Soviet-type thinking. He said: 'There are elements close to the Soviet Union within the CCP. They disapprove of Soviet foreign policy but think that Soviet domestic policy is just and socialist. We do not deny that from Stalin to Khrushchev and Brezhnev the Soviets have made economic progress, and that some reforms might be seen as constructive. But these reforms have not changed relations between the bureaucracy and the masses. Domestically there are no forces capable of opposing the Soviet bureaucracy's expansionist foreign policy. Oppression by the bureaucrats and the technocrats is preventing the Soviet masses from expressing their views on this question. Naturally, no-one in China supports Soviet foreign policy. But since our whole system stems from the Soviet Union, the same system is still in force here. So who can guarantee that China will not one day become hegemonistic too? We should oppose not only Soviet overseas aggression, but also the Soviet system's internal anti-democratic practices.'

After this statement, Xu Wenli answered our questions. He is 36-years old, married with a seven-year old daughter, and an electrician — 'not a technician or engineer', he specified. He was born in Anhui Province, son of a doctor and great-grandson of an official in the old regime. After finishing his secondary education he joined the army and was therefore not a Red Guard during the Cultural Revolution. He said he could have gone to university but preferred to pursue his own studies. I asked him the following more general questions.

What is the present state of the democratic movement?

Since the suppression of Democracy Wall and the sentencing of Wei Jingsheng the movement has been curbed. Many young people were deeply wounded by what happened, and their enthusiasm has been crushed. Publications are becoming rare, but at the same time some new publications are appearing in the provinces (in Anyang, Baoding and Shanghai). Although people don't dare express their views freely, they don't believe that the movement can be completely suppressed. After developing in the open, it has gone underground...

You deny that you are dissidents like in the Soviet Union. How do you define your relationship to the regime and to the CCP?

In China most young people in the democratic movement have a basically marxist viewpoint. We want to make China a democratic and socialist country. From a theoretical standpoint, our aims are the same as the CCP's. The democratic movement is formed by young workers and intellectuals, while in the Soviet Union the dissidents are famous intellectuals. Nonetheless the aim of the young people in the democratic movement is humanitarian socialism, and so they have some points in common with certain movements in the Soviet Union and with the Eurocommunists. But I don't like the word 'dissident', which means 'enemy' in Chinese.

You have pictures of Zhou Enlai and Mao Zedong in your room. What is your assessment of Mao?

Opinions in our movement differ on this question. Personally, I think Mao was a great man but that he made serious mistakes. These mistakes result in large part from the fact that he was born among peasants. This tendency is not exclusive to Mao, it's found throughout the party. I agree with the view that Mao's policy was correct up to the Eighth Congress of 1956. But a large part of his later work was already forshadowed in his thinking even then.

What are the main obstacles to democracy in China?

The main obstacles are economic. Political democracy presupposes economic competition. For example, if you don't like your newspaper, you can buy another one. Not in China. Here, individual autonomy is very limited. The people have to eat and cannot rock the boat too much. However, competition here would not necessarily be the same as in the capitalist countries. In the Chinese society of the future it will be limited by the state plan.

Is the low level of education of China's 800 million peasants not also an obstacle to democracy?

Yes, but the peasants have a spontaneous leaning towards democracy. For the past twenty years they have opposed several centralising stages in agricultural policy. The leaders are aware of that, and that is why they are now agreeing to extend the peasants' autonomy.

What are the similarities between the Chinese and Soviet systems?

This is a heavy burden for the democratic movement. It will take several generations to achieve scientific and democratic socialism. At present we are paving the way for the future. This is necessary in all spheres. It is vital to prepare the ground.

What are the most serious violations of human rights in China today?

China is very sensitive about this question at the moment. Deng Xiaoping refused to discuss it when he was in the United States. The situation now has nothing in common with the one under the Gang of Four. However, I prefer to talk of 'civil rights', since if you say 'human rights' you are regarded as an agent of Carter. Some people say that the main thing now is to work to modernise China; and that there will be time to discuss civil rights after that. For the time being we should not bother about affairs of state. But in that case, how could the people express their power? Is the aim to turn the Chinese into conveyor-belt workers like in Chaplin's *Modern Times*? What then would be the point of human intelligence? Ever since there has been a more open policy towards the outside world, Chinese intellectuals have been able to go abroad. Many have not come back. That is a very clear sign. A person who cannot think freely feels wounded. Only a minority are allowed to express their views. It is impossible to modernise the country unless you let the intelligence of a thousand million individuals unfold. So the problem of freedom of thought is more serious than that of physical attacks on people, although it is true that such attacks are very widespread in the countryside... Carter is not going to solve this problem. We must rely on the Chinese people themselves to do it.

Much is said about cadres' privileges. Is this an important problem? Can it be solved by the present campaign?

The problem of privileges is a major obstacle to the country's modernisation and to the movement for democracy. The leaders are aware of that. But this problem cannot be solved by directives. For instance a recent ruling says that those who use official cars for private purposes must pay. But what driver would dare to ask his boss for money? This is a typically stupid decision.

It is wrong to say that all society's faults are due to the Gang of Four. It's like the mother of an extremely ugly child denying she gave birth to it... What produced the problem of privileges? Partly it's a carry-over from the old society, but above all it's due to the present system. If our cadres are dismissed, they have no redress. So they take care to protect their personal power in order to safeguard their private interests... Cadres must be replaced and monitored by the people, and if they are sacked they must be able to find another job. Like teachers, for instance, or like Mr Kissinger. But if privileges grow, there is a risk of a serious popular back-lash. Take housing, for instance; a department chief with a small family has an apartment of seventy to eighty square metres. But workers sometimes live, boys and girls together, as many as ten to a room no bigger than that.

Several newspapers have mentioned a 'crisis of conviction' and a 'crisis of confidence' among the people. Why is this?

There is such a crisis, and it affects not only young people. I don't think this crisis is such a bad thing, since it is bringing about a reappraisal. The main reason for it is that in the past many projects were not carried out. This is not only true of China. Other socialist countries have also met enormous problems in building up their societies. Things have been drifting since the fall of the Gang of Four. People are better informed about the outside world and are inevitably asking questions. It is repeatedly said that Marxism-Leninism-Mao Zedong Thought set out the most correct path, but how can people help doubting this? It is vital to examine the faults of the system, even those of Marxism-Leninism. The Eurocommunists have encountered this problem in seeking solutions appropriate to conditions in their own countries. If the Italians Communists had not made these changes, they would never have got so much influence.

Does this crisis not also have a moral aspect?

Some moral crises are necessary. It is useful to make people understand that practices like 'getting in by the back door' must be eliminated, since otherwise cadres who resort to them will no longer inspire confidence. Privileges are the cause of the moral crisis. If it were not for these privileges, people would be less inclined to seek influential friends. However, the circle of privileged people has grown quantitatively since the fall of the Gang of Four.

Xu Wenli

A Reform Programme for the Eighties

Xu Wenli drew up this programme in the autumn of 1980. It brings together in one place a whole series of reform proposals raised at different times and in different places by supporters of the democratic movement. Wojtek Zafanolli, writing in *Esprit*, where this text was first made available outside China, draws a telling parallel between Xu and the Qing dynasty reformer Kang Youwei. Just as Kang tried to save the declining imperial system by urging it to modernise and democratise its institutions, so Xu urges the party to renew its mandate by carrying out fundamental political and economic reforms. Certain of Xu's proposals are even directly inspired by Kang's programme.

Chinese society has reached a critical point in its history, and further progress is only possible at the price of a thoroughgoing political reform...

The democratic socialist movement that grew up in late 1978 across China and whose main components are the young workers, the democratic ferment at the Third Plenum of the Fifth National People's Congress (NPC) and the Fifth Consultative Political Conference (CPC), and the movement now developing around the student elections shows that the desire of the younger generation for national renewal is irrepressible.

There can be no doubt that China must change. Head-in-the-sand conservatism will not resolve our problems, and nor will tinkering with the system.

The issue boils down to this. What road should the reform movement take? Should it be from above, from below, or both?

At present reform from below must be ruled out, since the Chinese people will tolerate no more public disorder. On the other hand, history shows that the bureaucratic resistance of the old structures will prove too strong for a movement that relies entirely on forces for change at the top. So only a combination of reforms from above and from below can be really effective.

The management of our affairs can no longer be left to a tiny minority. Government must hand power back to the people. The reform process must become an occasion for uniting and strengthening the nation.

Therefore, despite their rough and ready nature, I am presenting these few proposals on reform for the consideration of the Central Committee (CC), the NPC, the CPC, the State Council and the Chinese people as a whole.

1. The general elections now taking place at *xian* and *qu* level are undemocratic and should be annulled. The Twelfth Congress of the Chinese Communist Party (CCP) as well as the Sixth NPC and the Sixth CPC should be adjourned.

The point of democratic consultation is that the power to select candidates should lie with the electors. But in the present elections this right has been withdrawn. Our electoral law is unscientific. Our society has no tradition of democracy. We lack experience of democratic consultation. Above all, antidemocratic forces have interfered with and sabotaged the elections. The result is that in most places the electors have not even had a chance to meet the official candidates, let alone to ask them questions or give their own opinions. So these candidates can in no sense be said to have received a mandate, since they have not even bothered to explain their political programme (which they could easily have done during their free time). In fact the campaign was carried out not by the candidates but by officials of the electoral commissions.

Moreover, in many places normal electoral competition was suppressed. This is not true democracy. The right to vote is a right, not a favour, and it must be exercised without constraints. Otherwise we have only a parody of elections, amounting to authoritarian rule under another guise.

We must use democratic electoral campaigning as a scientific method for promoting social progress. We must abolish the pyramidical structures we inherited from feudalism, by which officials are responsible to their superiors but never to the people. These structures mean that political rights are stratified according to social group. We must progressively ensure that the people's representatives are responsible to the electors and can be dismissed by them. We must realise a new democratic socialist system in which the people are the country's true masters, through a new anti-pyramidical structure in which the NPC, the organ of supreme authority, will supervise the administration at all levels.

2. A consultative committee for the reform should be immediate-

ly set up, drawn from the Central Secretariat of the CCP, the Standing Committee of the NPC, the State Council and the Chinese Guomindang, as well as political parties, groups and experts from all sectors. This committee should be invested with independent authority.

Under its direction a six-month discussion should be opened in the press so that the opinions of the masses on the reform can be concentrated. A reform project should then be drawn up based on the views of the majority. After genuine elections, it should be presented to the Sixth NPC and the Sixth CPC for implementation.

In drafting the reform plan we must draw the lessons of the constant left-right zig-zags that have plagued us since the crushing of the Gang of Four. We should publish plans for raising the standard of living of citizens. These plans should be realistically attainable year by year, so that our policies are both credible and corruption-free.

3. Before the reform is carried out the old legislation and the old rules must be followed to the letter.

4. We should stop venerating only Marxism-Leninism and Mao Zedong Thought and practise freedom of belief. We should consider the progressive thought of all human civilisation as our heritage, and rescue marxism from deductive scholasticism by letting a hundred flowers bloom and a hundred schools of thought contend.

Marxism is a science, but science must be continually developed and does not fear the open competition of conflicting theories. That the CCP holds to marxism as its guiding ideology should in no way debar other parties and groups from holding their own beliefs and points of view. In pursuit of truth we should adopt the democratic principle that while the minority must submit to the majority, the majority has no right to suppress it.

5. Replace the 'Four Modernisations' slogan with that of integrated modernisation.

6. The CCP should re-register its members, but without turning this into a political campaign. The party's main source of finance should be its members. This will reduce the burden on the exchequer and on the people. After the reform is implemented

the CCP, along with all other parties, should get a state subsidy proportionate to its membership.

The CCP has glorious traditions. It is without doubt the only party in China capable of carrying through the reform programme. Its political qualities will decide the success or failure of the reform. The proposal to re-register its members should open up new perspectives for it.

7. Leave historical balance sheets to the historians, including the balance sheet of the conflict between the CCP and the Guomindang.

8. The four powers should be separated in the Chinese political system. The structure should be restored whereby the President presides over the State Council and commands the armed forces. Appointments for life should be abolished and no individual should hold the same office for more than two successive terms.

'Separation of the four powers' means that the CCP is the guiding power, the NPC and the CPC are the legislative power, the state organs are the administrative power, and the courts have judicial independence.

9. The present system, in which power is concentrated at the centre, should be progressively replaced by a federal one that combines central direction with local, regional and city autonomy. Taiwan should be treated as a special area in order to arrive at a peaceful solution of the Taiwan problem.

10. The Chinese armed forces are the defenders of the state and the people. They should stay out of politics, and if they don't, they should be severely punished. No soldier should serve in a government post. The minister of defence should be chosen from the civilian personnel. This measure is necessary for society's stability and the people's security. It permits military professionals to concentrate on developing military science and modern strategy and tactics.

11. The present conscription system should be progressively changed so that compulsory military service is replaced by a combination of volunteers and career soldiers. The system of people's militia should be extended. The research and teaching of modern military science should be strengthened. The quality of the troops should be improved and their numbers reduced.

12. We should continue to restrain military expenditure while

increasing investment in qualified personnel. Part of the funds released from military spending should be used to raise the standard of living of the lower and middle ranks or allocated to the parents of military personnel from the countryside.

13. The Sixth NPC and the Sixth CPC should be convoked to revise the present Constitution and draw up a new one based on popular sovereignty. The law should be revised in line with a modernised form of government so that citizens have the right to publish, associate, form political parties, strike and demonstrate.

14. All prisoners of conscience like Wei Jingsheng, Ren Wanding and Liu Qing should be immediately set free. People imprisoned in the past for political offenses should be given retrials. The vague and ambiguous articles of the penal code dealing with counter-revolutionary activities should be amended. The administrative ordinances that permit the Public Security Bureau to exercise judicial powers should be abolished. The freedoms to speak, assemble, associate, publish, march, demonstrate and strike, which citizens have on paper, should be guaranteed in practice.

The focal point of all reforms should be human liberation, and the respect for human value and human rights. The free development of each individual is the basis for all social progress. Military-style authoritarianism must be replaced by government by moral persuasion; all government must act strictly within the law. Adminstrative units should no longer have control of dossiers on individuals. Instead, there should be a system of passports, and the state should set up archive bureaus from which individuals can get their identity papers. Employment agencies should be set up, and staff should be engaged on the basis not of unified appointment but of job advertisements, exams and proper selection methods, with the signing of short- or long-term contracts. Provision should be made for job allocation in case of unemployment. Restrictions on residence permits should be progressively relaxed so as to eventually guarantee freedom of resettlement.

15. In all enterprises apart from state organs directly dependent on the centre, it should be the administrative committee nominated by the assembly of representatives of the workforce

that exercises administrative power, takes care of its own accounting, and takes responsibility for profits and losses, taxes and free competition. Cultural and educational bodies should be grant-aided and should gradually carry into effect a system of free universal education. After fulfilling its quota as set out in the Plan, each unit and enterprise should have the right to decide its own provisioning, production and marketing. As long as no employee earns less than the national minimum set by the state, each unit should have the right to fix its own wages, bonuses and social security provisions.

Income tax should be introduced after salaries have been increased on a broad scale. Invisible deductions from salaries should be explained. Those who work harder should get higher wages and those who are more able should make a greater contribution, so that each citizen recognises his or her own worth and cherishes his or her democratic rights.

The workforce and property of firms bankrupt as a result of lack of competitiveness should be put at the disposal of the people's government at the relevant level which will, acting in accordance with the relevant legislation and in consultation with employees' representatives, take the necessary measures.

16. The problem of the countryside is essentially that of the land. A new agrarian law should be drawn up to put an end to the present chaos. Popular assemblies should be set up in each village and each *xiang* and these should become organs of supreme power. They should be made up of people from all backgrounds (families with much labour power, families with little labour power, intellectuals, parents of martyrs and soldiers, families benefiting from the five guarantees, pensioners...) and should create permanent bodies to exercise administrative power in the villages and the *xiang*.

17. In accordance with the various periods into which the history of modern China is divided, cadres who were dismissed or retired early, military personnel who were honourably discharged and other deserving people should get certificates of merit and material benefits according to a system centrally administered by the state.

18. As an experiment a four-hour working day should be introduced for married women so that they can cope with their

household tasks and with bringing up the younger generation.
19. Education is the foundation stone of modern society. We should progressively establish free and universal education, encourage higher education on a half-work half-study basis and introduce a trial system of grants. Adult education, professional education, cultural education of a social nature, recreation centres and sports facilities should figure in the administrative programmes of the various units and of the people's governments at each level.
20. Reduce the number of deputies elected to the various levels of the NPC and the CPC. Deputies at all levels should be released from production so that they can devote themselves to serving society. At every level of the NPC and the CPC permanent bodies and specialised commissions should be established to listen to citizens' opinions and maintain organic links with the people.

The state belongs to everyone, and democracy is everyone's business. If everyone thinks that nothing can be done, then our nation will accomplish nothing. But if everyone believes that something can be done, then we will accomplish great things. As long as the youth and the people as a whole retain the will to work hard towards the goal of national prosperity, there will be great hope for China.

Yu Guangyuan

Socialist Construction and
Lifestyles, Values and Human Development

Yu Guangyuan, born in 1915, is concurrently Vice-President of the
Chinese Academy of Social Sciences and Director of the Academy's
Marxism-Leninism-Mao Zedong Thought Institute. During the winter
of 1979-80 this prominent member of China's intellectual elite became
known as an unofficial patron of the youthful democratic movement.
IIe was criticised for allowing young people to publish 'different
political views', even where he did not agree with them, and for allowing
a controversial journal called *Qingnian wengao* ('Youth Draft Articles')
to be published internally by the Academy. This journal, which only ran
to one issue, published an article on freedom of the press by Hu Ping,
who in October 1980 was elected against party wishes as people's
representative for Beijing University (see pp. 88-97 below). Yu is also
said to have expressed strong dissatisfaction with the party committee at
Hunan University for interfering in student elections. According to the
pro-Deng Xiaoping Hongkong journal *Zhengming* ('Contention')
(1 May 1981), Yu's connections with the democratic movement,
together with criticisms of his personal life (he is said to have arranged
for his daughters to study abroad and to have a taste for expensive
hotels) cost him the presidency of the Academy when Hu Qiaomu was
preparing to retire in 1981.

Yu's article, here abridged, shows him as a marxist with an independent mind and strong humanist inclinations. It first appeared in
vol. 2, no. 2 of *Social Sciences in China*, a quarterly journal published in
English by the Academy of Social Sciences in Beijing.

Professor Uzawa has asked me to speak today about the influence of socialist construction upon lifestyles, culture, values
and human development.

Lifestyles include both a material and a spiritual aspect.
Material life can be divided into time for labour and time for
leisure; or, from the material angle, it can be divided into production and consumption. Leisure time and the consumption
part of material life include all the various activities of survival,
enjoyment and growth. Spiritual life includes political life,
scientific and artistic life, religious life (for those who believe in
a religion), and all of our various ethical relationships. This kind
of analytical framework will allow us to move beyond vague

generalisations to a discussion of lifestyles with real substance.

In simple terms, 'values' refers to the particular viewpoint that a person brings to his or her appraisal of the variety of social practice (of course, the most important of which is their appraisal of various lifestyles). A person may ask: Which social goals and lifestyles should be given a high evaluation and deserve being struggled for and which social goals and lifestyles are not worth fighting for? In answering this question, there will be a definite social and philosophical viewpoint and this viewpoint is what people call values.

According to my understanding of these two terms, I want to share a few thoughts with you today.

What is socialism? If we are talking about scientific socialism, it was first a doctrine and then a movement; later, it became a system and, finally, a culture...

Generally speaking, the development of scientific socialism has undergone these four stages. Socialism began to affect lifestyles, values and human development from the very first stage; those who founded and accepted scientific socialism had their own values, and arranged their lives more or less according to these values, thus changing and forming their own lifestyles. The growth of their knowledge, talents, thinking, and moral character also began to merge with the doctrines of scientific socialism. As scientific socialism developed into a mass movement, moving gradually towards victory, there was a huge increase in the number of people influenced by the values of scientific socialism. Certain aspects of the lifestyles of these scientific socialists were different from those of others. It was in the socialist movement, consequently, that generation after generation came to maturity under the influence of scientific socialist thinking.

Of course, people can never transcend the society in which they live. For instance, in capitalist society, even though certain individual socialist revolutionaries may be supported by their comrades, the great majority must sell their labour power or come up with some other way to make a living. Furthermore, in a country where the socialist victory has not yet been won, any changes in material and spiritual life can only be the affair of a small minority. Only in socialist countries, through socialist construction, can lifestyles and values be changed society-wide.

Lifestyles are multi-faceted and each facet has its decisive factor. Certain elements of a person's lifestyle and value system are determined by the material environment; some are formed historically; others undergo major changes as a result of changes in the social system. I don't agree with geographical determinism, but the impact of the geographic environment upon lifestyles, especially its effect on clothing, food, housing and transportation, are obvious and long-term. Nor should we underestimate the influence of historical and cultural traditions upon lifestyles. These are the conservative elements in a person's lifestyle. However, that which exercises a 'directional' and 'motive' role in lifestyle changes are improvements in society's economic and cultural levels and the establishment, consolidation and development of economic and political systems... In studying the influence of socialist construction upon lifestyles, values and human development, we must explore the directional and motive forces within them. We are now in a position to carry the analysis a step further.

There are some elements of a lifestyle that are directly related to rises in society's economic and cultural level; a society's level, composition and pattern of consumption fall into this category. The poor have poor lifestyles, and the rich have theirs. This requires no explanation. Because one of the main results of socialist construction is the raising of economic and cultural levels, following the advance of socialist construction, labourers' incomes will increase and the level, composition and pattern of consumption will all change, and this expresses the relation between socialist construction and this part of lifestyle. Of course, similar situations occur under other social systems. The difference is that under the socialist system, if no serious calamities, natural and human-made, occur, the incomes of workers should steadily increase. Furthermore, under the socialist system the distribution of income, 'to each according to their work', is different from any system in history. Therefore, under socialism, changes in society's consumption have their own unique features...

It should be emphasised that social structures and consumption patterns are not only determined by cultural and economic levels; the social system can also play a major role, but only after rises in economic and cultural levels have exercised their influence. The influence of social systems on consumer lifestyles occurs as a matter of course, and can also be the result of conscious action. Under the socialist system there is the problem of guidance in consumer lifestyles. Individual consumption should be decided by the individuals themselves; others should not interfere. This principle is entirely correct, but it does not mean that we cannot or should not study this question and think of ways to carry out guidance through propaganda and education...

As the material lives of the Chinese people gradually become more and more prosperous, what will be the most rational composition and style of consumption? Should we seek the consumer pattern of Western societies today? Or should we creatively develop our own consumption pattern? In studying these questions, we should first consider economic feasibility. In China of the 1980s, is it possible to take the same road as that taken by the Western countries? Can the China of the future have the same consumer lifestyles that exist in Western societies today? For example, is it possible to achieve an automobile for each household in a population of one billion (by the end of the century it may increase to 1.2 billion)? Or, lowering our sights, a car for every two or three households? If so, how many millions of tons of steel would China have to produce each year? Is it possible for the Chinese people of the future to have the lifestyles of Americans today, each person consuming the the equivalent of 15 tons of standard coal in fuel and power? To attain that level, China would have to produce the equivalent of how many millions of tons of coal and fuel? These levels of consumption are clearly out of the question for the next twenty years, and will be very difficult to achieve even in the more distant future.

Chinese economists are asking themselves: Looking at the contemporary world situation and China's concrete conditions, what composition and level of consumption would constitute the best objective for China's modernisation? What is both possible and necessary? What would be most beneficial for the development of China's economy and society? These questions involve values. Are the composition and patterns of consumption in Western societies most suitable for China as a developing socialist country? Are their consumer lifestyles worth our pursuit?...

I think that Chinese scholars should, on the basis of in-depth studies of China's economy and society, formulate plans for a rational social consumption pattern that is suitable for our country, and according to this plan carry out education in socialist values among the people. Experience indicates that people are not usually conscious of their own consumption patterns and are easily influenced by others. 'Keeping up with the Joneses' applies not only to individuals but also to countries. We must recognise the importance of carrying out correct guidance regarding social consumption, paying particular attention to scientific research in this areas, and we must initiate a long-term education program; otherwise there will be much blindness in social consumption. And because consumption is the goal of socialist production, it will affect society's production for a long time to come.

Leisure activity, a very important part of lifestyles, is directly related to society's economic and cultural levels. Rising economic and cultural levels bring positive results in two ways: they make possible increases in social products and increases of leisure time...

The increase of leisure time has an extremely important and manifold significance for human life. If we divide life, as Engels did, into survival, enjoyment and growth, and don't count the time expended for survival as leisure, then leisure time is the time used for enjoyment and growth.

Enjoyment not only requires the means of enjoyment, it also requires time. Enjoyment activities can be integrated with the goal of improving health. Leisure time can be used to regulate and modulate one's life. For example, a change of environment, travel, swimming, skating and other physical recreation are all essentially enjoyment activities. This kind of enjoyment is commendable, but not all uses of leisure time are healthy. In Western societies this is a problem of serious concern to sociologists, as well as the general public. Besides physical health, there is also the question of mental and emotional health. Leisure time should also be used for mental and emotional release and enjoyment.

This again involves the question of values. As far as the values of scientific socialism are concerned, healthy physical and mental development is an excellent social goal. The goal of socialist society is people's happiness; mental and physical health is thus one of the most important aspects of socialism's ultimate goal. Enjoyment that is not healthy is not compatible with the nature of socialism. In socialist construction we should carry out correct guidance regarding leisure time for enjoyment.

Besides enjoyment, there is still the question of growth, the cultivation of one's talents and character... Under the socialist system, we should encourage each worker to use his or her leisure time to cultivate their character and develop their potential in every sphere to the fullest.

From the angle of production, the increase of leisure time is both the result of and a factor in economic and cultural development. 'In relation to the whole of society, the creation of *disposable time* is then also creation of time for the production of science, art, etc.' (Marx, the *Grundrisse*)...

There are some aspects of a person's lifestyle that, although directly connected with the social system, are only distantly related to rising economic and cultural levels. This segment of people's lives, which includes work life, political life, and so on, changes rapidly with the construction of socialism. The amount of time spent in labour occupies a big proportion of a person's lifetime. In the labour process, a person's overall life situation should be given full consideration. Part of the labour process is the physiological aspect, e.g. the intensity and conditions of labour, etc. As the basic nature of socialism, this aspect of the labour process should receive special attention. But this aspect of the labour process is conditioned by the level of economic development. As far as the worker is concerned, there are also the psychological and political aspects of work life. The victory of the socialist revolution enabled workers to rise to the position of masters, a transformation that is primarily expressed in the production process and entails a fundamental change in the nature of the labourer's work life. It gives the workers a certain satisfaction to know that they are not working for a capitalist but for themselves. This can occur immediately following the establishment of socialism. At the same time, the workers' position in political life also changes very rapidly. By rapid change I don't mean that there is not a transitional process before workers can be masters in their own labour and in the political life of society or that this process is not related to economic and cultural development. On the contrary, the growth of democratic life depends on economic and cultural conditions. A lack of leisure time, busy all day long with work and housework, is bound to seriously affect a person's enthusiasm and initiative for participation in social activities. But this aspect of lifestyles is, after all, different from the consumer life which I mentioned earlier. It is directly connected to the social system and changes directly as a result of changes in the social system.

There are other aspects of lifestyles that although related to economic and cultural levels are not directly determined by them, and can be improved through sustained education under the socialist system along with efforts in other fields. I am mainly referring to people's spiritual lives, which are affected by socialist ethical relations. We can observe in social life — and also in literature and art — many typical cases that illustrate that material prosperity does not necessarily mean happiness...

We want a prosperous life for the people because poverty is misery. However, there are countless examples under every social system in history of prosperous people who lead unhappy or miserable or even tragic lives. Unhappiness in family, marriage and love relationships is the theme of many famous novels and plays. Princes, nobles and rich men have often led wretched lives because of infelicitous ethical relations. This is a glaring problem in Western societies today...

China is economically and culturally very backward. We must devote ourselves to the realisation of socialist modernisation and propel the national economy onto a path of steady and sustained growth so that the material lives of all our people may prosper. However, at the same time we should also devote ourselves to the creation of a socialist spiritual civilisation. We must develop socialist human relations between parents and children, between husbands and wives, among siblings, friends, neighbours and even strangers. This kind of relationship is different from relationships in feudal patriarchal society or capitalist society. Absorbing all of the fine traditions of the past, it transforms and improves them according to socialist principles. The ethical relations promoted in the old society, the kind father, the filial son, the loving elder brother, the respectful younger brother, the genial husband and the tender wife — these relationships must be deprived of their feudal content and transformed. We must establish among the members of socialist society relations which are based on mutual understanding and help, affection, love, equality and democracy. Because socialism has eliminated classes and the labouring people have become masters of society, there no longer exist fundamental differences of interest among people. Therefore these comradely, fraternal and cooperative relations can be spread to all ethical relations. The establishment of socialist ethical relations can bring the people spiritual happiness. Of course, in the real world of socialism today, some people lead very happy lives and others, for a variety of reasons, are not completely happy; others because of misfortune and adversity are even unhappy. But if we are successful in building a socialist spiritual civilisation, every member of society will be affected.

The problem of the relationship between social systems and lifestyles, values and human development is both a practical social problem and a philosophical question. As a philosophical question, there is the problem of the relationship between marxist and non-marxist philosophies and the relationship between Eastern and Western philosophies. As a marxist, I believe that marxist philosophy can play an extremely important role in seeking solutions to the many problems of contemporary reality. At the same time, as a Chinese, as a son of an ancient country of the East, I believe that the fine traditions of countries like China and Japan embrace many things that will be useful in curing the ills of modern society. Of course I certainly don't approve of restoring the old. I only mean that when studying the advanced science and technology of the West, we must also realise that Eastern countries have many fine traditions that must not be casually discarded.

Editorial Board, Renminzhi lu

A Statement of Clarification

Guangzhou, the capital of Guangdong Province in South China, was a stronghold of the democratic movement and the home-city of Wang Xizhe, one of its most persuasive and brilliant writers. Students from the two universities in the nearby British colony of Hongkong often visited Guangzhou to meet Wang and his comrades, and to exchange views and opinions with them. Back in Hongkong these students organised an energetic campaign to publicise the views of the democratic movement, and to defend it when it came under attack. Although these was nothing unconstitutional about these links, the Guangdong provincial government accused the democratic movement of illegally liaising with abroad. The 'four principles' mentioned in the provincial government's warning were announced in Beijing in March 1979. They required adherence to the socialist road, the dictatorship of the proletariat, Communist Party leadership and Marxism-Leninism-Mao Zedong Thought. Most unofficial journals paid lip-service to these four principles, but in reality the logic of their campaign was fundamentally at odds with this strongly Stalinist conception of socialism. The provincial authorities also accused the unofficial journals of violating the ordinances on publications. This issue is discussed in more depth in the text 'Democracy and legality are safeguards of stability and unity' (see below pp. 74-77).

The democratic movement and the unofficial journals, born in late 1978, are now both more than a year old. Although still infants, they have come under intense pressure, yet they persevere. Young people in China have come to recognise their duties to nation and people, and strive for democracy and reform. But the struggle spares none, and permits no illusions. Now our movement is being suppressed throughout the whole country, including here in Guangdong. On 4 April 1980 *Nanfang ribao* ('Southern Daily') published a warning by Comrade Xi Zhongxun, Governor of Guangdong Province, in which he told the democratic movement:

> Anarchism and extreme individualism are masquerading under the banners of democracy and human rights. In the past, these people were keen on writing wall-posters and publishing magazines. Now, they even secretly liaise with abroad. They are violating the ordinances on publications, and continue to publish wrong and even counter-revolutionary

articles. It is clear that they have deviated from the Four Principles, damaged stability, harmed the Four Modernisations, and virtually placed themselves on the opposite side to the party and the people.

Readers in Guangzhou will know that after the suspension of *Renminzhi sheng* ('Voice of the People'), there only remain *Renminzhi lu* ('People's Road'), *Shenghuo* ('Life') and *Hongdou* ('Red Bean') (this latter published by students of Zhongshan University). We believe that it is our duty to clarify our position on the points raised in Xi Zhongxun's statement:

1. Ever since we split from 'Voice of the People' in September 1979, we have been publishing bi-monthly. We have published four issues in all, and we have sent each issue to the Publications Bureau and other relevant government departments. On 18 December 1979 the Provincial Committee told us via the Communist Youth League that we should no longer sell our journal publicly, and so we stopped. But at the same time we affirmed that we would continue to publish, and we stressed that the 1952 regulations on the registration of publications, which require guarantees from two private shops, are clearly outdated, since shops are now publicly owned. These regulations do not conform with present social conditions and they contradict the Constitution, which guarantees freedom of the press. But the authorities replied that it was not possible to change the law. This means unofficial journals cannot be registered...

2. It is only natural that young people who are concerned about their nation and committed to the democratic movement should liaise with and support one another. It is entirely legal to do so, and it is wrong to call such liaison 'secret coordination'. The freedom of correspondence stipulated in the Constitution gives individuals the right to keep certain things secret. Our correspondence is legal and above-board, although our letters are frequently opened and inspected. We deeply regret the charge of 'secret coordination', a term inherited from the period of the Gang of Four's reign of terror.

3. Since its emergence in 1979, the democratic movement has had much impact in Hongkong and Macau, particularly among patriotic students disillusioned by the downfall of the Gang of

Four and the collapse of the Maoist faction in the student movement. These people feel that their liberation from colonial rule — Hongkong is a British colony — is intimately bound up with China's progress. They see hope in the democratic movement.

In August 1979, students at Hongkong University organised a 'discussion camp' in Guangzhou so that they could contact people here and see what changes are taking place... Since then Hongkong students have frequently visited us to discuss politics and the democratic movement. Through them we have deepened our knowledge of world affairs, of the international Communist movement, and of new developments in marxism in the various countries. Young workers and teachers as well as students have contacted us. We feel encouraged by these gestures of solidarity... Needless to say, we cannot investigate the background of every person we meet, and it is possible that we may have come into contact with people of a political background. But we insist on restricting our communication with such people to the democratic movement, and we will never agree to take instructions from others or to accept aid to which conditions are attached...

We affirm the Four Principles and marxist teachings. We welcome criticism so long as it is directed at specific points raised in our magazine. We believe that dialogue is useful both to us and to our readers. Finally, we believe that socialist democracy and the legal system will develop under party leadership. The road is hard, but the new generation, baptised by the Cultural Revolution and led by the party, will bravely follow it.

Commentator, Zeren

Democracy and Legality
are Safeguards of Stability and Unity

Zeren ('Duty') is the name of the journal published by the National Federation of Unofficial Journals, set up in the autumn of 1980. The following article by 'Commentator' was published on 16 January 1981 shortly before the government's final crackdown on the democratic movement in April. It is a brave and forceful protest against the quickening turn towards repression. Despite the crackdown *Zeren* has continued to appear, published from bases within the underground.

Is our country stable and unified today, four years after the fall of the Gang of Four? Most people think that things have improved, since at least they no longer need worry that they will be suddenly searched, arrested, put before a criticism meeting, or sent to gaol merely for voicing an opinion. Most people think that the situation has stabilised, and that the country has become more unified. These changes are the result of a long, hard struggle, and people cherish them. Now that people are awakened, they will never agree to a revival of the sort of social fascism that plunged China into turbulence and disaster, and that brought them great suffering and despair.

But some officials feel uneasy when they see our freedoms even slightly widened. In their view ordinary people should be voiceless, like beasts or machines. In their dictionary, democracy means they speak, we listen.

What a masterpiece is Commentator's article in *Jiefang ribao* ('Liberation Daily') of 10 January 1981!... It lays bare the contradictions in the thinking of some people at the top. We would like to ask the author of this explosively-charged article a question. Mr Commentator, you talk much about 'illegal organisations' and 'illegal publications', as if you yourself were some heroic defender of the law. But this law that you worship — is it royal law, or constitutional law?

The Constitution says that citizens have the freedom to meet and associate. Any organisation of citizens is therefore constitutionally legal. Specific provisions on how to organise should have been clearly set out in a Law of Association and

Organisation, so that citizens can act according to them. But even though China has had the name of 'People's Republic' for the past thirty years, no such law has ever been enacted. Similarly, the Constitution says that citizens have the freedom of speech and publication. Constitutionally, any publication that citizens produce is therefore legal. But unfortunately no Law of Publication has ever been decreed.

It seems that Commentator is only concerned with royal law — the law that might is right. So he denounces as illegal any organisation that, although constitutional, has not yet won the approval of the authorities; and he refers to publications started by the people as illegal, even though they have tried repeatedly to apply for official registration.

Commentator's authority is apparently even above that of the National People's Congress. One word from him and many organisations and dozens of unofficial publications are trapped in the law's net. But a closer look shows that this net is woven by royal law. When royal law rules supreme, the royal labels factory will have no lack of markets: old labels like 'counter-revolutionary' will be joined by 1980 and 1981 models like 'extreme individualism', 'the Democracy Wall Gang', 'turbulent agitator', 'dissident' and 'hostile element'. If this goes on much longer Commentator will begin to match the Gang of Four, and could even leave them in the shade!

Commentator also takes a swipe at grassroots elections, which he calls 'so-called elections' and views as a mere pretext for reactionary speeches. If Commentator had a longer memory, he would recall that 'Liberation Daily' itself carried many reports on elections and election campaigns, and made a great fuss about the need to strengthen people's awareness and sense of initiative through them. How can he deny it? If this goes on much longer, 'Liberation Daily' will become like newspapers were during the last years of the Gang of Four — fit only for wrapping paper.

Without election campaigns there can be no real elections. And what if a counter-revolutionary does stand for election? As long as the people themselves are not counter-revolutionary, such a person will simply be exposed and isolated. Only those without guts and who are opposed to the people fear election campaigns. Commentator is very hostile to elections. Doesn't that say something about his politics?

Commentator muddles together publishing and speaking with crimes like robbery and causing explosions. His method is all too familiar. Our country is now on the point of perfecting its legal system. Criminals who cause explosions or commit other crimes will be dealt with by law. Ordinary Chinese, unlike our anxious Commentator, are confident that the legal system will safeguard social order. But what does Commentator have in mind when he puts publishing and speaking on a par with criminal acts? Can we expect a new round of 'literary hell' and of manufactured public opinion? We hope not. We would prefer to view Commentator as a second-rate scribbler and self-advertiser than as the harbinger of a new wave of repression.

Commentator is deeply worried about our national economy. Of course, we share his worry. But we are diametrically opposed to him on how to change things. He says that in times of difficulty we need stability and unity. What he really means is that ordinary people should be gagged. Why doesn't he just say out straight, 'We cadres botched things, but we forbid you to grumble about it! Keep your mouths shut! We big-shots will put things right. You must believe that the future is infinitely bright and beautiful!'

But unfortunately for him, the people are no longer wrapped in ignorance. Without their active participation the national economy will never prosper. So much money has been squandered — money earned by the hard toil of the people... Why should they not complain? If we rely only on some saviour and make no effort to win the enthusiasm of ordinary Chinese, we are on the road to disaster. Is that so difficult to grasp? If ordinary people are not allowed to discuss things, and if everything is left to people like the Oil Minister (who wasted huge sums of money and was responsible through his incompetence for workers' deaths), then it will be truly difficult to maintain 'unity and stability'.

Our position is: practise democracy, win people's enthusiasm, pool all talents, share out responsibility — and then there will be no difficulty that we cannot overcome. Every citizen should be encouraged to speak out boldly and often. The people are the masters of the state. Only when they give of their best will China prosper and stability and unity be strengthened.

We think that particular attention should be paid to election campaigns. Only through such campaigns can citizens become aware of the value of their own existence and work hard for the country. Only then will they ditch the time-servers and chair-warmers so that skilled and talented newcomers can take up public posts. Only then will people's potential be fully tapped. As for Commentator, he will be able to exchange his blunt pen for another job more suited to his talents. Otherwise, a few more lousy articles like that and the world will be in a right mess.

We have repeatedly asked the authorities to draw up and promulgate laws of speech, association, and election, so that citizens have something to which they can refer. Otherwise, people with ulterior motives will exploit the confusion. Commentator's article in 'Liberation Daily' is a good example of this.

We should also recognise that China's unofficial publications, which have been appearing for two years now, have achieved much and are on exactly the right course. Again and again ideas and proposals that first appeared in unofficial publications have ended up part of official government policy. Of course there are people who would like to deny our contribution, but history will sneer at their efforts.

As an unofficial publication we risk much by speaking out like this. We are not like Commentator, who presents himself as 'always reasonable, and stable as Mount Tai'. We refuse to earn our living by bending before every wind; our own security means nothing to us. We long ago weighed the value of our lives: if we can help China overcome poverty and backwardness and achieve civilisation and progress, and if we can help to win lasting happiness and true stability and unity for our beloved people, then our consciences will be clear and even if we die, we will die content.

Ge Tian

A Guangdong Youth Forum on Wall-Posters

During the Hundred Flowers campaign of 1957, the Cultural Revolution and the winter of 1978-79, critics of the regime or of factions in it could express their opinions through wall-posters. The government, particularly its radical element, used such posters to give the appearance of spontaniety to its campaigns, but courageous individuals could use them to publicise dissident views, although many were persecuted for doing so. Wall-posters became particularly associated with the Maoist faction in the party, and the Four Greats — speaking out freely, airing views fully, holding great debates and writing wall-posters — were seen as Mao's policy. The Deng government's decision in February 1980 to erase the Four Greats from the Constitution (where Mao had put them) dismayed the democratic movement, which saw it as a betrayal. The government argued that wall-posters, being anonymous, could be used to spread slander, and that in any case they were no longer necessary now that China was restoring democracy and opening the official media to public opinion. But this argument did not convince oppositionist youth, who rightly reckoned that views like theirs would never be officially published. It is interesting that the forum described below was organised by the Communist Youth League. The democratic movement had friends in the party throughout China, and would otherwise never have come so strongly into the public eye. This article, here excerpted, first appeared in *Renminzhi lu* ('People's Road'), Guangzhou.

On 4 April 1980, the Guangdong Provincial Committee of the Communist Youth League held a forum on the Communique of the Fifth Plenum of the CCP Central Committee. Those invited included Li Zhengtian, Chen Yiyang and Wang Xizhe, authors of the famous Li Yi Zhe wall-poster; student representatives; members of the editorial boards of the four non-governmental journals *Renminzhi sheng* ('Voice of the People'), *Shenghuo* ('Life'), *Langhua* ('Spray') and *Renminzhi lu* ('People's Road'); cadres of the Ocean Shipping Bureau; and reporters of the official journal *Zhongguo qingnian* ('Chinese Youth')...

The teacher Xu X X from Zhongshan University said: Most students cannot see why the Four Greats should be abolished. They think that if the Four Greats are abolished, it will be impossible to make proposals. Are the central authorities scared of criticism? Can't they tolerate a few suggestions?

Liu Guokai (of 'Voice of the People') said: Most of our workers feel that if the Four Greats are abolished, there will be no way left to supervise the bureaucrats. They dare not post their joint letter exposing the serious problems of bureaucratism in their factory because none of them believes that such a letter will have any effect.

Student Cai X from the Chinese Department of Zhongshan University said: Some people say that those comrades on the Central Committee who supported abolishing the Four Greats are probably those who were lashed by wall-posters in the past. If the meeting had been attended by ordinary people, there would have been no mention of this issue. No one at our student meeting supported abolishing the Four Greats. After all, there are laws, so everyone who uses wall-posters to spread slanders can be punished.

A representative of Huanan engineering students said: our students' faith in the party vacillated recently. Some demanded a rational explanation of the rehabilitation of Liu Shaoqi. Some said that all these things were the result of a power struggle. They said that they do not understand the handling of the four people [Wang Dongxing, Ji Dengkui, Wu De and Chen Xilian, the Maoist old guard that was dismissed from the leadership once Deng Xiaoping had tightened his grip on it]. In the past, we said that Wang Dongxing contributed to the struggle against the Gang of Four. Now we say that he made mistakes in opposing the Gang of Four. How can we account for this sudden switch? Some students do not understand why Liu Shaoqi was rehabilitated. They say that to remove Liu Shaoqi from power was the main aim of Chairman Mao's Cultural Revolution. But now the party claims that Liu's rehabilitation is aimed at restoring the true features of Mao Zedong Thought.

Most students disagree with abolishing the Four Greats. They think that with democracy weak in China, the Four Greats have an important role to play. Why aren't we allowed to use the Four Greats as weapons against bureaucratism? The demonstrations of 5 April 1976 [against the 'gang of four'] also made use of the Four Greats. But now it's alleged that the Four Greats never played a positive role.

Students from Shaoguan, Zhanjiang and Meixian reported

that there was a serious trend towards dividing up the fields among the peasants... They said that the central authorities should spend more time studying social problems, for if such trends spread unchecked, problems will emerge, and the images of Chairman Mao and premier Zhou Enlai will be besmirched.

A representative of the students of Huanan Teachers' College said: None of us sees why the Four Greats should be abolished. Without wall-posters, what other means are there for us to show what we think? In the past, students could use wall-posters to reflect problems. Now they no longer dare to write them. We think that the party should guide us in the right way to use wall-posters rather than just abolish them...

The secretary of the Communist Youth League at the Ocean Shipping Bureau said... Since we Communists are fearless and dauntless, what reason is there to be afraid of wall-posters? As for the four dismissed leaders, I also fail to understand their treatment. Why weren't their mistakes made public? Did Wang Dongxing not render outstanding services? Why treat him badly now? If he made mistakes, then his mistakes should be made known to the public. Some young people believe that the party always follows this rule: Whoever wields power dominates everything...

Li Min of *Langhua* ('Spray') said: Many articles eulogising Liu Shaoqi have appeared in the press. It seems as if this is another movement to create a god. All this publicity implies that Chairman Mao's Cultural Revolution was aimed merely at overthrowing Liu, and that it was just power-play. But I believe that things were not that simple... As for the Four Greats, I have neither a bad nor a good opinion of them. However, I am sure that people in our socialist society would still find them useful.

Wang Xizhe said: [Wang Dongxing and his supporters] should not have been removed from power. They should be allowed to make statements and speeches. Why aren't they allowed to explain their position and talk about their problems?... As for the Four Greats, I think that Deng Xiaoping is not respecting the Constitution. In 1978 he told some foreign visitors that the people have the constitutional right to put up wall-posters, and that no one has the right to stop them. But now he says that the Four Greats have never played a positive role... Although wall-posters have been abolished, the people still do not know how to apply democracy. So the people now have even fewer democratic rights. Non-governmental journals should be allowed to exist.

Li Zhengtian said: Before the National Peoples' Congress discusses abolishing the Four Greats, our leaders should try to get it to discuss a new publications law. Every society needs some way of reflecting public opinion. To embody democracy in our society, we need a publications law.

The Polish Crisis: Solidarnosc and China

Since 1949 radical Chinese have followed new movements in Eastern Europe as closely as the available sources of information permit. Titoism and the Hungarian Revolution of 1956 inspired dissident currents in the Hundred Flowers campaign, and recently there has been a lively interest in Solidarnosc, especially in the democratic movement. The following two documents show the impact that the growth of the Polish trade unions had in China. The first document, written before the crackdown, is still quite optimistic about China's future course. It appeared as an editorial in Qingdao's *Lilun qi* ('Theoretical Banner'). The second article, 'Solidarnosc and China', was commissioned by the Polish journal *Rabotnik* ('The Worker'), but the issue in which it was scheduled to appear could not come out because of General Jaruzelski's military take-over. Since then the Deng government has given de facto support to the coup against Solidarnosc.

The Death Knell Tolls for the Bucreaucratic Class: China and the Polish Crisis

After the 1953 Berlin uprising, the 1956 Hungarian Incident, the 1968 Prague Spring and the Czech Charter 77, now the independent trade union movement, Solidarity, has emerged in Poland. But whereas previous movements were crushed by the joint forces of their own bureaucratic privileged classes and Soviet social imperialism, Solidarity has been granted legal recognition. Is this because the bureaucrats have 'dropped their cleavers and become Buddhas', or is there some deeper reason?

Clearly the bureaucrats have not become Buddhas, and nor will they ever do so. It is in their nature to murder and deceive. They embody in distilled form the venom of centuries of class exploitation... Now, after thirty years of atrocities, the people are starting to see through them. 'Workers now realise that officials' wages are thirty times their own minimum wage. They see special cars deliver luxury goods to the mansions of these bigwigs.' 'We ordinary folks die in the hospital corridors, but these bureaucrats are cared for by the best doctors, and get their own individual wards. They even have their own special shops and sanatoria.' One in six of the three million party members in

Poland enjoys some privilege. 'The manager of a small import-export company got over US$1 million in bribes from his company's trading partner in the West, and he embezzled DM 473,379 and US$310,000. He had a bank account and a flat in London, where he kept a mistress. He even built a luxury villa for the Minister of Construction on the pretext that it was a training centre for the building industry.' It is interesting to see that 'when Vice-Premier Pyka was negotiating with strikers in Gdansk and was asked how many country villas he had, he gave evasive answers and became acutely embarrassed'.

And here in China, even though the economy is about to collapse, it has become common practice since the fall of the Gang of Four for bureaucrats to build themselves private villas. At a time when farmers are short of food and building workers are without houses, mansions are being built for party secretaries and generals, and even for their sons. Is this socialism? Is this 'to each according to his ability'? Surely the exploited people will rise up against these 'red dignitaries' who, while boasting of the superiority of socialism, are unrestrainedly corrupt, spend wastefully and seek privileges...

Moscow's tanks rolled over Berlin, Budapest and Prague. But they can no longer roll into Warsaw, where the headquarters of its military pact is sited. This is partly because the Soviet Union is bogged down in Afghanistan and kept busy by younger brothers like the Vietnamese, so that it lacks the material resources to influence events. There are few people in the world today who do not despise the Soviet Union as a main centre for the suppression of human rights. In its scramble for world markets and resources the Soviet Union has apparently gone onto the offensive, which annoys its imperialist rivals. As for the world's people, they wholly reject the system and class represented by Soviet social imperialism...

The problem is: with what shall we replace the bureaucracy's rule? Shall we replace it with capitalist private ownership or some doctrine such as Catholicism? Absolutely not! It would be just as wrong to replace bureaucratic rule with bourgeois rule as it would the other way round (although as things now stand, people would find bourgeois rule slightly more acceptable). The only right way is to build a system of proletarian democracy appropriate to this period of transition, a system that organically links true public ownership with true democracy, so that each complements and guarantees the other on the path to true socialism.

No so-called socialist country can ignore the existence of a free trade union movement in Poland. Solidarity may alarm the bureaucrats, but it inspires the people. It is an acid test for evaluating the political positions of the various social groups in China. The Chinese Communist Party, sensibly, is still reporting the truth about the events in Poland. But if it were really wise it would not just try to restrict bureaucratic corruption, but it would side with the people and fundamentally reform the social and economic system. The feudal bureaucracy that has ruled China for over 2,000 years can only be overthrown by revolution; reforms will have no effect. We have not yet completely despaired of the ruling party. After all, He Qiu and other members of the National Federation of Unofficial Journals have been released from their illegal detention; the Changsha student movement has been fairly treated; and the elections at various universities have not yet been suppressed. So it is still conceivable that China will get radical change without going along Poland's road. But we should not wait too long, for the more the pressure is allowed to build up, the greater will be the eventual explosion; in which case China's road will be even more chaotic than Poland's. Which road China goes depends largely on which course the authorities adopt... We hope that the party will not let the people down, but will follow the logic of recent reforms and carry through to an end the revolution for proletarian democracy...

Gregor Benton

Solidarnosc and China

When Solidarity made its recent appeal to workers in socialist countries to get organised, one country it failed to mention was China. This is a shame, since Solidarity — *tuanjie gonghui* in Chinese — has probably won more public expressions of support from Chinese workers than from workers in any Soviet-bloc country.

After Mao's death and the fall from power of his supporters, political life in China became very lively for a while, and dissent was freely expressed both inside and outside the party. China's dissidents, unlike Russia's, are young and lowly placed. Most work in factories, although a few are students and teachers. The events in Poland excited them enormously, and were a main topic of debate in the unofficial movement and its press. Some oppositionists drew the lessons of the Polish experience and tried to apply them in their own factories.

Changjiang ribao ('Yangzi Daily'), published in the sprawling industrial city of Wuhan on the Yangzi (Yangtse) River, warned that a small group of people was planning to organise Polish-style free trade unions and wanted to 'lead our country into chaos'. On 18 February 1981 the editor of Beijing's *Gongren ribao* ('Workers Daily') revealed that workers in Shanghai and Xian were also demanding Polish-style independent unions, and that some had even gone on strike to air their complaints.

This movement to copy Poland greatly alarmed the authorities in China. Even though the Constitution officially guarantees the rights of free association and free speech, they are not allowed in practice. Only state-run unions are tolerated, and these represent the party's view rather than the workers'.

Life is not easy for a Chinese factory worker. Wages are low, and health, safety and living conditions are poor. Security of employment — what the Chinese call the 'iron rice-bowl' — is a compensation of sorts for poor pay and conditions, but by no means every worker has an iron rice-bowl. In China you can easily spend the whole of your working life on a temporary contract. Some work is seasonal, and those hired to do it are dismissed once the season is over. Not surprisingly, these people are frustrated and resentful, especially when they see party and union chiefs getting big salaries and all sorts of perks and privileges.

They are therefore fertile soil for ideas like those from Poland. Small wonder, then, that the Chinese leaders cracked down ruthlessly on Solidarity supporters in the unofficial movement. Ever since dissenters first appeared on the streets in China many leaders argued that they should be immediately suppressed, but for some months the more liberal wing stayed the hands of these conservatives. It was partly the spectre of a Chinese Poland that finally persuaded the moderates to abandon their liberal stance and join the hardliners in curbing the unofficial movement.

On and around 10 April 1981 twenty-five leading dissidents and an unknown number of lesser ones were arrested in a nationwide swoop. They included Xu Wenli, who on 14 November 1980 wrote an Open Letter to Lech Walesa praising him as a 'shining example for working classes in socialist countries the world over'; and Wang Tanyuan, who in December 1980 put up posters in his home-city of Tianjin in solidarity with the Polish labour movement and against the threat of a Soviet invasion of Poland.

As far as is known, these people were not put on public trial and were not formally charged with any crime. They are now in gaols and labour camps.

China and the Soviet Union are anything but friends, and some people might therefore have expected Beijing to support Solidarity. But for all their criticism of Moscow, the Chinese leaders have rarely supported Soviet-bloc dissenters. This is partly because Eastern European governments are in Beijing's eyes potential allies against Moscow, and therefore not to be offended. But a deeper reason for not supporting them is that to do so would strengthen the position of China's own dissenters. So Beijing has made only a few muted criticisms of Moscow's bullying of the Polish labour movement, and it is unlikely that Solidarity will ever get the support of the Chinese government; but it will continue to enjoy the admiration of China's brave unofficial democrats.

11 November 1981

Open Letter to Lech Walesa

Dear Chairman Lech Walesa, and members of the National Consultative Commission of the independent and autonomous trade union Solidarity.

My friends and I learned with great joy that your independent and autonomous trade union Solidarity has successfully accomplished the legal formalities for registration. Thanks to your courage, your intelligence and your perspicacity, there is now a shining model for working classes in socialist countries the world over. This opens a new era in the world socialist workers' movement.

We congratulate you from the bottom of our hearts, and we wish you even greater victories! Poland belongs to the Polish people! Long Live the Polish people! Long live the friendship between the peoples and the working classes of China and Poland!

With the respectful compliments of Xu Wenli, veteran founder of the alternative Beijing journal *Siwu luntan* ('April Fifth Forum'), electrician on the Beijing railways.

Message of Greetings to the Polish Workers

Dear brother workers of Poland, your strikes have won a great victory which has impressed people throughout the world. It shows the tremendous power and new class consciousness generated by working class solidarity. It shows clearly that the revisionist bureaucratic privileged class and expansionism are mere paper tigers in the face of the people's revolutionary power. It shows that proletarian democratic revolution is an inevitable trend in history. It breaks through national boundaries and achieves a wide international significance. We, the young generation of the Chinese working class, congratulate and salute you! We hope you will continue to progress in the direction of democratic socialism! Workers of all countries, unite!

Siwu luntan ('April Fifth Forum') editorial board,
Beijing, China, September 1980.

Gong Bo

The Wind Rises from Among the Duckweed: Elections at Beijing University

Normally elections in the People's Republic are strictly controlled by the party, which permits only officially approved candidates to win. The elections of 1980 were different in that in some places unofficial candidates insisted on standing against the official ones. Where the authorities did not intervene, electors could therefore choose for the first time ever between genuinely different points of view. One place where the authorities were particularly tolerant during the elections was Beijing University. Candidates and voters played their parts with great gusto, and the history of the campaign was recorded with loving care by a commission specially set up for the purpose. But the Central Committee of the Communist Party was not happy about this, and forbade the publication of the writings of Hu Ping, the successful candidate, on the grounds that he had 'resorted to a Cultural Revolution-style movement' (*Zhengming* ('Contention'), 1 May 1981).

This account of the elections was first published in the Beijing University students' journal *Sixu* ('Train of thought'), no. 1.

The election: an overall sketch

...The election campaign lasted for six weeks. There were 6084 electors and 29 candidates. Most of the candidates organised teams of canvassers, although the way in which they did so varied. People like Xia Shen and Wang Juntao set up election committees before announcing their candidatures, while Hu Ping formed his team only later. Other candidates like Zhang Manling did not set up any stable support group, although they never lacked people ready to work for them. In some groups people already knew each other from school or university; in others, they were drawn together for the first time by their commitment to the election.

Each team explained its goals and viewpoints on hoardings set up at points specified by the university. Candidates also organised open forums in the canteen, the hall and the lecture rooms, where they answered voters' questions. There were altogether eighteen such forums during the six weeks of campaigning, attended by twenty thousand people. Some committees held regular consulting sessions where they received voters or comrades from other units who came with questions. Many candidates visited student voters in their hostels and discussed with them formally and informally. During the campaign, many voters volunteered to help candidates copy out and put up wall-posters, and to publish and distribute information. As a result, some ten publications were produced, with names like 'Election Affairs', 'Election Short-Wave' and 'Reporter Station'. These publications were non-aligned and carried general campaign reports. Together with some of the election committees they conducted a dozen or so opinion polls and general investigations. Students from the Department of History and the Department of Chinese volunteered to set up a Board to Edit and Collect Election Information in order to preserve documents and recordings of the campaign... During those six weeks the whole campus was in a lively ferment. Even unenfranchised students expressed their views and preferences. Everywhere there were wall-posters, leaflets, opinion polls, investigations, advertisements for forums, and candidates' opinion boxes. Everywhere people were arguing, discussing, asking naive questions and making stirring speeches.

On 1 December 1980 the first round in the election resulted in the elimination of all but three candidates. On 11 December the first round of the main election was held, resulting in the election of Hu Ping. The turn-out was 5509, or 90.55 per cent. The voting was 3457 (57 per cent) for Hu Ping, 2964 (48.72 per cent) for Wang Juntao and 2052 (33.77 per cent) for Zhang Wei. The second round of voting was on 18 December. Since 198 electors were out of the district at the time, the number of potential voters fell to 5976. Of these 4778, or 81.63, voted. Wang Juntao got 2934 votes (49.1 per cent) and Zhang Wei got 1456 (34.36 per cent); neither was elected...

How the electors viewed the election

...An opinion poll conducted early on in the campaign revealed that 8.6 per cent of the electors thought that the election was an empty formality, 52.6 per cent saw it as a first step towards socialist democracy, and 37.9 per cent thought that it might have some positive effect, although not a lasting one. Voters were also asked what their attitude was towards political life in our country: 5.6 per cent neither cared about it nor participated in it;

46.2 per cent cared little and did not participate much; 48.2 per cent cared much and participated actively.

The apathy revealed by these statistics can be partly explained by the powerlessness of people's congresses at all levels, particularly at county level. But most electors expected something of the elections, and this roused them to action. They hoped that the people's congresses would acquire some real power so that they could represent at least some of the people's interests; that it would be an election, not an 'appointment'; and that members of the people's congress at county level could also become representatives at a higher level. What particularly heartened them were the frank discussions. Discussions of this sort were a novelty, and threw new light on a number of theoretical, social and political issues...

The candidates' views

(1) Wang Juntao alone among the candidates made a critical assessment of the last thirty years of Chinese history. He believed that:

(i) If Liu Shaoqi's line of 'consolidating New Democracy' had been followed in the early years of the People's Republic the economy would have developed more quickly, society would have developed more healthily, and the subsequent switch-over to socialist construction might have had some real meaning. But as it turned out, socialist construction simply meant superimposing advanced forms of ownership on underdeveloped productive forces.

(ii) Agriculture was collectivised too quickly and without regard to what was objectively possible, thus slowing down agricultural growth. The same is true of handicrafts. Producers' interests were neglected and city-dwellers suffered great hardship. However, the reform of capitalist industry and commerce was more successful.

(iii) The 'anti-rightist struggle' of 1957 was based on a mistaken view of the state and the class struggle, and should not have happened.

(iv) The Greap Leap Forward was a leftist initiative. For reasons of vanity some party leaders wanted China to be the first country to reach Communism, and they manipulated the masses accordingly. The result was disaster.

(v) The 1959 Lushan Plenum led to the frame-up of Peng Dehuai. We should criticise Mao's wrong treatment of dissenters.

(vi) The anti-revisionist campaign correctly opposed the idea of a 'father-party' and Soviet great-power chauvinism, but irreparably weakened its whole case by promoting Stalinism as the alternative to Khrushchev.

(vii) The 'general-line' led to a new and more dangerous phase of leftism. The theory of uninterrupted revolution under the proletarian dictatorship was anti-Marxist.

(viii) Corruption was a product of Mao's wrong line and of the irrational cadre system. But the Four Clean-ups Campaign tried to deal with it simply by purging lower officials.

(2) On the Great Proletarian Cultural Revolution, Wang Juntao believed that it was a mass movement directed by Mao's wrong line, but he also thought that it had produced some valuable new ideas. Fang Zhiyuan thought that the Cultural Revolution was an unsuccessful anti-bureaucratic revolution, but that reactionary forces like Lin Biao and the Gang of Four had tried to exploit it in their own interests. Most candidates had rather simple ideas about the Cultural Revolution. The majority thought that it was reactionary. A large minority saw it as a complex affair that required further analysis. A few saw it as a failed revolution. But so far there has been no deep or detailed discussion of it.

(3) On 29 November Wang Juntao and nine others held a discussion on whether or not Mao was a marxist. Wang pointed out that the core of marxism is historical materialism, and that marxism starts by analysing the productive forces and only then analyses productive relations, the productive mode and the mode of social development. But all along Mao based his analysis of Chinese society on class relations, and consistently ignored the determining role of productive forces... Second, Wang pointed out that marxism stresses the role of the masses in history and opposes historical idealism, whereas Mao ran a sort of oligarchy both inside and outside the party and was a historical idealist who refused to learn from the experience of advanced democracies. Third, Wang pointed out that marxists

have always emphasised that people should critically accept and preserve their cultural heritage, but Mao denounced a large part of that heritage as bourgeois and feudal, and so did great harm to Chinese culture. Wang concluded from his analysis that Mao was not a real marxist. In three subsequent essays he elaborated these views. Among other things he said that... if Mao was not a marxist, then perhaps other leaders like Liu Shaoqi and Zhou Enlai were also not marxists. He criticised Mao's view, formed in his old age, that a new class of bourgeois had grown up inside the party. But not all candidates agreed with Wang's assessment of Mao...

(4) Most candidates, in discussing the nature of Chinese society, used terms like 'socialism in the broad sense', 'semi-socialism' and 'near socialism'. Xia Shen said that society's intangible interests had superseded the practical needs of individuals. Abstract ideas of the collective had come to dominate over personal values. The high degree of centralisation in politics, economics and ideology had become a serious obstacle to social progress. Fang Zhiyuan pointed out that collective ownership of the means of production does not equal socialism, and that socialism must also embrace democracy. Democracy is both a means and an end. Without democracy, collective ownership is illusory. Wang Juntao pointed out that after the crushing of the Gang of Four, at first only the most extreme manifestations of Mao's wrong line were discarded... Since then there have been some good developments and some bad. The people and some leaders have come to realise that bureaucratism is a problem of the system, and that it would be sensible to adopt certain aspects of the political system of capitalist societies. But at the same time Democracy Wall, which mapped out China's path for the eighties, has been closed down. Yang Peikuai said that intellectuals are the most progressive force in society. Wang Juntao said that intellectuals, supported by youth and students, provide the main impetus for reform. The peasants enthusiastically support reform, while the workers are already its main beneficiaries. The main obstacle to it comes from sections of the cadres. Tian Cheli said that the middle cadres were the main obstacle, and that they should be pushed into action from two sides (the Central Committee, and the rank and file).

(5) There were various views on how reforms should be carried out. These views can be summarised as follows:

(i) Xia Shen and others said that China's shortcomings originate in the extreme centralisation of political, economic and ideological control, and that this centralisation must be destroyed. The achievement of a modern economy and modern thinking are intimately connected to the achievement of political democracy. Chinese society will be reformed throughout or not at all.

(ii) Fang Zhiyuan and others said that the further liberation of thought is the main precondition for successful reform in any sphere.

(iii) Hu Ping and others said that democracy and the legal system must be strengthened. Democracy means not only that the majority should rule, but also that the rights of minorities are properly protected and that the powers of the leaders are checked. Genuine democracy is therefore impossible without the separation of powers and free public opinion. Other candidates said that the main task now was to interpret and elaborate the law, so that it becomes clear.

(iv) Yang Peikuai and others said that the economy is the basis of society, and that without economic development there could be no political democracy. Economic reform should come first, since without it no other reform was possible.

(v) Wang Juntao proposed four goals of political reform: inner-party democracy, separation of party and government, a system of checks and balances, and supervision of government by society...

(6) The question of freedom of speech was widely discussed ... Hu Ping said that free speech was beneficial both to the ruling class and to the ruled. The reason it was suppressed was that the low level of awareness of the masses. Others replied that free speech must be class-specific, and that counter-revolutionaries should not have it. But most candidates believed that the problem was not whether counter-revolutionaries should have free speech, but whether the rulers alone should have the right to decide who is revolutionary and who not. Some candidates said that in the absence of freedom of the press, Democracy Wall and the Four Great Freedoms were the only outlets for free speech,

and with their abolition even the most minimal free speech was wiped out.

(7) The case of Wei Jingsheng also became an issue in the election. Some said Wei's entire prosecution was wrong. Some said that the sentence was too harsh. Some said the trial was improperly conducted. Some said they were ignorant of the background and circumstances of the case. An opinion poll of eighteen candidates found none who thought the trial was completely correct.

(8) All candidates called for the reform of tertiary education. It was generally thought that tertiary education should aim to give students an all-round education and develop their abilities to the full, rather than turn them into instruments or machines. Many candidates favoured the credit system and open-book examinations. Some said that the administration and process of learning should be democratised and that students, teachers and other staff should form a representative council to which the Chancellor and other administrators would be directly accountable. Graduates should be assigned to jobs on the basis of a combination of their own personal wishes and the country's needs. Many candidates said that the main problems facing youth in China were the crisis of faith, unemployment and the difficulty of getting an education. But many thought that present-day youth have many good attributes, including scepticism, independent thinking, enthusiasm for new things, a zeal for reform, a commitment to democracy, a strong desire for learning and an awareness of their own interests. They are a thinking and exploring generation...

(9) A main point in Xia Shen's manifesto was the need to respect human individuality, and to allow it to develop freely and to the full. The female candidate Zhang Ailing raised the same question from another angle. She called for women's liberation and said that the beauty of eastern femininity must be restored and issues concerning Chinese women should be further studied. Towards the end of the campaign she set up the Chinese Women's Study Association. (For further information, see Anita Rind's article below, pp. 195-201.)

Voters' political views and tendencies

Asked what sort of candidates they would like to see elected, voters replied as follows:

Radical social reformers	36.6 per cent
Moderate social reformers	19.5 per cent
Gradualists	18.8 per cent
Non-political candidates	10.2 per cent
Others	14.9 per cent

Most favoured moderate reform, although some wanted 'major surgery'. As to who should have responsibility for carrying out reform, many felt that they themselves were impotent, and looked for reforms initiated from above. Other felt that the leadership and the rank and file should act in concert, with the latter exerting pressure on the former, and that reforms would only be effective if the masses (especially their advanced sections) had a stake in them... Many voters voiced varying degrees of opposition to the closing down of Democracy Wall, the abolition of the Four Great Freedoms and the sentencing of Wei Jingsheng. Some students from the faculties of economics, law and politics drafted an Ordinance on Publication, Printing and Distribution which is now being circulated for signatures and will be submitted to the law commission of the National People's Congress. Those elected to represent the constituency would be asked to bring the matter to the regional people's congress and ultimately to the national one...

'Particularities' versus 'generalities'

Candidates tended to concentrate on local issues or 'particularities', whereas from the very beginning of the campaign voters showed an interest in overall political, theoretical and social issues — the so-called 'generalities'. The wider the campaign ranged, the more these 'generalities' come to the fore. This is partly because the electors were in this case students, who are more interested than most people in ideas, politics and broader culture. But there are more general reasons too. First, county-level congresses have little power and what power they do have is ill defined, so that they rarely take up local issues.

Second, people tend to judge candidates by their general political stand and theoretical competence, for if these are lacking, then what chance have they of fulfilling their 'particularistic' promises? Third, successful candidates at county level stand the chance of being elected upwards into congresses at higher levels, in which case what were previously 'generalities' would become 'particularities'. Fourth, China has too little experience of democracy, and in the past people have had little chance of voicing their opinions on important social issues. It is therefore only natural that with the deepening of the reform movement some people should seize the chance to make their general needs known, and that candidates should tend to discuss these broader issues. The party and government leaders should pay attention to this trend. Finally, it should be noted that student voters also voiced concern over various 'particular' issues such as the shortage of shops and services in the area, the inadequate cultural facilities, the traffic congestion and the noise pollution on the roads around the campus.

Guiding the election

Before the election the university administration indicated that it would not interfere in the proceedings. The local electoral authority abided by the electoral laws and provided various facilities to ensure the smooth running of the election, including places to put up posters, paper, and halls and lecture rooms. Campaigning was organised by the students themselves. But a free election was not what some party and government leaders wanted. Some top leaders outside the university accused various candidates of being 'dissidents'. The wall-posters were torn down immediately after the first round of voting, even though the results had not yet been announced and there was still another round to come.

The campaign was too narrowly conducted

Various important questions were raised during the election campaign, but they were not discussed in enough depth. For example, the assessment of the Cultural Revolution was too simplistic, and there was no real discussion of the causes of the absence of free expression in China. There are five main reasons for this. First, some voters were simply not interested in broader issues, and especially had no time for radical views. This reflects China's political and theoretical tiredness. Second, some voters are still bound by the orthodox ideology that had dominated them for all these years, and counter original opinions simply by parroting the official textbooks... Third, some of those who were interested in discussing broader and more important issues did not research them deeply enough. Fourth, an election campaign is not the most appropriate forum for a serious and detailed discussion of sensitive issues. Fifth, the election was conducted in too gentlemanly a way. Candidates rarely confronted one another's views, although when they did so, the exchanges were serious and substantial...

The implications of the election

This and other elections showed that the Chinese people have a certain basic grasp of politics and are no longer satisfied with letting party officials speak in their name... These elections also showed that the people want to make the congress at various levels the sole legislators and the sole source of the executive, and to place them under popular supervision...

He Nong
Election Scandal in a Rural Commune

The democratic movement was mainly confined to the cities, but here and there it made pinpricks into the vast countryside. This complicated account of shenanigans in a Shanxi commune shows some of the problems of introducing democracy to the Chinese villages. The story is further confused by the fact that the four men named in it have only two family names between them: Meng and Liu. This suggests that lineage ties may even today still cut across political divisions in the brigade. This article first appeared in *Fengfan* ('Boat's Sail'), December 1980.

Up to 1974 Comrade Liu Xijian was secretary of the party branch of Xiangshanzhuang brigade in Xi County, Shanxi Province. While he was secretary members of the brigade got lots of food and a good income, and the three fixed quotas (for production, purchase and marketing of grain) were fulfilled for twelve years running. In 1974 Liu was promoted to commune level, and Meng was appointed brigade secretary in his place. Under Meng the brigade's performance worsened and individual income dropped catastrophically to 0.5 yuan a day and 200 catties of food a year. Naturally brigade members were dissatisfied, and during the democratic election of cadres at the beginning of this year they urged Liu to stand as candidate for the brigade leadership. Liu felt that he could work better in the brigade than in the commune, and agreed to stand. The commune secretary, also called Liu, was away at a meeting in Taiyuan at the time, but Liu Xijian first discussed his decision with other commune leaders. Officers of the commune disciplinary board and the commune military board also stood as candidates in the brigade election. The result was that Liu Xijian was elected brigade secretary in Meng's place, a youth was elected brigade officer and Meng was elected as brigade vice-secretary. On his return from Taiyuan the commune secretary said: 'Liu has returned to the brigade and pushed out the incumbent secretary. He did not give others a chance, so he won't be given a chance either. All he's done is to create trouble in the brigade.' In the brigade study-group that the commune had organised the commune secretary, far from promoting unity, deliberately set about creating splits. The ten cadres in the study-group lined up for and against their new brigade secretary, and were so deeply split on this issue that they even refused to eat together. Brigade secretary Liu was under intense pressure and could only remain at his post because of the support he got from brigade members and from a section of the cadres. After his election he worked closely with the brigade members, stood firmly on the party line, and applied it with the necessary flexibility. The result was that despite a summer drought the harvest was good, and the three fixed quotas were once again fulfilled. By the end of the year average pay was expected to rise to between 1.3 and 1.5 yuan a day. The county radio even did a report on the brigade's achievements. This greatly annoyed the commune secretary, who could only swear and deny the facts.

The commune secretary's meddling was not without effect. Of the brigade's five teams, from now on only three could be counted on to attend brigade discussions. The other two teams, which were led by brigade vice-secretary Meng, did not dare attend for fear of offending him. If he wanted to he could easily make difficulties for them... For example, the former officer of the brigade women's federation was beaten and cursed as a traitor simply because she had voted for Liu Xijian in the election. During the summer drought the brigade organised the repairing of wells, but Meng's two teams refused to send anyone to help. Nonetheless they jumped the queue for water after the repairs were done. To avoid conflict, the other three teams gave way.

There was another Meng in the brigade whose father had some historical problems and who was treated as a 'bad element'. He had several times requested the commune to remove this label in line with the new party policy. The commune's organisation board asked the brigade for a report and then passed on an announcement that Meng's label should be removed. Since Meng was in a team led by brigade vice-secretary Meng, this announcement could not be made at a meeting of the brigade, for both 'bad element' Meng and vice-secretary Meng were boycotting these meetings. Therefore the brigade officer, who had been asked by the commune to relay the announcement as soon as possible, broadcast it over the radio. Vice-secretary

Meng's mother and wife then took to the streets reviling 'bad element' Meng and proclaiming that their family had been ruined by the brigade officer. When the brigade officer's wife went to work that day, she was surrounded in the brigade square by six members of the vice-secretary's family, who cursed her and severely beat her. Since things were getting out of hand, the brigade officer asked for a meeting with the commune secretary. The commune secretary said: 'I refuse to take any further action. You were wrong to make the announcement about Meng's label. You should apologise to the brigade vice-secretary. That man Meng has been labelled a bad element for more than twenty years now, and your broadcast was very damaging to the vice-secretary. If I were him I would have beaten you even worse. You've never had any respect for me. If you had, there wouldn't be so many conflicts in your village. This would never have happened if you had not been brigade officer.' The brigade officer said: 'I'm not brigade officer just because I want to be, I was elected to the post.' The commune secretary said: 'You could still have refused. If you'd refused, then Meng could have been elected.' The brigade officer said: 'Well, you can always sack me and appoint him.' The commune secretary did not appear at all worried and still refused to act on the matter of the beating. Later the brigade officer appealed to the county disciplinary board and the consultation board, but they did not dare take action because the commune secretary was a member of the county standing committee and vice-officers of the revolutionary committee. Later the brigade officer took his wife to the home of the commune secretary, who grudgingly promised to ask his assistant to deal with the problem. This assistant sent for brigade vice-secretary Meng five times but each time Meng failed to show up, so the assistant had no choice but to transfer it to the county court. The court in its turn transferred it to the Public Security Bureau. But despite all this transferring, the case was not resolved. In the brigade work came to a standstill. The brigade members were very angry, and said: 'The policies of our elected representatives can never be carried out as long as we only have the right to elect lower cadres. If the leading cadres don't control the elections, those who are elected cannot work.'

Zheng Xing

The Election Movement is in the Ascendant

Where the democratic movement was represented in the factories, its supporters tried with varying degrees of success to stand in factory elections in 1980. Little is known of these campaigns, except that where dissidents were not prevented from standing, they got big votes. But many obstacles were placed in the way of their campaigns by factory managers and party bureaucrats.

This account of factory elections first appeared in *Zeren* ('Duty'), no. 3, 14 January 1981.

In 1980 the word 'election' officially entered China's political vocabulary. This was an event of great consequence, joyously welcomed by many. Only a handful cut off from the people by an abyss fear this change, and are seeking ways to reverse it. But they will never succeed; however much they may resent and resist the progress of history, elections are spreading everywhere across this vast, ossified land.

After the elections in several of Shanghai's major universities, there was a spectacular chain reaction in universities throughout China, particularly in Beijing. Even more spectacularly, workers all over the country have followed the example of workers at Shanghai Motor Factory, who set a precedent by holding their own elections.

On 17 November 1980 He Defu, a young worker at the Organic Chemical Factory who is also an editor of *Beijing qingnian* ('Beijing Youth'), and Gong Ping, a worker at an oxygen factory, stood for election as people's representatives in Chaoyang district. They wrote a joint manifesto: 'The Chinese people suffered for ten long years from the ravages of the Cultural Revolution. This was clear proof that because the people did not rule the country or control their own destinies, power fell into the hands of a small minority whose mistakes have cost us dear...

'We view this election as a test of how far democracy can be implemented, and we view the electoral process as a struggle for democratic rights. At the same time, this election is a test of how far popular awareness has grown. Habit and tradition suggest that elections are a mere formality and that the representatives will have been secretly chosen in advance. We believe that this was true of previous elections. But now we must resolve that from now on things will be different. We have the protection of the law (although it is still far from perfect). We have support from inside and outside the country. And most important of all, the people are more aware. As long as we dare to struggle and know how to struggle, we can win recognition for the people's democratic rights. Voters should be confident and determined.

'At present the positions of master and servant are reversed in China. But the people strongly want those that they elect to truly represent them. The role of people's representatives is to defend and fight for the people's basic interests, to ensure that government works in the interests of the people, and to supervise the policies and measures of the ruling party. A people's representative must understand the people's wishes, dare to express them, fight to realise them, and firmly resist policies and measures that contradict them. We view this as our duty and obligation, whatever the consequences for us personally; which is why we want to be elected. If voters support us, we will fight to the end for their basic interests...

'The long-term aims of our struggle are as follows: a rise in the people's living standards must be a first priority, and should be written as such into the Constitution; we must realise socialist modernisation in all spheres, including in democracy, ideology, consciousness and people's livelihood; all these are interrelated aims, and none can be omitted. We view this election as a test of the ruling party. Does it believe in the people and stand together with the people? Or does it stand against the people?'...

In the first round of 'discussion and negotiation' He Defu got 202 votes; in the second round he got 451 votes, and came third in the election. In the oxygen factory Gong Ping came fourth; but in his case leading cadres held 'individual discussions' and 'greetings sessions' with each voter, so there were many abstentions...

Early this month, there were also elections for people's representatives in Qingyuan, Hebei Province. After the officially approved nominations had gone through, Wang Yifeng, a young worker in the sales department of a hardware factory, courageously rose to his feet to announce his candidature. He distributed and posted up an election manifesto headed 'Citizens, you must control your own fate'. In it he wrote: 'People's representatives, as the name shows, should represent the people's wishes and interests. To be a people's representative is not to wear hero's laurels, nor to carry official rank, nor to be in a position to pursue fame or to repress the people. People's representatives should be militants and servants of the people. They should dare to fight bureaucracy, to speak up for the people and to work for the people. They should be neither selfish nor self-effacing.

'Citizens! The nomination of candidates is now closed, but what do you know of those who have been nominated? Are they prepared to accept your mandate? Do they stand for reform of the state, and are they capable of carrying it out? Obviously you do not know, since the candidates have not explained their views and aspirations to you. But experience shows that without campaigns there can be no elections, especially not elections for people's representatives. What is a campaign? It is a competition among those up for election. It is the process whereby candidates (nominated or self-nominated) try to get elected by making the best speech or writing the best manifesto, and by demonstrating their ideological level and their aspirations.

'I was born on 4 October 1954 into a peasant family in Qingyuan County. My family was poor. After a serious illness I became poverty-stricken and had to beg for my living. The endless bleakness stimulated my young ambition, and I studied hard to change the world. I had no money to enter school, but I managed with the support of others to study for five years, although it was not easy. That was during the Cultural Revolution. At the age of sixteen, I went to work in commerce. At eighteen, I joined the army. This experience tempered my ambition and character. It also taught me that poverty is general, and that it is caused by the underdevelopment of the social system of production. And so it became my burning ambition to help liberate the people of the whole world and build a world of peace and happiness. From then on I began to pay attention to social issues, to study history, politics and philosophy, and to look for ways of changing the world. By the age of 20, I had learned that the science of marxism is the ideological weapon with which to transform oneself and society. Since then I have always used marxist theories as my guide, transformed myself through practice, and learned from others in order to improve my knowledge and skills. I devote my spare time to the theoretical study of Chinese society and of the world. In April 1976 I was discharged from the army and worked for a while in a native products factory. In 1978 I was transferred to the sales department of a hardware company. Since the party's Third Plenum issued the call for the liberation of thought, I have put all my energy into researching theoretical questions of the Chinese Revolution. In October 1980 I submitted my article "Socialist revolution: a special transitional period" to the state theoretical institute.

'Although the electoral law has been drawn up and general elections have begun, some bureaucrats have tried to control the elections, and have failed to explain their true meaning and procedure. The result is that when it comes to voting, many people are still in the dark. Even worse, the candidates are chosen by the leaders. I believe that this is wrong, that it breaches electoral law, and that it defiles public opinion. I hope voters will fully understand the meaning of their vote. If we all vote for someone who genuinely represents our views, such lawless acts will lose their point: for what is small will become big, and few will become many. All power will return to the hands of the people. As a start, here are three proposals that will benefit the people of our area: (1) A procedure must be worked out, and immediately implemented, for electing and dismissing leaders of the administrative units. (2) Units must be autonomous, accounting must be done at unit level, and workers must get a share in profits. (3) A procedure must be drawn up at once to shorten the working hours of women and to protect their health. Electors, please vote for me. I will speak and work for you.'

Wang Yifeng put up his manifesto on the north wall of the County Committee building on the night of 6 January, but by the next morning it had been torn down. The same day Wang protested that the election was being 'barbarously and illegally sabotaged'.

Mr Guo of the County Committee phoned the head of the

hardware company on the 6th to inform Wang Yifeng that his manifesto had been torn down in line with the recent constitutional ban on wall-posters. On 7 January Wang replied in an open letter:

> 1. The Four Great Freedoms, which include the freedom to write wall-posters, were struck out of the Constitution on the grounds that Article 45 already guarantees the freedom of speech, to which category wall-posters belong. So striking out the Four Great Freedoms does not make wall-posters a crime.
> 2. It is not against the law for people to write wall-posters. If it is, then please tell me what law, since I know nothing of it. If wall-posters were illegal, then so would be all propaganda put up on walls. Are notices put up by the Judicial Department wall-posters? Are commercial adverts wall-posters? Are the black-on-yellow notices outside the County Committee wall-posters? If so, why are they not banned?

On 9 January Wang Yifeng wrote out a 'Proposal for disallowing official candidates who have been illegally nominated'. In it he pointed out that in his electoral constituency 'nine candidates had been reduced to three; there was no proper discussion — voters were simply instructed to raise their hand in support of the three people decided on by the Commercial Bureau. No particulars of the other six nominees were presented for discussion, and I, as a self-nominated candidate, was completely ignored. This is not election but a disguised form of appointment, and as such a serious offence against the law'... Wang ended his proposal as follows: 'I shall wait three days for an answer to these points. If I do not get one, I shall join with other voters to complain directly to the Legal Committee of the People's Congress, and I shall call on all voters to rise up and struggle against this lawless bureaucracy, and to fight for the rights of which they have been deprived.'

Needless to say, no answer came, so after three days Wang Yifeng lodged a complaint with the Central Committee...

The Student Movement in Hunan

In the early spring of 1927 'an unknown young man called Mao Zedong' (as Victor Serge described him at the time) wrote a report on the Peasant Movement in Hunan that was destined to become a classic of the Chinese Revolution. Perhaps the author of 'The Student Movement in Hunan' had Mao's report in mind when he wrote this interesting account of events in Changsha in the early winter of 1980. The account shows that it was still possible even after the first crackdowns of 1979-80 to persuade the national leadership in Beijing to intercede on the democratic movement's behalf against conservative provincial leaders. Tao Sen, the leader of the Changsha students, was later arrested and imprisoned as a dissident.

This article here abridged, first appeared in *Renminzhi sheng* ('Voice of the People'), no. 6.

On 9 October 1980 two thousand students of the Hunan Teachers' Training College marched to the office of the provincial party committee. They were protesting against the college administration, which had broken the Election Law. They organised mass meetings, processions, petitions and a hunger strike. This finally led to victory. Students from other colleges supported them, and strikes were organised in colleges and factories... There follows a report of this struggle.

On the evening of 20 September Liang Heng, a student at the Hunan Teachers' Training College, announced that he would stand for election to the local government. He said: 'I do not believe in Marxism-Leninism. I favour democratic socialism. I want to reform the university's distribution system.' The students Liu Zhongyang and Tao Sen also announced their candidatures. All three organised forums and put up posters. But the college's vice-president, Su Ming, said that this was bourgeois electioneering, and that since the Four Greats (including wallposters) had been banned by the national leadership, the posters were illegal. Tao Sen protested to the provincial party that these activities were in no way 'bourgeois'.

Between 22 September and 6 October three primary elections were held to determine who would go forward into the final round. But the college authorities were unhappy with the outcome, and organised a fifth and even a sixth primary. The electors boycotted the fifth round. On 6 October the authorities nominated their own candidate for the final round of voting... On 8 October the fourth round ended and the college administration said that the names of the six official candidates would be announced the next day.

Next evening the college radio said that the election committee, in line with majority feeling, had chosen seven official candidates (including Tao Sen and Liang Heng). This attempt by the election committee to impose its will on the voters angered the students, thousands of whom marched spontaneously to the college office singing *The Internationale* and other songs. Three representatives demanded to meet Su Ming, and asked for an explanation. Su Ming responded rudely and refused to give an explanation. He accused the students of acting like in the Cultural Revolution, of disturbing social order and of behaving illegally. Saying that he was going to sleep, he returned to his office.

The students were furious at his bureaucratic attitude. Two thousand of them marched to the office of the Hunan party provincial committee. They called on Tao Sen to come out and lead them, and Tao Sen did, his eyes filled with tears.

The marchers shouted 'Down with bureaucratism!', 'Down with feudalism!', 'Let the people be the masters!', 'We want democracy!' and 'No to autocracy!' They arrived at the provincial office at midnight. They elected sixteen representatives (including Tao Sen), three secretaries and two special secretaries. These people marched into the office. At 2.25 a.m. local party leaders... negotiated with them. Reporters from *Guangming ribao* ('Guangming Daily') and two provincial papers were present. Two hours later the provincial party committee conceded that the students' petition was legal and promised to send a work-team to investigate.

At 4.30 a.m. the negotiators left the office. Tao Sen said: 'We've won!' The two thousand waiting students cheered and lifted the representatives onto their shoulders. After Tao Sen had reported on the discussions, the students marched back to the college. It was by now six o'clock in the morning.

Early on 10 October the students' union executive held an emergency meeting. In the afternoon the party and youth cadre of every department also met. At the same time, the students were celebrating their victory. At the party meetings, members were told to trust in marxism-leninism and the party leaders, and to stand firm and not join in illegal activities. One party leader... in the Chemistry Department said he would find out the names of the students who had signed the petition, and that he would educate these people and help them.

That afternoon the provincial party work-team arrived. They met with the student representatives, but concluded that the college election committee had acted legally in adding one more name to the list of six final candidates. This only encouraged the college administration. On 11 October Tao Sen sent the following telegram to party General Secretary Hu Yaobang, and to Peng Zhen, Wang Zhen and Yuan Renyuan:

> Some leading cadres have suppressed the democratic election at our college. Two thousand students protested spontaneously. Their protest was well organised and disciplined. As a citizen, a candidate and a students' representative, I ask you to send a work-team to Changsha. Please reply at once.

On 12 October Tao Sen, Liang Heng and another announced their temporary withdrawal from the election in protest against the college's action. They demanded that the election be postponed, but the voting went ahead on 14 October. Again the students petitioned the provincial party office. This time there were three thousand of them. They arrived at 11 o'clock in the evening. Two hours later the provincial party turned down their demands.

At 2.40 a.m. eighty-seven students, including Tao Sen and Liang Heng, went on hunger strike. While expressing their determination, they began to weep. The other students wept too. Their tears were a protest against bureaucratism.

The next morning Tao Sen telegrammed Hu Yaobang and the Premier, Zhao Ziyang, asking them to intervene. Four out of five of the college students came to the provincial party office to show their support for the hunger-strikers. As a result, the election planned for 14 October could not go through.

The same day 800 students of the Hunan Medical School marched through Changsha in support of the Teachers' Training

College students, and three thousand marched that afternoon... On 15 October the students went on general strike. The famous writer Ou Yangshan went to visit the hunger-strikers. He gave them his support, and said he would go on hunger-strike too if necesary. Thousands of students at other Changsha colleges also went on strike. In the meantime Wang Zhen, of the central party leadership in Beijing, telephoned Tao Sen twice, but his calls were intercepted by a local party leader... Finally Wang Zhen got through to Tao Sen. Wang told Tao that the central authorities [in Beijing] had already sent an investigating team to the college, and told him to end the hunger strike. Tao Sen refused to do so until the students' demands were met. By 7 o'clock that evening, twenty-one hunger-strikers had fainted.

Students from all over Changsha... and ordinary citizens gathered to show their support, and even representatives of Beijing University flew into the city. Later that evening students' and workers' representatives decided to organise a city-wide general strike and march.

But then disaster struck. Tao Sen decribed what happened:

> Some bourgeois rightists and splitters emerged from the ranks. Together with the college and provincial authorities and gangsters, they undermined the struggle. On 16 October the hunger strike collapsed. I was the last to leave, in the cold wind. Tears flowed down my face as I looked at the workers, students and newspaper reporters who had come to show their support. The flame of socialist democratic reform was out. Intellectuals are so weak!

The next day the investigating team... sent by the National People's Congress arrived in Changsha and met with Tao Sen, and on 19 October the Party General Secretary Hu Yaobang arrived in the city. However, by deception the provincial officials prevented him and other central government officials from meeting the students' representatives.

When negotiations with the investigating team produced no results, the students decided to send representatives to Beijing to report on what had happened. The Provincial Party Secretary, Mao Zhiyong, warned them not to go to Beijing, and said that if they did, they would be arrested by the security police. But at

9.50 the next morning the twenty-one students got on the train bound north. En route they were feted by student union officials and representatives.

On 27 October the Hubei provincial party committee sent some officials... on board the train to listen to Tao Sen's story. Their leader said:

> If the Hunan committee can solve your problem, they should do so quickly. Otherwise, it's quite legal for you to petition the Beijing authorities. That means that you trust the party centre. We did not know that you were coming, so we were unable to prepare lodgings and meals for you. We must apologise. But we will take you by car to the Hubei Provincial Lodging-House no. 2. We will help you with daily necessities. If you have any request, let us know. You are our country's hope and future. We must take good care of you.

...The Hubei committee sent cars as promised but the students decided to continue the trip to Beijing, so they turned down the offer... The Hubei students said they hoped a students' federation would be set up on a national level to truly represent students' interests. They said they wanted to maintain contact with us...

Back on the train, the students explained to the head conductor what had happened. He was very concerned, and reported to the Railway Department. The Railway Department told the head conductor and all stations along the line that they had known that Tao Sen was travelling north and that he and the other representatives had difficulty in paying their fare. The Railway Department told all stations that they should be allowed to pass.

The petitioners arrived in Beijing early on 29 October. They were received by the Central Committee and the State Council, and welcomed by democratic militants and by college students in the capital. They sent the following telegram to their college: 'The situation is fine. The Central Committee leaders are very concerned. Unite against the bureaucrat, resolutely carry out reforms, learn the lessons and continue the struggle.'

In Beijing the petitioners were received several times by

Central Committee officials. The government finally decided that Su Ming had to make a self-criticism and permit a new election. The team returned to Hunan on 11 November.

Chen Ding

Youth Disturbances in China's Far West

Cities in most Third World countries have grown at an alarming speed in recent years as birth-rates soar and peasants leave the villages in search of a better life. But the urban economy is unable to absorb all comers, so that many stay unemployed or semi-employed. City-born educated young people also find it hard to get jobs in societies where the education system and the labour market are often badly matched. As a result urban society becomes tense, violent and unstable.

For many years China has been called the exception to this pattern. Between 1968 and 1975 China's urban authorities sent twelve million school-leavers 'up to the mountains and down to the villages', and at the same time stopped peasants from resettling in the towns. For most of these urban youth the transfer to the villages was meant to be lifelong. The aim of this programme was to control the growth of the towns, help develop the villages and reduce the 'three great differences' — between town and country, worker and peasant, mental and manual labour.

Sent-down youth have often organised to protest at their exclusion from the cities. During the Cultural Revolution groups of them called for the system of permanent resettlement to be turned into a system of rotation, and some even wanted to abolish it altogether. Others called for an end to abuses in the implementation of the programme. Many believed that the procedure by which they were chosen for rustication was arbitrary or discriminative, that it was used to punish rebels and that young people with good family connections could usually managed to stay in the towns.

The word 'youth' is quite elastic in People's China. Officially it refers to those between the ages of fifteen and twenty-four, if you take eligibility for membership in the Communist Youth League as your criterion, but there are often difficulties in getting over-age members of the League to retire from it. Some of the people called 'youth' in Chen Ding's article are in their thirties, but this is because they are still officially seen as belonging to the category of 'sent-down youth'.

After the fall of the 'gang of four', the government recognised that the rustication programme had largely failed. Living conditions for sent-down youth are hard, and it is clear that most will never accept the idea of a lifetime among the peasants. Because they are in the villages by compulsion and not by choice, their morale is low and they contribute little to village society, so that most peasants see them as a burden rather than as a vital part of the community.

The government therefore took steps to improve the conditions of sent-down youth and allowed many to return home — some 400,000 in Shanghai's case. But many are still refused permission to leave the villages. According to an official of Shanghai's labour bureau, more than half million young Shanghainese sent to the countryside have not returned, and there are no plans to let them return (*The Guardian*, 29 September 1981).

This article, here abridged, first appeared in *Zhengming* ('Contention'), Hongkong, 1 May 1981.

In late 1980 disturbances broke out in Xinjiang, involving as many as 70,000 people. When the incident reached its climax, some government offices were taken over. Finally, the local authorities got the situation under control, but they had to make concessions. The incident touched off a general shock whose repercussions have not yet completely died down even today.

Nine out of ten of those who took part in the disturbances were young men and women from Shanghai or local people married to them. A handful of local ruffians joined the crowd and tried to fish in troubled waters, but they were few in number. Nonetheless, they caused some trouble, thus giving the authorities the excuse to use force.

This incident happened in the city of Aksu, in western Xinjiang. Disturbances continued for more than a month. It was one of the most serious incidents in Xinjiang since the founding of the present regime. This protracted and widespread commotion may be compared with the incident in early 1960s when the Soviet Union incited minority nationalities on the frontier to flee in large numbers. The bloody conflict in the last stage of the disturbance was not entirely unavoidable. Unfortunately the young people were too stubborn and went to extremes, and local authorities handled their case wrongly.

As early as last autumn, youth on farms near Aksu began to discuss returning to Shanghai with the local authorities. They established ties among themselves, formed an alliance, and elected scores of representatives to conduct negotiations...

At these talks, the party committees said that they had no authority to make a decision on this important issue, but must first ask the Aksu Prefecture Administrative Office for instructions.

The instructions ran: 'It is difficult to accept the demands of the Shanghai youth. It is up to the grass-roots units to enlighten these young people.' But the party committees on the farms knew well that as long as the basic problems of the Shanghai youth remained, it would be difficult to persuade them ideologically... They therefore tried to shift the responsibility back to the higher level. They told the representatives that they had done their best to present the case to the higher level and that if the Prefecture would accept the delegates' demands, they would create no obstacles. This was a hint to the representatives to go to the Prefecture for a solution.

The representatives took the hint, and decided after consulting the masses to approach the Aksu Prefecture Administrative Office. When they arrived for negotiations, the office made an emergency call to the Xinjiang Autonomous Region Party Committee in Urumqi, which telegraphed back that the problem should be dealt with on the spot. The Prefecture party committee knew that the Shanghai youth would make trouble if they were not allowed to return to Shanghai, but they had no choice but to try to negotiate...

During the negotiations the representatives found that the two sides held incompatible views and that talks would not resolve the matter, so they decided to force concessions. Instead of marching to far-away Urumqi to present their case, they decided to create disturbances in Aksu, where all the Shanghai young people gathered...

During the negotiations, the authorities stressed that Shanghai youth who had immigrated to Xinjiang before the 'Cultural Revolution' were not included among those who were allowed by the central government to return to the big cities. They explained that if the government made an exception of the Shanghai youth, then people who had been sent to the villages would strive for the same thing everywhere. They warned that Xinjiang stood on the frontline in the struggle against the Soviet Union, and that any reckless action would harm China and its people. They therefore asked the delegates to refrain from any rash move. At the same time, they recognised that the Shanghai youth had a real problem and promised that the government would gradually resolve it.

But... the representatives held radically different views and said that the official position merely repeated the cliches of the past twenty years, and did nothing to improve their conditions

They had waited patiently for twenty years; would they now have to wait another twenty? They alleged that... many young people with good connections managed to get their residence registration transferred to big cities. This was a major complaint of the Shanghai youth.

Moreover, a small handful of people hated the socialist system and poured oil on the fire, so that negotiations broke down. By mid-November, the two sides were like fire and water. After mid-November Shanghai young people began to leave their farms and go to Aksu city to support their representatives; meanwhile, representatives returned to the farms to consult with other young people. The party committees could do nothing to stop them leaving. Most young people were determined to stage a mass demonstration in Aksu, and vowed not to give up until they got satisfaction.

By late November, about 10,000 Shanghai young people had gathered in Aksu, and their numbers grew daily. The representatives were ready to take extreme action.

They organised a protest rally and a hunger strike in front of the Prefecture Office. As the young people were leaving their farms, they heard rumours that the authorities had allowed the ringleaders to transfer their residence back to Shanghai, so they sold their belongings and hurried with their wives and children to march on Aksu...

The news spread quickly, and they grew to as many as 70,000... The situation soon got out of control.

These young people, having sold all they had and cut off all means of retreat, were strong in fighting spirit... They were a pitiful sight. They thought that the time had come to burn their boats and fight with their backs to the river.

Of the tens of thousands of people who took part in the hunger strike, about a hundred, including women and children, died of exhaustion. During the demonstration the Aksu authorities did much ideological work, several times sent delicious food, and tried to persuade the demonstrators to end their fast. But the demonstrators were determined to fight to the bitter end, and the organisers called on the young people not to take food offered by the authorities. When some died, tension mounted and disturbances broke out. The demonstrators held the authorities responsible for the deaths, and pointed the spearhead of their struggle at the local government offices.

They elected a leading group and set up a command of seven members... Under the slogan 'Die at Aksu or return to Shanghai alive!' they took military-style action against government offices in Aksu. The authorities sent forces to suppress the attackers, but neither the troops nor the security personnel opened fire. The confrontation was limited to hand-to-hand fighting and scuffles...

The riot leaders decided to risk everything in the hope of gaining the attention of the Xinjiang Regional Party Committee and even of Beijing. They organised a 'dare-to-die corps', a 'pickets team' and a 'dog-beating team', and tried for an all-out attack on the government offices.

The 'dare-to-die corps' were dauntless and quick in action. Whenever the security forces slackened their vigilance, the corps would lead a large group of followers to charge forward and take over a building. The 'pickets' were to maintain order and prevent people from fishing in troubled waters. The 'dog-beating team' was a unique invention. The riot leaders knew that when the struggle escalated many would try to back out even though they had sworn that it was 'better to die in glory than live in dishonour'. To enforce internal discipline, prevent defections and deal with outside opponents, a special 'dog-beating team' was therefore organised. The 'dog-beating team' was cruel and very unpopular.

According to an old Chinese saying, 'An army burning with righteous indignation is bound to win'. The demonstrators with their superior numbers and organisation were in a good position. The members of the 'dare-to-die corps', the 'pickets' and the 'dog-beating team' were determined fighters who acted swiftly and effectively. Even more important, the local authorities and the military had shown extreme self-restraint and never once opened fire. The demonstrators soon occupied all important government offices in Aksu.

Between late November and early December, all government offices, including the Administrative Office, the Bureau of Agriculture and Reclamation and the Bureau of Public Security, were seized by rioters. The government leaders slipped away in an effort to avoid further conflict. Even the security personnel went into hiding. All political functions were paralysed, and the entire city seemed in the hands of the demonstrators.

But most demonstrators were not against the socialist system, and had started the riot mainly as a way of getting back to Shanghai. They committed no outrages and maintained fairly good discipline. Some lawbreakers wanted to stir up trouble, but they were too few to have any effect. The demonstrators made no move and waited for the local authorities to come to the conference table.

The prefecture party committee understood the intentions of the demonstrators, and agreed to send them back to Shanghai by rail. They even announced that those who were determined to return home could have their residence registration transferred back to Shanghai. This removed the cause of grievance, and pacified the demonstrators.

As a result, the young people withdrew from the government offices, and made preparations to depart. They were sent back to Shanghai in batches. But on arriving in Shanghai, they were not welcomed, not even by their own parents. This was not really surprising. After more than twenty years, family members had become estranged. In Shanghai living quarters are very restricted, and could hardly accommodate the returned young people with their wives and children. Worse still, even though the Xinjiang authorities had sent their residence registration back to Shanghai, the Shanghai authorities refused to accept it. This was an especially hard blow.

The returnees refused to accept their fate and tried to repeat what they had done in Aksu. Once again they held street demonstrations. But this time they met with failure. They had not the support of local people, and even their families wanted them to return to Xinjiang. Their parents and brothers gave them some money to buy articles for daily use back in Xinjiang. When things reached this stage, only a few young people from rich families could stay in Shanghai; all the rest knew that they had played a losing game. They realised that they should not have sold their belongings on leaving Xinjiang, since now they had to return there. Had they known beforehand what they now knew they would never have gone to Shanghai.

Meanwhle, on instruction from the central government, the Xinjiang authorities made preparations for resettling the Shanghai youth. They repeatedly announced that those who had taken part in the disturbances would be treated no differently from the others. But for the seven ringleaders and those who had committed crimes, the outcome was not so fortunate. Early in December 1980, when all the demonstrators had left Aksu and were preparing to depart, the local authorities arrested these people.

By then, the disturbances in Xinjiang were over. On 23 January 1981 New China News Agency published the following report: 'Recently Wang Zhen, member of the CCP Central Committee's Political Bureau, paid a visit to Xinjiang and urged cadres and young people of all nationalities to carry forward the glorious tradition, continue their hard struggle, step up the frontier construction and bring benefit to future generations.' ...According to reliable sources, the Party Secretariat and the State Council held a joint conference to discuss ways of dealing with the consequences of the policy of sending young people to the countryside. The conference held that the past policy of persuading young city people to settle down for good in frontier regions is harmful to China, to the peasants and to the young people, and could lead to social unrest. Undoubtedly, the Xinjiang incident proved this point.

The conference recognised that China will have to continue sending large numbers of people to remote frontier areas, but they agreed that there must be changes in the way in which this policy is implemented. Experience shows that the young city people cannot be the main force for this policy. They find it hard to settle down, and each year the central government has to spend big sums of money on their resettlement. Economically, the loss outweighs the gain.

Finally the conference decided to mobilise peasant families in densely populated provinces such as Shandong, Henan and Hebei to migrate to remote frontier areas. But this migration should be voluntary, and proper material incentive should be given, e.g. each peasant family should get 500 yuan rehabilitation expenses. On arrival at their destination they should be given large private plots of land, and no grain tax should be levied on newly reclaimed wasteland for five years. Peasants in Shandong and Hebei Provinces can now move of their own accord to Heilongjiang Province, and peasants in Henan can move to Xinjiang. Since Heilongjiang and Xinjiang are on China's border and both have large areas of virgin wasteland, resettling people there is strategically advantageous. Moreover, peasants in densely populated provinces lead hard lives and gladly move to these regions. According to reports, the CCP Central Committee considers this project both practical and effective, and is planning to send 100,000 peasant families to Heilongjiang and to Xinjiang over the next year or so.

Fengfan

The Reawakening of the Chinese Working Class

The democratic movement tried hard to widen its social base by organising, publicising and defending struggles for higher wages and better conditions in the factories. One particularly disadvantaged group are the single workers: workers who, although married, live apart from their families. Their conditions are described in this article. In February 1981 Reuters and AFP reported that according to the 'Taiyuan Daily' steel workers in Taiyuan, Shanxi Province, launched a struggle against the 'privileged bureaucratic class' and called for a 'struggle for democracy and freedom'. They demanded an end to the dictatorship and the power to determine their own future. The newspaper announced that the authorities had smashed a 'counter-revolutionary clique' of political dissidents, and would put them on trial. It is likely that those arrested included the author of this article, which appeared in December 1980 in the inaugural issue of the unofficial Taiyuan journal *Fengfan* ('Boat's Sail').

Recently the single workers at the Taiyuan steel works spontaneously demonstrated for improved conditions and in defence of their rightful interests... The single workers in our country are the worst treated of any category of workers. They earn very little, and enjoy few social benefits. They eat every day in the staff canteens, which are invariably badly managed. In theory they are entitled to fixed food rations, but in practice they never get more than 80 per cent of their rations. They pay twice as much in the canteen as workers living with their families, and for worse food. They spend their lives in cramped single quarters that are seldom properly looked after. Some of these quarters are falling apart through neglect or are poorly lit and dirty, just like the capitalist slums they show us in the films. These single workers are separated from their families for years on end, and only have twelve days' leave a year in which to visit them. Although they are married, they live like widows or widowers. They too create social wealth, just like the worker-cadres. But their families get no medical care insurance. Other workers whose families are here in Taiyuan get coal allowances, but not so the single workers. Female single workers are often reduced to tears because their husbands are not there to help them with their problems. The single workers at the Taiyuan steel works are right to put forward their ten demands.

The leading cadres at the steel works should canvas opinions and devise long-term solutions to the problems of these single workers, so that they can forget their worries and commit themselves wholeheartedly to the Four Modernisations. But instead, some of these leaders range themselves against the people's interests, denouncing legal meetings as 'Black Gatherings' and criticising people even for visiting one another...

The actions of these single workers are proof that the working class of our country has reawakened. On the surface it would seem that they are merely out to protect their own legal rights. But in reality they have voted for democracy, whether they are aware of it or not. They know that if they want change, they must rely on their own power of organisation and on their own elected representatives, for no messiah will achieve change for them. And if those they elect no longer represent them, then the election must be reheld. The demands of broad sectors of the people are the social base upon which democratic change in our country will be founded...

Fu Shenqi

In Memory of Wang Shenyou, Pioneer of the Democratic Movement, Teacher, Comrade

Fu Shenqi was born in 1954 in a workers' family in Shanghai, and on leaving middle school went to work in a Shanghai generator factory. In 1977 he entered Shanghai Number Four Normal College, and returned to his factory the following year. He was a member of the Communist Youth League. In 1979 he joined with others to found Shanghai's unofficial journal 'Voice of Democracy'. When 'Voice of Democracy' declared its support for the 'strikes of Polish workers fighting for democracy and against bureaucratic tyranny', the authorities branded it as 'anti-party and anti-socialist'. When the National Federation of Unofficial Journals was formed in the autumn of 1980, it started its own journal, *Zeren* ('Duty'). From issue No. 3, Fu Shenqi became its chief editor. In October Fu stood for election in a factory in south Shanghai. Factory officials threatened that people who voted for Fu would not get a wage rise and the Communist Party branch flouted the regulations to stop his election. Still he got 43 per cent of the vote. In April 1981 Fu went to Beijing to petition the authorities for the right to publish freely, but he was arrested.

Fu's article on Wang Shenyou, an early martyr of the democratic movement, shows that even after the fall of the 'gang of four' the regime continued to repress and even execute dissidents. Because Wang Shenyou was a critic of the Maoists and an admirer of Deng Xiaoping, Fu hoped that his work would be made public and his name rehabilitated; but it is unlikely that this ever happened.

Today [28 April 1980] is the third anniversary of the death of Wang Shenyou, whom I mourn deeply. Although I have no time to write more than a brief recollection of him, having spent the day giving out leaflets at my factory and campaigning in the election, I am convinced that he would approve of my priorities. I dedicate my commitment to his memory.

I first met Wang in May 1976, shortly after the suppression of the demonstrations in Tiananmen Square against the Gang of Four. China was then under a dark cloud, and menaced by 'Red Terror'. In the thick fog, people were numbed, depressed and frustrated. But underground the fire was still burning, and people were seeking their way out of the darkness. Foremost among them was Wang Shenyou.

Wang grew up in a working-class family. His father was a cadre in the Jiabei district committee, and many of his relatives and friends were also officials or party members. Wang was intelligent and thirsty for knowledge. While still in his first year at Huadong College of Education, at the age of 18, he had already begun to formulate his independent standpoint. At college he excelled in all subjects.

Besides studying, he kept his 'never-ending' diaries. In these diaries he discussed current affairs and recorded his views on social injustices and on China's domestic and foreign policies. These writings revealed his youthful talent. Although not yet familiar with marxism, he was a revolutionary by instinct, who criticised the present and looked forward to the future.

When the Socialist Education Campaign began in the early sixties, Wang's diary-writing attracted the attention of the 'professional organisers of class struggle'. Wang was summoned to talk with cadres of the Communist Youth League, who said he should apply to become a League member; but while he was with them his drawers were searched and his diary was photographed. Secretly, the authorities began to concoct evidence of his 'crimes'.

Not long after this the Cultural Revolution broke out, and the attack on Wang Shenyou was temporarily postponed. At first Wang took no active part in the Cultural Revolution, but later he wrote some outstanding articles... It was during this time that he discovered marxism, particularly the classical marxist writings on the Paris Commune. He accepted Mao's later ideas, and saw the Cultural Revolution as an attempt to realise the Paris Commune. In his writings he defended the Cultural Revolution. One of his best works was *Follow Chairman Mao and Move Forward Bravely Amid the Great Wind and Waves*. Many university libraries probably still have copies of this tract.

But history is pitiless. Once Lin Biao, Jiang Qing and Kang Sheng took the reins of power, strict discipline was imposed, and the Red Guards, once the fearless defenders of the revolution, were ruthlessly crushed, and tossed aside like broken tools... Wang Shenyou also came under fire. He was labelled a counter-revolutionary and evidence collected during the Socialist Education Campaign was used against him. The authorities staged a display of his diaries and organised a criticism forum against him on the local radio. But they did not succeed in convicting him.

For a time, he was sent to labour camps. Later he was detained by the Public Security Bureau for interrogation. Finally, he was sent for re-education. During all this time he was kept jobless. And yet he never once gave up. He kept physically fit, learned foreign languages and studied marxism, equipping himself as an outstanding marxist and revolutionary. He made constant notes on his reading — his notes on *Capital* alone amounted to a million words. It was during this time that I got to know him. It was the evening of 6 May. I went to the Huangpu public library, with a book by Engels under my arm. I sat down to read. Wang Shenyou was sitting opposite me. His keen, deep eyes studied my young, naive face. He seemed to be interested in me. He smiled at me, and said something. I moved my seat nearer to his and we began to talk in whispers. In a short while we became close friends.

From then on we met and read together almost every day. We went for walks together, and discussed all sorts of problems. We were surprised to find that we shared similar views on many subjects. But his ideas were invariably more systematic, more profound and better grounded than mine. We spent numerous evenings together in the People's Square, the People's Park and the Shanghai Municipal Library.

For him marxism, though not a perfect or absolute truth, was a systematic and well-rounded scientific theory, and there was no alternative theory that could transcend it. He particularly praised Marx's theory of historical materialism, and used it to analyse present-day society. He criticised the theory of social leaps, and believed that Marx's successors had corrupted the revolutionary essence of marxism and turned it into a rigid dogma. He felt that the dogmas that Mao proposed in his old age were simply a cover for feudalism. Since China lacked a mature working class, the Communist Party developed as a peasant party led by revolutionary intellectuals, and the revolution it carried out was not proletarian-socialist but peasant, with a strong feudal tinge. After the revolution Chinese society therefore gradually evolved into a new form of oriental despotism. Once Wang said, 'Mao is just a peasant with a military cap'. Wang even challenged Mao's claim to be a marxist. He advocated a new approach to marxism and the need for a critical review of so-called Mao Zedong Thought. He founded a marxist study group, and was determined to revitalise the revolutionary spirit of marxism. He felt that ever since the Stalin era there had been a confrontation between feudal and scientific socialism in the world Communist movement, and that Mao and Stalin were both typical representatives of feudal socialism. At the time he believed that the reforms following destalinisation in the Soviet Union were a sign that scientific socialism was gaining ground. He therefore approved of comrade Deng Xiaoping's ideas and policies although they were not yet fully formed, and considered Deng a representative of scientific socialism. Even though the Cultural Revolution Group [the 'gang of four'] was still at the height of its power, Wang confidently predicted that it would fall, and that it would be succeeded by an era of scientific socialism represented by Deng. Then China would be able to assimilate Soviet experience and work out its own plans for reform. Wang particularly valued the April Fifth Movement that ultimately brought down the Gang of Four. He anticipated that this new political development would differentiate China from the Soviet Union, and equip it with its own unique identity.

I have none of Wang's theoretical works to hand, and what I have written is based simply on my recollections of our conversations. But fortunately Wang put his views on paper shortly before he died, and if I am not mistaken they will shortly become available to the public, which can then judge for itself the accuracy of my summary. Wang set out his ideas in a long letter to his girl-friend, and it was mainly on the basis of this letter that he would later be sentenced to death.

Wang had had more than one girl-friend, but for various reasons, mainly political, his relationships never lasted long. In July 1976 he was introduced to his last girl-friend. She was no ordinary woman, and had strong ideas of her own. After a few meetings Wang and she fell in love. Later, because she was somewhat pessimistic about the future, Wang wrote her his long letter, to lighten her spirits.

On 2 September 1976 I met Wang outside the Municipal

Library. At the time he was busy writing articles. Before we parted, I held his hand and warned him to be on his guard. I had a feeling that he was in for trouble. We arranged to meet again on 10 September at the South Library, but this meeting never happened, since the library was unexpectedly closed that day due to Mao's death. Three days later, I went to his house. His mother told me that he had left home, and was unlikely to return. I realised that something must have happened. I guessed that with Mao's death, anyone with a background like Wang's would be put under surveillance. It turned out that his letter to his girl-friend had fallen into the hands of the authorities, and that he had been arrested. But at the time, I was convinced that he would be set free.

Very soon, the Gang of Four fell from power. I was delighted at this historic change, and I hoped I would soon meet my teacher and comrade again. I joined in the criticism of feudal socialism, and in November 1976 I sent an article to *Hongqi* ('Red Flag') headed 'The Deceptions of Left Opportunism as Revealed in the Essay "On the Absolute Dictatorship of the Bourgeoisie" '. But feudal socialism did not easily quit the stage of history. Its supporters still wielded great influence, and used it to oppress the people.

In the municipal party committee there were various views about Wang Shenyou, but at the time some big-shots wrote that 'It would be disloyal to Chairman Mao not to kill this person', and with those few words his death warrant was signed.

On 21 April 1977, six months after the fall of the Gang of Four, the verdict on Wang was announced: 'Guilty of an extremely evil crime. If he is not killed, the people's anger cannot be assuaged.' I held the verdict with shaking hands. I was in an agony of grief and rage. Just a few words from these people could send a man to his death! There was nothing I could do to avert this tragedy, but I was deeply convinced that things could not go on like this, and that change was bound to come...

Today, it is possible that the municipal party committee will review the case of Wang Shenyou. Some people may continue to revile him, but most will see that he was a young man of great talent once they have read his last essay, and they will recognise him as a committed revolutionary, an outstanding marxist theoretician, and an eminent fighter for democracy. Even if the power elite refuse to admit this, history will prove that they are wrong.

If Wang Shenyou were alive today, I do not believe that his ideas would remain unchanged. If he had lived, he would have produced even greater ideas. But that was not to be. As for me, what is important is to look to the future and to realise my plans and dreams, and to do what is necessary. The road to democracy is long and winding. Perhaps new blood must be shed, in which case I offer my own for the shedding.

On 28 April 1977 Wang Shenyou sacrificed his young life for the truth of marxism, social progress and the people's happiness. He was only 32 years old. He never flinched from the truth, and he never bowed his head even in the face of death. He lived his life with his eyes turned towards the democratic future. His body is destroyed, but his spirit lives on, in me and in every other young marxist. Over these past three years Wang's smiling image has constantly appeared before me. It is as if every day he studies, discusses and struggles with me. His kind and tender manner, his industriousness, his sincere and realistic way of working and his devotion to truth will always be fixed in my memory, and will be reflected in my work.

Interview with Yang Jing

Yang Jing, born in Jiangling, Hubei Province, and in his mid-thirties, was a worker in the Beijing Steel Rolling Plant before his arrest in April 1981. Yang Jing became editor of *Siwu luntan* ('April Fifth Forum') after it began publishing for the second time in November 1980. This interview, conducted in March 1981, appeared in the Hongkong *Guanchajia* ('Observer') No. 42, 20 May 1981; it is among the most important and informative documents to survive the democratic movement. It shows Yang Jing to be on the left of the movement and without illusions in the party leaders.

This interview was translated by He Fu.

Why did 'April Fifth Forum' stop publishing in March 1980, and begin publishing again in November of the same year?

Producing 'April Fifth Forum' is a service to society, it is a service to the cause of true proletarian democracy. We stopped publishing in March 1981 for external and internal reasons. It is not necessary to explain the external reasons; you can draw your own conclusions from what you know about the political situation at that time. Nor do I want to dwell too much on the internal problems. To use a Chinese saying, 'one should not publicise family disputes'. During the period when we stopped producing, we had some wrong ideas internally that we believed would be resolved. Throughout that time, we received many letters of support, urging us to carry on and to re-issue the journal. We strongly agreed with this, because 'April Fifth Forum' is the social product of specific historical factors, and fulfils certain needs in society. None of our readers suggested that we should stop publishing. They even exaggerated 'April Fifth Forum's' worth, saying that it is the angel of marxism, and the sacred word of the suffering people of China. This made us re-think our hurried decision to cease publication, and encouraged us to overcome some internal problems that we had not thoroughly worked out. And so the journal eventually reappeared.

How does its reappearance relate to the development of the democratic movement nationally?

Today the trend throughout society is towards progress and democracy, so the more people involved in the struggle the better.

The reappearance of 'April Fifth Forum' will naturally make some contribution to the movement, and consolidate the forces seeking democracy. Re-issuing the journal will help us clarify some confusions, get us away from unhealthy influences and widen our support, so that we can make a better contribution to the development of the democratic movement.

What was the situation before and after the reappearance of 'April Fifth Forum'?

Around the time it reappeared, most unofficial journals in other parts of China were still publishing. Unfortunately, due to internal and external problems, we did not take part in that movement. We must take responsibility for that. We can only hope that we will work harder in the future, and make further progress.

In September 1980, in Guangzhou, a meeting was called of representatives of unofficial journals from all over China, and subsequently a National Federation of Unofficial Journals was set up. What was the effect of this development on the democratic movement nationally?

This meeting took place thanks to the comrades in the South, who took great risks and developed the democratic movement, which was at first quite primitive, to a higher level. I personally believe that this was an historic event. The setting up of the Federation was a historic contribution to the democratic movement. So our position is quite clear — even though we could not take part in it for various reasons, we support the Federation, we completely agree that we should work together to increase the internal solidarity of the democratic movement and to fight as a united body for democracy in China.

It is now more than four months since 'April Fifth Forum' re-appeared. How have the unofficial journals developed in other parts of China?

You can sum the situation up in one sentence. It has only just begun. The democratic movement represents the general demands of society, and arose out of the internal demands of society, so it is as wide and deep as society itself. In spite of barriers and pressures, and differences between one place and another or one journal and another, in the long run these are problems that can be resolved. The democratic movement has not only influenced all social layers, but has even had some response from within the party. There can be no doubt that it has support among all layers of society.

Some friends think differently — they say that the unofficial journals have big problems of distribution, and only produce between one and two thousand copies, and sometimes just a few hundred. In that case how can the democratic movement be said to influence all levels of society?

There are two aspects here. First, external pressure. Because of the restrictions on democracy, the dialogue between us and the masses came up against big obstacles. Earlier, when Democracy Wall was still tolerated, we could sell thousands of copies in five minutes. Now things have changed. But we are still workers living at the bottom of society, so even if we had no publications, our aspirations would still be the same as those of the masses. If our social existence is the same then so will be our social consciousness. But we must still introduce ideas to our readers. They are precious comrades. By contacting us they run great risk of persecution. They do not just read our publications, they pass them around and exchange ideas with other people. Some of them cannot work with us because their ideological or theoretical level is low, but we believe that their thinking and their ability to draw conclusions will improve through propaganda and through our publications, and they will eventually work together with us.

Can you say something about the struggle of the democratic movement for a Publications Law?

We believe that all civilised countries should have a Publications Law, but up to now our country does not have one. This means that democratic publications have no law to follow. This is a tragedy. So by fighting for a Publications Law we hope to change things, so that democratic rights can be realised in the Constitution. But the government has responded equivocally, even though some enlightened people in the party feel, like the democratic movement, that there is a need for such a law. For example, in October 1980 the State Publications Bureau said that unofficial journals objectively existed, and that they should be authorised, but this was opposed by the State Council.

What about Liu Qing?

The Liu Qing affair has been at the centre of attention of unofficial journals throughout China. Even Hongkong Chinese and Overseas Chinese are demanding that the government release him. However, the government's position is again unclear. It is still using the same old methods. We believe that the Liu Qing affair will only change if the social environment changes. If the social environment remains backward, the lot of individuals is hardly likely to improve much. So we see saving Liu Qing as the collective responsibility of the democratic movement.

We heard that democratic movement activists stood for election to the People's Congress in Beijing, Shanghai and Shaoguan. What were the results?

To stand for election is a constitutional right. But today a bureaucratic layer has already formed or is forming everywhere, and ordinary citizens who stand for election will inevitably clash with the interests of this privileged stratum. The results therefore depend on the level of awareness and determination of the citizens. In areas where awareness is high, quite good results were achieved in the elections, for example, at Beijing University [see above pp. 88-97], Fudan University and other places. But in places where people's consciousness is not high enough, and where bureaucracy is strong, all sorts of obstacles were put in the way of candidates, and in some cases even the right to stand was taken away. At Beijing University Hu Ping was successful. He was the editor of an unofficial journal called *Wotu* ('Fertile Soil'). He emphasised freedom of speech especially. He is famous for saying that to have freedom of speech is not to have everything, but to lose freedom of speech is to lose everything; and that to recognise freedom of speech is not necessarily marxist, but to deny freedom of speech is not even half marxist.

It now seems that the authorities want further restrictions, and even want to eradicate unofficial journals altogether. What is your feeling?

It is obvious that we are about to go through a difficult time. Ever since we started the movement, we knew there would be many difficulties, so today's tensions are not unexpected. If there were not factors in society to create this pressure, what would be the point in our movement? Are we to take up a Taoist position, and simply let things run their own course? I don't think so. China has aspirations, and so does the democratic movement. No matter whether there are difficulties or not, we still have to continue the struggle for a brilliant future.

Recently, the CCP proposed a rectification of party work-style. Do you think that this could bring any change for the better?

To know the root of the problem and to remove it are two different things. They might just as well be 108,000 li apart. [This was the distance that Monkey could leap in Wu Chengen's Buddhist classic *Xiyouji* ('Pilgrimage to the West'); it is a great distance!] Some people in the party can see the root of the problem, and know how serious the problem is. Of course, all citizens welcome this. But we believe the leading layer lacks the will. They try to deal with the social evils produced by the old system with methods preserved from the old system. This is a dead-end. Of course, it would be even worse if they went backwards.

Does the Polish workers' struggle encourage the Chinese democratic movement and Chinese workers? In the past, many people felt that in 'socialist countries' workers don't even have the right to open their mouths, let alone set up independent trade unions.

We feel close to the Polish workers. The conditions we live under and our personal feelings are quite similar. This is because we are all workers, and we all live in a so-called socialist country. The struggle of the Polish workers is an encouragement and a model for us and for workers in similar countries. There can be no doubt about the historical and international meaning of the Polish workers' struggle.

We see from some unofficial journals that some democratic movement activists admire Yugoslavia. But Yugoslavia represses its dissenters.

We are living in a closed society, we know little about what happens abroad. It may be that we have illusions because our understanding is deficient. In any case, our position is that if there is a movement in Yugoslavia that seeks socialist democracy, then we support that movement with all our strength and without hesitation. What workers most admire in Yugoslavia is workers' self-management. No matter how limited, that self-management is progressive. But nowadays most workers are more inclined towards the Polish struggles, since in those struggles workers' power and authority are affirmed by facts.

What is your view on the government's policy of 'economic readjustment'?

Premier Zhao Ziyang says that thirty years after the establishment of the People's Republic we have finally drummed a little sense into the economy. For people like us at the bottom of society, all we can say is, thank god, you finally realised. With or without 'readjustment', ordinary Chinese never had any power, and they were never able to take part in this process. The system in China today is that politics and the economy are organically merged and highly centralised, so that economic policy is decided by the political power. The workers have no say in planning, so they have no chance to become expert or to work out better policies for the country and the people. So now that past mistakes are being recognised, our first reaction is of course, thank god. But we must go further than that. If the workers can't participate in economic policy and decision-making and can't become masters of production, work enthusiasm will not improve. For them to become the masters would imply a radical innovation in politics. But without such an innovation any economic readjustment can have only limited results. Without radical changes in the political system, it is impossible to ask the masses to commit themselves to economic readjustment.

Since late 1980 a pro-Soviet group calling itself Beijing qingnian *('Beijing Youth') has been active in the Beijing democratic movement. What is the weight of this group and what is its influence?*

What is the attitude of the democratic movement towards it?

The pro-Soviet current is a small minority in the democratic movement. Of the dozens of unofficial journals only 'Beijing Youth' is pro-Russian although they do have another theoretical journal called *Zhexue* ('Philosophy'). Their numbers are very small, and their influence is very limited. We do not agree with their position on Russia, but this reflects a problem, i.e. the authorities have blacked out information, so that it's difficult to know the facts. Even though we don't share some of 'Beijing Youth's' views, we obviously agree with their support for the Polish workers' struggle. But if they are suppressed for publishing their views, then it's our duty to defend them, because we shall stand or fall together. Where it's a question of views or standpoints, we can only raise consciousness, clarify differences, and resolve problems through public debate.

What is your view of the future of the democratic movement?

In a word, I'm optimistic. There may be difficulties, perhaps even big ones, and the cost may be high. But even though individuals may be silenced, views that represent a historical tide desired by the whole of society can't be stifled. That's why we're so confident.

The Case of Liu Qing

Liu Qing, a machine technician in his late thirties, was an editor and co-founder, with Xu Wenli, of *Siwu luntan* ('April Fifth Forum'), and one of the first and most influential members of China's democratic movement. Like many other high school graduates, he was sent to work in the countryside in 1965. He probably returned to Beijing when the Cultural Revolution began in 1966. From 1973 to 1977 he was a student at Nanjing University, and was then sent to work in a factory in the region. Later he moved back to Beijing again.

The following three documents describe Liu Qing's arrest and imprisonment after publishing a transcript of the trial of Wei Jingsheng in November 1979. In October 1980, a National Committee to Save Liu Qing was set up by sixteen unofficial journals from different provinces in China. Many of those who joined in this appeal were arrested in April 1981.

Liu Qing managed to smuggle out from a labour-camp a 196-page account of his detention. He attached three covering letters, dated January 1981, in which he appealed for justice to his fellow citizens, to the Chinese press, and to leading public figures. The prison testimony and the letters are said to have been written on paper provided by the prison authorities for the purpose of writing self-criticism. The Chinese authorities have dismissed the testimony as a forgery but reliable sources, including Liu's friends, have authenticated the manuscript by comparing its calligraphy with earlier writings by Liu.

Liu Qing calls on the press to have the courage to 'protect the truth and uphold justice'. He calls on Deng Xiaoping and other leaders to be faithful to the trust the public has in them. He reminds his fellow citizens of the Dreyfus case and tells them: 'Our democratic system cannot develop from the benevolence of an emperor but depends on the efforts of society itself.'

In this testimony Liu Qing reports instances in which he and other prisoners were maltreated. Torture and maltreatment of prisoners was common during the Cultural Revolution, but reports of it now are rare. However, Liu Qing himself was badly beaten, and he describes how Zhang Wenhe, a member of the Human Rights League, had his hands locked behind his back for several months and how Wei Jingsheng was held in solitary confinement.

Since Mao's death and the fall of the 'gang of four', the Deng government has promised to guarantee citizens' rights and to safeguard these rights by appropriate judicial procedures, but arrests on political grounds are still happening despite the Constitution. According to the Constitution, offenders who go through a complete judicial process, from arrest to trial, should pass through the hands of the Public Security (police), the Procurates (who review cases) and the courts. Parallel to this system are organisations like the party and the army which have their own internal control organs. Penalties for political offenders can be either informal (i.e. 'persuasive') or formal. For serious offences there are two sorts of penalties, 'administrative' and 'criminal'. 'Administrative' penalties can be inflicted by police order or by one's neighbourhood, work or party unit, but may still mean that the offender is sent to a labour camp.

For a thorough analysis of the law, the judicial process, penal theory and prison conditions as they affect political prisoners in China, see *Political Imprisonment in the Peoples Republic of China, an Amnesty International Report*, London 1978.

At the time of writing, no integral Chinese text of Liu Qing's 'Prison Notebooks' is available. Moreover, the excerpts that appeared in various Hongkong journals show a number of significant discrepancies. It is therefore pointless to indicate gaps and omissions.

Xiao Rui

Eye-witness Account of the Arrest of Liu Qing

On 11 November 1979 I arrived in Xidan's Democracy Wall at 2.30 p.m. to buy a copy of the pamphlet *On the Course and Outcome of the Trial of Wei Jingsheng*... As it turned out, I wasn't able to buy the pamphlet; but I saw some amazing scenes.

There was a big crowd of people waiting to buy the pamphlet, but everything was quite orderly: the crowd had organised itself and was waiting in an orderly line. A few minutes later, a squad of police arrived; they pushed people around, shoved aside the onlookers, and carried out a brutal charge against those selling the pamphlets. The next minute there was chaos. Several people started shouting: 'It's forbidden to arrest people like that!', 'The police are picking people up!', 'They're taking our comrades away!' Many young people threw themselves at the police, shouting. But they could not hold their own against highly trained policemen: the people buying pamphlets and the crowds surrounding them were drowned in an ocean of blue uniforms and visored helmets. Then the scuffles began. One policeman punched a foreign journalist, who was adjusting his lens to take a photo. Another foreign journalist, a woman, very tall, was struggling with policemen who were trying to tear from her the pamphlet she had just bought. Yet another foreigner who had climbed on top of something to get a better photograph was sent sprawling after a cop had knocked away the object he was perching on...

Afterwards, the police left quickly, and a few fainthearts also went away. Those who stayed began to discuss what had happened. Everyone was seething with indignation. Then several people wanted to go to the Security Bureau to get news of those arrested. Along with Liu Qing (who had published the pamphlet), we went to the Xicheng office. The officer on duty claimed that they knew nothing of what had happened, so we went to the police station in Xi Chang'an Street. First of all the police there refused to see us, claiming that they too knew nothing of the matter. But then we recognised one of the policemen who had taken part in the arrests, so they had no choice but to let us in.

A policeman: 'What's your name?'

'Zhao XX.'

'Where do you work? Are you a worker or a cadre?'

'A worker.'

The policeman turned to someone else:

'And you, what's your name?'

'Yang XX.'

'Where do you work? Where do you live?'

'I was in the crowd and I am a witness to what happened. I refuse to say where I live or where I work. If you think you have no business with us, we will leave. If you need us as witnesses you only have to ask Liu Qing to come and fetch us.'

'Hm.'

The policeman turned to Liu Qing:

'Your name?'

'Liu Qing.'

'What is your work unit?'

'The third unit at the Ministry of Industry.'

'Are you a worker or a cadre?'

'A cadre.' (The policeman was taking notes). 'This afternoon you arrested some of our people. I'd like to know what they were doing that was illegal. If you can't show that they broke the law, you must release them and give them back the things you confiscated.'

The policeman, after a moment's hesitation:

'We do what we're told; I'm going to speak to my superiors.' He went out.

A moment later, he came back with a 'veteran policeman' whom he introduced to us as the commissioner. This commissioner noticed Liu Qing and hurried over to him.

'Ah!' he said warmly, 'Liu Jianwei! Is it you? When did you change your name?'

'More than a year ago. Liu Qing is my pen-name.'

'How are you? Where are you living now?'

'In Dongcheng.'

'Is your mother well?'

'Let's not talk about that for the moment, please. We'll have time later to discuss my family.'

'But what do you expect, it's so long since we saw each other, we can chat a little, can't we?'

'For the moment I'm very worried, we should talk about what brought me here.'

The commissioner took Liu Qing and comrade Zhao to one side so that they could discuss together, and the rest of us were made to go into another office with other policemen. They avoided giving us information. They only wanted to know our names, addresses, and work units. We refused to give them.

The conversation did not last long, and was a pure waste of time. They could tell us neither why they had arrested people nor what they had done with those arrested. They simply repeated that they had acted on orders from above, but they refused to say where these orders came from. We then went to the door of the floor above, which housed the municipal Security Bureau.

We announced the reason for our visit to the man on duty at the reception desk. He handed us a form. Liu Qing filled it in — name, work unit, address, age, sex, purpose of visit, etc. The man on duty then asked us to wait while he went to get information from his superiors. A moment later he came back with another man (like him, in plain clothes) and the two began to question us. The man on duty asked Liu Qing:

'Are you responsible for this pamphlet?'

'Yes. I'm responsible for publishing it and for selling it.'

'Your journal is "April Fifth Forum"?'

'That's right.'

'How many of you are there?'

Liu Qing acted as if he hadn't heard. The policeman went on:

'Is this pamphlet published by "April Fifth Forum"?'

'It has nothing to do with "April Fifth Forum". I published it myself, with the help of friends.'

'What is the pamphlet based on?'

'I had a tape-recording of Wei Jingsheng's trial.'

'When did you finish printing it?'

'Several days ago.'

'Have you sold it everywhere?'

'Of course. We have subscribers all over the country.'

'Foreigners too?'

'Yes. In the whole world people will know.'

One of us:

'A while ago, there were a lot of people in Xidan, including foreign journalists. They all bought the pamphlet, how could they not know about it? I was just passing by and saw police arresting people, just like that, for no reason! Those arrests were arbitrary. There are laws, aren't there?'

'Do you not know that you must distinguish between China and abroad?'

'Wei's trial was a public trial, the "People's Daily" talked about it to the whole world. What are the differences between China and abroad? What divine law are we breaking? What is there about it that's illegal?'

'What is there about it that's illegal? We arrest who we want to, that's what.'

When he said this everyone shouted: 'Ah, you arrest who you want to! What sort of world are we in?' 'What about the law, who is the law for?' 'You've really shown your true colours!' Just then four people arrived and took two of our comrades away with them. Liu Qing and I waited. It was already gone eight o'clock in the evening.

They interrogated us separately, but they replied to none of Liu Qing's questions. When it was gone nine o'clock, Liu Qing became impatient: 'Why won't you discuss? I am the person responsible for this business. Won't you listen to me? Fine, I'm off then.' The policeman on duty said hastily: 'Wait! Wait a bit!' He then went back to reading his newspaper. Liu Qing again: 'If you won't answer, I'm off. Tomorrow I'll tell people what happened.' The policeman stood up. 'You wait here', he said, and disappeared. At once new people began arriving, and asked Liu Qing to go into another office. The rest of us waited outside. We could hear snatches of conversation between Liu Qing and the police, but we could not make out what they were saying. We could only guess from the tone of their voices that they were arguing. Then the policeman on duty said to us: 'Off you go, you've no further business here.' But we insisted on waiting for Liu Qing.

Soon it was gone ten o'clock. They had already changed the men on duty twice, but Liu Qing was still inside.

At eleven o'clock we went to ask them to finish their interrogation as quickly as possible, since there would soon be no more buses. They did not answer. Then one of us said: 'The rest of you go home. I'll stay here and wait for Liu Qing.' At first we refused, but after he had repeated his proposal several times, we left, in spite of our misgivings. The next day, still worried about Liu Qing, I went looking for news, and I finally learned that he had been arrested.

The Family of Liu Qing

Liu Qing is Innocent!
The Public Security Bureau is Breaking the Law!

The Beijing Municipal Public Security Bureau acted rashly and recklessly in detaining, trying, sentencing and disposing of Liu Qing. The legal procedure they followed was chaotic, and had no firm basis in law. On the principle that laws must be observed and wrongs must be righted, we demand that the Beijing Public Security Bureau annul its verdict.

On the afternoon of 11 November 1979 members of 'April Fifth Forum' were selling transcripts of Wei Jingsheng's trial at Xidan Democracy Wall. The Public Security Bureau intervened to stop the sale and made arrests. Liu Qing, although present, was not arrested. After the incident, at about five o'clock on the same afternoon, Liu Qing and several others went along to the Public Security Bureau to ask on what legal grounds their colleagues had been arrested. They stayed there until eleven o'clock, arguing with the officials who received them. Then the Public Security Bureau suddenly announced that 'Liu Qing cannot return, he is detained'.

Clearly the decision to arrest Liu Qing was taken on the spur of the moment, and had no basis in law. Law does not permit muddling, yet comrades in the Public Security Bureau acted quite arbitrarily. At the time, they did not explain to anyone the legal grounds for Liu Qing's arrest. Two days later they told Liu's family that he had breached the State Council's Law on the Dissemination of Information, and that he was being 'administratively detained'. First the arrest, then the fishing around for charges — this makes a mockery of the legal system.

Liu Qing made no secret of editing and publishing the transcript of Wei Jingsheng's trial. He had put up posters announcing its sale several days in advance. If the Public Security Bureau considered this unlawful, it had time enough to warn him. In fact it was its duty to do so. Sadly, it neglected to carry out its duty.

The State Council has issued may regulations, but the Security Bureau has carried them out only selectively. Liu Qing was detained according to the Law on the Dissemination of Information, but the State Council has also stipulated that 'administrative detention must not exceed fifteen days'. The Bureau, however, violated this regulation. Which regulations the Bureau enforces and which it does not clearly varies from person to person and from case to case. 'Regulations' are merely pretexts behind which lurks the real reason: Liu Qing was editor of 'April Fifth Forum'...

Before the verdict, i.e. during the nine months of so-called administrative detention, the Bureau refused all along to say where Liu was being held or to allow his family to visit him. This is inhumane. Even after the verdict the family was not informed of Liu Qing's whereabouts, and he was secretly led away without meeting any of his close relatives. This is a violation of basic civil rights. Why this secrecy? Has Liu Qing met with some mishap? Has he been tortured?

After the marathon trial the Security Bureau finally came up with three legal 'grounds' for Liu Qing's arrest. In August 1980 they informed his family by word of mouth (not, as they are legally obliged to do, in writing) (a) that Liu had taken part in the petition, sit-in, demonstration and rally initiated by the gaoled woman activist Fu Yuehua, and that he was one of Fu Yuehua's chief collaborators; (b) that he had publicly sold the transcript of Wei Jingsheng's trial, contrary to the Law on the Dissemination of Information temporarily enacted by the State Council in 1950; and (c) that over a long period he had improperly obtained sick-notes. As a result, Liu was sentenced to three years' re-education through labour.

Liu Qing actively supports the spirit of the party's Third Plenum. He hopes that the motherland will thrive and prosper, and realise the Four Modernisations before the century is out. But he believes that without true democracy and a healthy legal system such goals can never be achieved. Therefore, despite his ill health, he has risked his whole future by plunging into the movement spontaneously initiated by the people for democracy and a legal system. He long ago foresaw the consequences of his actions, but he has not retreated one step from his aims. He even foresaw the verdict against him. Is that not ironic, when democracy and legality are so vigorously advocated?

Article 45 of the Constitution unequivocally specifies that each citizen has the freedom of speech, publication, association, demonstration and strike. This is the most basic of all civil rights, and guarantees the character, dignity and personality of each citizen. It also guarantees the right of every citizen to supervise and address enquiries to the state, the government and officials at all levels. If this right is upheld, we have democracy; if not, we have autocracy. Nothing Liu Qing did went beyond the limits set by the Constitution. He merely exercised his constitutional right to propagate the need for democracy and legality. Law should not be an empty word or mere window-dressing. It should be the very pillar of society. It should place the same constraints on heads of state as on ordinary citizens... What, then, does Liu Qing's imprisonment show? It shows that we are being stripped of what we treasure. Do you want to express your views without contraint? To uplift your spiritual life? To openly criticise the bureaucracy when it violates your civil rights? If so, Article 45 is your guarantee of freedom from retaliation, persecution or imprisonment. We are pained to see this freedom violated. We are told that all are equal before the law. If so, this violation means that no one can be sure that he or she will not be gaoled for acting within the Constitution...

By collaborating with Fu Yuehua and publishing the transcript of Wei Jingsheng's trial, Liu Qing did not violate Article 45 of the Constitution. The Security Bureau based its case on regulations issued by the State Council thirty years ago, at the founding of the People's Republic. Even if we discount the fact that these regulations are thirty years old, that they were never published in official documents or circulars, that the Bureau did not cite them at the time of Liu Qing's arrest, and that they were clearly a temporary enactment, it still remains that they contradict the Constitution, and as such cannot be used to prove Liu Qing's guilt...

As for the third charge, Liu Qing's work unit and hospital can prove that he has been ill. First he was hospitalised in Guiyang and Shaanxi. Then he came to Beijing for treatment, with the approval of his work unit. At the time it was very difficult for people living outside Beijing to get treatment in the capital. Liu Qing's sick-notes can be verified by his factory; in any case, this is outside the jurisdiction of the Security Bureau. Shortly before he was arrested he had agreed with his work unit that he would return to Shaanxi for treatment, and he was preparing for the journey. How could he know that at the same time the Security Bureau was preparing to arrest him?

Liu Qing

Sad Memories and Prospects:
My Appeal to the Tribunal of the People

On the tape-recording of Wei Jingsheng's trial

On 14 October 1979 I heard that the public trial of Wei Jingsheng was to begin the following morning. I passed the news to some journals and groups in the Beijing democratic movement, and we arranged to meet at seven o'clock the next day outside the court-house at No. 1 Zhengyi Street and to try to attend the trial. When I got there, there were already a few foreign journalists and people from the democratic movement shivering in the fresh morning wind. A notice had been pasted up on the fence in front of the court building: 'Wei Jingsheng's trial has been postponed.' When we asked at the reception how long the trial would be postponed, we were told that it was not yet known. We assumed from previous experience that it would be postponed indefinitely. But to our surprise we learned the same evening that the trial would begin at 8 o'clock the following day (the 16th). At the same time we heard that only a hand-picked audience would be allowed to attend the trial. Why so much secrecy surrounding a public trial?

The whole country was closely following what would happen to Ren Wanding (of the Human Rights League), Wei Jingsheng, Fu Yuehua, Chen Lü, Zhang Wenhe and others arrested in March 1979. Even the world press was interested, and it seems that the United Nations and Amnesty International corresponded with the Chinese Government about them. Why this concern about the fate of a few ordinary Chinese? It was because the arrests had created a cold March wind that was blowing across the Chinese political horizon. It was not only a question of these few individuals. Even more important was what the arrests implied for the political situation as a whole in China.

Now the authorities had filled all the seats in the public auditorium where the trial was to be held (why was that necessary?), we had to work out another strategy. That same evening I visited an acquaintance who was among those officially invited. I gave him a tape-recorder to record the trial.

On the evening of the 16th I got my tape-recorder back and together with a few friends spent four or five hours listening to the recording. We all thought that Wei Jingsheng had been sentenced for leaking secrets, but it turned out that the court had found him guilty of two serious crimes and had sentenced him to fifteen years in gaol and three years' deprivation of political rights. We were not going to take that lying down. It was an attack on democracy and in open contempt of the principles of legality that were just beginning to win ground in China. This sentence shows that in China it is still not possible to speak one's mind. Genuine freedom of conscience and expression remains something for the future. Progress in this direction will depend on the efforts of individuals who have the courage to challenge injustice. If everyone averts their eyes and pretends that nothing is happening, there can be no progress. A people that acquiesces in injustice will be destroyed, and deserves to be. But the Chinese people has thrown up individuals who even in periods of darkest dictatorship speak the truth fearlessly.

As a result of the wide interest in the case and the obvious irregularities in the judgement, Wei Jingsheng's trial became a main topic of conversation. All the democratic journals in Beijing shared the view that it was our job to publicise the truth and get more people interested in the affair. We hoped in this way to exercise some influence on those national leaders who were serious about wanting to reform the Chinese system. Duplicating the entire recording turned out to be less work than we expected, so that it was not necessary to call on the assistance of people from the various Beijing democratic journals. Moreover, it was rather dangerous to expose the authorities in this way. Later we discovered that our premonitions were justified. It was essential to involve as few people as possible in this work. I therefore took responsibility myself, and used the help of a few good friends.

My differences with Wei Jingsheng

From the very first time *Siwu luntan* ('April Fifth Forum') hit the streets we have always openly stated our political views, and these differed in significant ways from the views expressed in Wei Jingsheng's *Tansuo* ('Explorations'). As editor of 'April Fifth Forum', I repeatedly debated Wei Jingsheng. When 'Explorations' published Wei Jingsheng's 'Democracy or a New Dictatorship' I answered with a critical article.

Although the authorities were very irritated by Wei Jingsheng's articles, to my knowledge they never once seriously countered them. At Democracy Wall some people honoured Wei Jingsheng as a hero, while others cursed him. I am probably the only one who, however clumsily, actually criticised his arguments in an article. And I was not thanked for doing so. One friend told me to my face: 'I'd like to tear that damned article of yours off the Wall.' So some people see me as an enemy of Wei Jingsheng, and at the very least I cannot be considered his co-thinker. Even my worst enemy would find it hard to put me in the same camp as Wei Jingsheng, so I was naive enough to think that I could go ahead and plead his case. The unofficial journals and groups in Beijing had set up a 'joint conference' at the beginning of 1979. In it all currents were represented, and they signed a four-point agreement the most important point of which was that in the case of individual or collective arrests on the grounds of opinions or beliefs the surviving groups would come to the aid of those arrested. They would then have the duty to mobilise public opinion, to console the relatives of those arrested and to support them financially as far as possible, and to approach the authorities with requests to visit those held prisoner. The participating groups named me as contact person. The job was actually too much for me, but when Ren Wanding, Wei Jingsheng and the others were arrested I had no choice but to carry out the four-point agreement. Although the 'joint-conference' no longer existed, it was up to me, the contact person, to do what had been promised.

Wei Jingsheng asks me to defend him

In June 1979 I heard from a court official, Luo Kejun, that Wei Jingsheng had asked whether I would defend him or find another lawyer to do so. I talked over his request with people in the law department of the University and with some other experts. At the time the penal code had not yet been promulgated, so I finally had to tell Luo Kejun:

Since there is no penal code, there is no basis for a defence.

That means that I cannot agree to Wei Jingsheng's request. But I am prepared to defend him if the court cooperates by announcing what legal provisions will be followed in this case. We request the court for permission to visit Wei Jingsheng and discuss the entire case with him, so that he can really defend himself during his trial. Finally I request the court in the name of all the democratic magazines and a great many individuals to conduct the trial in public.

Later the penal code was published, and with a few others we decided to set up a defence committee for Wei Jingshcng, Ren Wanding and the others. Unfortunately the sentence was already passed before we had the chance to tell the court that we now agreed to Wei Jingsheng's request. Our national sickness — the inability to make decisions — had struck once again; we had acted too late. Although the trial's outcome was obvious even in advance, it was my moral duty to stand by Wei Jingsheng and not to dishonour the trust that had been placed in me. In early November, with friends' help, I transcribed the entire trial proceedings. We carefully checked the transcript against the original, and the result can be considered a complete and literal rendering of what was said during the trial. The only exceptions are a few unintelligible words and short gaps while the tape was being changed. At first we intended to put the text up on Democracy Wall in the form of a wall-poster, but later we decided to make stencils of it, and to duplicate between one and two thousand copies.

Arrests during the sale of the trial report

In early November we put up a notice on Democracy Wall that the transcript of Wei Jingsheng's trial would go on sale on the 11th. That day several thousand people had gathered by the early afternoon. At the request of many of those present we began selling earlier than planned. We tried to keep order with the help of some twenty people, but things still become rather chaotic. Potential buyers saw that the edition was limited and everyone began to press forward to make sure of getting a copy. While I was busy trying to restore order a friend tugged at my sleeve and told me that he had some important news for me. I followed him to a quieter place and then he told me that the security police were on their way and would arrive within half an hour. I hurried back but it was already too late. The crowd had grown so thick that I could no longer reach the sales point.

Someone told me that there had been arrests and that the publication had been confiscated. This person took me to one side and I saw a lorry packed with people and a sort of ambulance which began to drive off with its siren on.

Later I heard what had happened after my departure. Suddenly the police had appeared on the scene. Some said that there were between 70 and 80, others spoke of a hundred. The street in front of Democracy Wall was sealed off and some of the agents forced their way into the crowd, seized the transcripts and arrested one seller, who was taken off in handcuffs. A few bystanders who protested at these arrests were also shackled hands and feet and put into a police vehicle. Altogether some four or five people were said to have been arrested. [Later Liu Qing was himself arrested when he tried to get these people released from custody.]

Experience in prison

Once you are in the hands of the security police you have no chance of struggling against their illegal behaviour. You'll always end up the loser, all the more so since you can count on no support from the outside world. My present situation is proof of this. I am not protected by any law. My voice cannot reach the outside world. I shall lose out every time, since they can do whatever they want with me and they're planning to give me a hard time. But I'll resist to the end and use every opportunity to show how they trample on the law.

Friends in need

After three days I was transferred from the special observation cell to a bigger cell full of other prisoners. I realised that this was a move for the better. Up to then I hadn't been allowed to speak to the gaolers. Now I was suddenly in a cell with more than ten people. The prison chiefs had realised that neither the soft nor the hard treatment would work on me, so they had obviously decided to try another ploy. I discussed my situation with a former Red Guard, and he thought that maybe I would now be officially arrested. That would be an enormous improvement, because it would give me the chance to plead my case in a court of law. Of course it was possible that this transfer was a trick, but if the cops thought they were going to defeat me that way, they were mistaken. Anyway, I decided to continue asking the prison authorities to request clarification from their superiors about my illegal imprisonment. I demanded correct treatment, and told my story to my fellow prisoners, so that as many people as possible would know what had happened to me. My account was so effective that the prisoners became restless. Some even asked the gaolers why I was being held prisoner. Needless to say, the gaolers went purple with rage, but there was little they could say to justify what had happened. They either said the case had not yet been clarified, or they argued that there will always be some cases that fall outside the rules.

But I was lacking in experience and knew too little of the tricks that the security police were capable of. They don't need the law; they can twist it just as they please. My companions in the new cell had the experience that I lacked, and they had rather a good insight into the workings of the security police. Yue Zhengping from Fangshan, who was serving five years for false accusation; Mai Mao, who had problems with rehabilitation and so was still in gaol; Li Anjiang, sentenced to six years for working on the black market — they and others told me what was what under the prison regime. Yue Zhengping said:

> You haven't done anything? Fine. You haven't broken a single law? Even better. Then we won't sentence you; we'll just send you to a camp for reform through labour. If we think someone needs reforming, we send them to a camp. It's for your own good. Even if you haven't done anything wrong, you're capable of it, because you're the type that easily turns to crime. By sending you to a camp we're preventing you from making a serious mistake.

He held up his hand in admonition and ended his little speech on an unctuous note: 'Please believe me, this is for your own safety and your own good. That's why I'm swallowing you up. You won't feel better until you're in my stomach, because there nothing can happen to you.'

And they were right. These friends in need meant a lot to me. Some had something on their conscience, while others were innocent, but that made little difference in the long run. Packed together in a small room, we all depended on one another. Their help came just at the right time. They prepared me for all the possible tricks of which the security police were capable, so that when I was confronted with them I knew what to expect. I kept my cool.

I'm also very grateful to my friends for their practical help. I'm very unpractical myself, and I didn't even know how to keep my things in order. Every now and then my cell-mates helped me tidy things up. They did my washing for me and even darned my socks, in fact they did so much for me that I was embarrassed by their concern. Thanks to them I even managed to get a bath every now and then. When you've had a good wash and your clothes are clean, you feel less vulnerable.

The most important way in which they helped me was by supporting me when I refused to live according to the humiliating regulations set by the guards. Suddenly, for no obvious reason, prisoners were ordered to fold their hands in front of their stomachs while they were out exercising, and at some points we were even expected to slow down and bow our heads. I refused to comply, and for two reasons: first, I had not been sentenced, but was being illegally held, so that guards' regulations were not binding on me; and second, even people serving official sentences should not be degraded, and the law says as much.

My cell-mates decided unanimously to join me in my protest. Naturally, under presure from the guards they were forced to bow their heads, but when they saw that I was punished for my disobedience they unanimously protested. Some said to the guards: 'How dare you torture someone who is being held illegally?'

Yue Zhengping was so angry that he asked for writing paper and planned to accuse the Beijing Security Bureau of kidnapping and maltreatment. The authorities found it advisable to transfer me out of this cell to a smaller room. But when my former cell-mates were let out to go to the toilet and passed my cell door, they would bang on it or shout out to show that they had not forgotten me.

At the time that I was transferred I was beaten black and blue, and I had a gag on so that I could scarcely breathe and handcuffs that cut deep into my flesh. I was not alone. There were two other prisoners in my new cell. One was called Luo Xinguo, a shoplifter who had moved illegally to Beijing from Shaanxi; and the other was called Wei Rongling. He claimed he was a deputy section-chief in the army's political bureau. He had worked for a long time as bodyguard for Zhang Chunqiao and Jiang Qing, I already knew him from the previous cell. He knew a lot about the prisoners awaiting death sentences for he had worked with them (in cell 23) the previous year. When he learned who I was he told me a few things about Wei Jingsheng and Fu Yuehua. According to him, Wei Jingsheng had not been sent to the unit where he was supposed to serve his sentence, but had been locked up by himself in a condemned cell. He said he had got a letter from Wei Jingsheng, who had asked him to pass it on to Lu Lin after his release. But the message was confiscated and he got a beating for it. I didn't give much credence to this story. Wei Jingsheng had been sentenced seven or eight months earlier, and normally he would long ago have been sent off to the camp. But the dictatorship of the proletariat is capricious and full of surprises, for I later learned that Wei Rongling was telling the truth. When I got back from exercising on 1 July 1980 I suddenly came across Wei Jingsheng, who was looking very pale and thin. He saw me too, and I could see from his face that he was uncertain about what to do. He was led past me by two guards.

Another activist I came across in prison was Zhang Wenhe of the Human Rights League. He was a militant as ever. He protested at everything and gave the guards hell, however much he suffered as a result. At one point he was so heavily shackled that he even found it difficult to do things like eat, sleep and go to the toilet. He was forced to wear a balaclava helmet and a gag, and he was repeatedly beaten. He was kept like this for months on end. For a while his cell was near mine. We were often let out of our cells at about the same time, and by deliberately slowing down our pace we occasionally got the chance to swap a few words and squeeze each other's hands.

My state of health

The period of my solitary confinement was not long and it has not affected me very seriously. But changes are already noticeable. One day I noticed a lot of loose hair on my sheet. When I looked at myself in the small mirror on the cell door, I discovered that part of my head is already bald. The dampness and coldness in the cell, plus my habit of curling up in a corner for long periods, must have been the cause of my swollen left foot, which still gives me great pain. My near-sightedness has got much worse. I started to talk to myself, sometimes loudly, debated with an imaginery opponent. I also tried to recall some mathematical or physical problems or did exercises against the wall. Please don't laugh at me. I think a lot about my mother, worrying about the anxiety I have brought her in her old age. This makes me very sorrowful. I looked through a broken window in the toilet and saw a small patch of grass near the foot of a high wall. The green blades seem to have just emerged from the dark, muddy soil. I was suddenly overcome by a strong desire — I wanted to get out there and be closer to the grass!

Lotus Temple Camp

On 21 July two policemen came to tell me to gather up my things, and that they were going to take me to a work unit in Shaanxi. Instead they took me to the Lotus Temple labour camp, in Hua district, Shaanxi. Only there did I learn that I had been sentenced to three years' re-education through labour. Having reached this final stage, the Public Security Bureau was forced to make up lies to justify its actions. No doubt the Public Security Bureau people are pragmatists for whom the end justifies the means, but in my view it is not so easy to separate the state of a person's soul from the means that he or she uses.

The Lotus Temple was originally a prison reserved for people sentenced to 'reform through labour', but nowadays all sorts get locked up there, and there are five main categories of prisoners: those sentenced to reform through labour (*laogai*), those sentenced to forced labour (*juyi*), those sentenced to rehabilitation through labour (*laojiao*), those detained for less than two months and required to work (*qianglao*), and finally the 'professionals' (*jiuye*) [convicts who, having served their sentences, ask to be allowed to stay on in the camps as 'free' workers]. The camp is surrounded by a grey wall, fifteen-feet high, with an electrified fence running along the top. At the four corners stand lookouts or soldiers, guns at the ready. When you enter the camp you go through four successive doors, all heavily barred, which slice up the prison compound like the squares of a chessboard. Each contains one category of prisoners — only the 'professionals' have no special area reserved for them. The work is very hard. It consists of carrying heavy stones about. Common criminals sentenced by a court do labour of a technical sort — in effect a sinecure. The worst jobs are given to those in the 'forced labour' category or those undergoing reform through labour, i.e. people who have not been convicted by a court. The organisation of the work teams is usually entrusted to prisoners who have been sentenced by a court. The warders trust these prisoners more than they trust the others. This is not only because they are especially obedient or because they have been given long sentences, but because they and the warders are engaged in all sorts of trafficking and swindling. And yet these are people who have gone before a judge for breaking the law, and have lost their rights as citizens. So what is the difference between them and those who have simply 'committed errors' judged insufficient to merit a legal conviction and who have kept their rights as citizens (even though they may have been sent for forced labour or re-education through labour)? As far as I can see, the difference is minimal and purely terminological. Those who are sentenced to reform through labour are told to 'recognise their crimes and submit to the law'; and those sent for re-education through labour are told to 'recognise their errors and submit to re-education'. I think that even the administration would find it hard to explain the difference between reform through labour, re-education through labour and forced labour, since when it comes down to it they are the same thing.

According to the Constitution there are two sorts of people in society: those who have their rights as citizens; and criminals, who do not. But in reality a third category of people has emerged — citizens who have full rights on paper, but no rights in fact. These are the people who are sent for forced labour or re-education through labour. It is no use looking up this third category in the Constitution. In law it is only the courts that, with the help of an official document from the State Council, can take away someone's civil rights, i.e. turn a citizen into a criminal. But the Public Security Bureau, if it so wishes, also has the power to turn someone into a criminal and treat him or her as such. In effect this is tantamount to installing a second type of court in our society: a court that dispenses of the usual paper-work and simply ships off those it doesn't like to the camps, where they are turned officially into criminals and 're-educated through labour'. It's all very easy. No public proceedings, no trial, no right of appeal, and absolutely no delay — the decision is immediately put into effect. In fact criminals are treated far better than these people. Criminals are dealt with by the Bureau of Detention. Only then can they be put on trial. Before the trial they can find out what the charges are, clarify points about their case and assert their right to a defence. They can also appeal against the verdict. But those sent for re-education through labour have no chance to defend or even to explain themselves.

One category you find in the re-education camps are those who have made the mistake of getting on the wrong side of the Public Security Bureau, or who have annoyed their bosses in some way, and were sent for re-education as a result. Take for example the case of Shi Jinsheng, an apprentice at the Hong'an works in Shaanxi province, who gate-crashed an evening of entertainment organised by his work unit. A trivial incident, you might think. But Shi Jinsheng was caught, badly beaten up and dragged before the Public Security Bureau, who took him back to the factory for a 'criticism and struggle session'. The worker Yu Zhonghai, seeing what was happening to his apprentice, got angry and insulted the chief foreman and the people from the works security section. The result: apprentice and apprentice-master both got two years in a re-education camp. Even if we concede that Shi Jinsheng disturbed the public order, at most he deserved to be arrested and cautioned. But two years of re-education! As for the way his master was treated, it is hard to imagine anything more childish. Even the camp guards were shocked when they heard about it.

A second category of prisoners are those who have broken

the law badly enough to get a really heavy sentence from the courts, but who have influential family connections and are sent for re-education through labour instead. These people have quite some clout. Inside the camp they do what they like. Often they are freed for 'medical treatment' and return home to work under another name. Or they get their sentences reduced. At the Lotus Temple there was a whole gang of these people who had carried out more than ten burglaries and stolen over half a ton of copper ingots from a factory. Not only did they get a mere two years' re-education, but they were freed well before the end of their sentence.

A third category are people who have committed 'crimes or grave errors' but who have been held so long in pre-trial detention that they are considered eligible for release, thus saving the expenses of a formal trial. But a year later their situation changes once again and they find themselves back in camp with 'an old bill to pay'. Take the case of Zhou Donglin, who was detained about a theft. Zhou spent a long time in the camp and was eventually freed without a trial. After his release he was filled with remorse and decided to go straight, even to the point of studying Lei Feng [a model soldier who sacrificed himself for the revolution' and whose conduct ordinary citizens are urged to emulate]. But a year later he was rearrested without the slightest justification and dragged off to the camp. The reason? The same theft for which he had been arrested a year earlier. 'Debts paid recently do not cancel old ones', he was told. As far as I can see this is a debt that he will never finish paying, at a usurious rate.

A fourth category are people who have committed grave errors or even crimes but whom the Public Security Bureau could not catch in the act. They are simply suspects; nothing has been proved against them. And in the absence of definite proof or a confession, there is no way in which they can be put before the courts. So the paper sending them for re-education talks of 'inner conviction' — backed up by suspicious circumstances — that they are guilty. This category includes some real criminals, but also some victims of judicial error. It is not good to treat suspects in this way. First, it makes the Public Security Bureau look incompetent, since they can't find solid proof and are forced to rely on presumptions. Next, it encourages the Public Security

Bureau to be lazy, to neglect procedures and to use bureaucratic manoeuvres. Last, if one lacks the means to convict, this creates a psychology of revenge and recalcitrance in the criminal, which is bad for society. Today life is insecure. Many grave crimes are committed by people who have been released from re-education. One reason for this is the irrational and illegal nature of re-education through labour, and the bad way in which the Public Security Bureau treats its prisoners.

Today, when the accent is on legality and when we have realised, thanks to the blood that has washed the dirt from our eyes, the importance of laws and institutions, it is still very easy to manipulate policing and the law so that people understand nothing of them. So: do the authorities sincerely want to clean up the legal institutions and strengthen them, or do they prefer to look upon them as amusing decorations (thereby deceiving both the people and themselves)?

Wang Fanxi
Chen Duxiu, Father of Chinese Communism

Chen Duxiu (Ch'en Tu-hsiu, 1879-1942) was not only a founder of the Chinese Communist Party but he was also the main leader of the 1919 May Fourth (5:4) movement, with which leaders of today's democratic movement, born on April Fifth (4:5) 1976, strongly identify. When the democratic movement insisted on the need for democracy as well as modernisation, they no doubt had in mind Chen's famous 1919 slogan: Democracy and Science. The present dissidents have had little if any chance to study Chen's writings, but the similarity between their views and his late and early ones is striking. Chinese society has changed radically since Chen died, yet methods of governing and of dealing with intellectuals are hardly less despotic, obscurantist and 'feudalist' now than they were then, and it is largely this that explains the similarity.

For decades the CCP had nothing good to say about Chen Duxiu, but since Mao's death he has been partly rehabilitated. He is now recognised once again as a founder of Chinese Communism. He is no longer held solely responsible for the defeat of the Revolution of 1925-27, which is now blamed partly on Moscow. But he is still described as a traitor for joining the Trotskyists, although the charge that he collaborated with the Japanese imperialists has been dropped.

The author of this article, Wang Fanxi (Wang Fan-hsi, born 1907), was a member of the generation of Chinese radicals awakened to political and intellectual life during the late 1910s and early 20s, when Chen Duxiu was still the undisputed leader of the Chinese Revolution. As a Trotskyist Wang worked with Chen in 1930-31 and again in 1938, both having spent most or all of the intervening years in gaol. Wang was more than once Chen's opponents on political and theoretical questions, but on the whole he sees himself as Chen's pupil and admirer. Wang's autobiography was published by Oxford University Press in 1980 under the title *Chinese Revolutionary, Memoirs, 1919-1949*. This assessment of Chen has not been previously published.

To many younger Chinese socialists the name Chen Duxiu means little, and to most socialists outside China it means nothing at all. Of China's main Communist leaders only Mao, Zhou Enlai, Liu Shaoqi and a handful of others have won fame in the outside world. How could Chen, a nonentity, stand alongside these great leaders? But in truth Chen was anything but a nonentity in the history of the Chinese Revolution. If judged not just by what he achieved directly but by his influence over an entire historical period, he ranks not only above Zhou and

Liu, but even above Mao himself.

In 1936, in conversation with Edgar Snow, Zhou and Mao frankly acknowledged Chen's influence on them, and Snow reported their remarks in his classic *Red Star Over China*. But Zhou and Mao apparently had second thoughts, for the Chinese translation of Snow's book was withdrawn from circulation in the spring of 1938. Zhou had told Snow: 'Before going to France, I read translations of the *Communist Manifesto*; Kautsky's *Class Struggle*; and *The October Revolution*. These books were published under the auspices of *New Youth*, which was published by Ch'en Tu-hsiu. I also personally met Ch'en Tu-hsiu as well as Li Ta-chao [Li Dazhao] — who were to become founders of the Chinese Communist Party.' Mao Zedong said: 'I went to Shanghai for the second time in 1919. There once more I saw Ch'en Tu-hsiu. I had first met him in Peking [Beijing], when I was at Peking National University, and he had influenced me perhaps more than anyone else.' So Mao was Chen's pupil, not just before the party was founded, but for a long time afterwards too.

Chen Duxiu was born on 8 October 1879, 35 years after the Opium War and 15 years after the defeat of the Taiping Rebellion. Outer pressure and inner dissension had already shaken the Qing dynasty to its foundations. The corruption and incompetence of the imperial system and the growing Western threat had awoken many Chinese intellectuals to the need for reform. So when Chen Duxiu was born, China was already in the first stages of political ferment and change.

But Chen was brought up in a strictly traditional way. Born into an Anhui gentry family, he lost his father in the first months of his life, and was raised and educated by his grandfather and his elder brother. They were both classical Confucianists and set out to train the young Duxiu for the imperial examinations, which were the sole path to bureaucratic office under the Qing.

Chen had no liking for the Confucian classics, and even less liking for the *bagu* or eight-legged essay, a stereotyped form of composition in which examination candidates were required to excel. However, to please his grandfather and his mother he took the first exam at the age of seventeen, and came top of the list with a *xiucai* degree. The following year, in 1897, he went to

Nanjing to take part in the triennial examination for the degree of *juren*. As a result of his experiences there he lost interest for once and for all in the imperial examinations and, more important, began to question the soundness of China basic institutions. He vividly described his feelings in his unfinished Autobiography. One candidate, a fat man from Xuzhou who paced up and down the examination pen naked but for a pair of broken sandals, chanting his favourite *bagu*, made a particularly deep impression on Chen. 'I could not take my eyes off him', he wrote.

> As I watched, I fell to thinking about the whole strange business of the examination system, and then I began to think about how much my country and its people would suffer once these brutes achieved positions of power. Finally, I began to doubt the whole system of selecting talent through examination. It was like a circus of monkeys and bears, repeated every so many years. But was the examination system an exception, or were not China's other institutions equally rotten? I ended up agreeing with the criticisms raised in the newspaper 'Contemporary Events', and I switched my allegiance from the examination system to the reformist party of Kang Youwei and Liang Qichao. And so an hour or two of pondering decided the course of my life for the next dozen years.

The Kang-Liang reformist movement was considered very radical at the time that Chen Duxiu joined it. It called for a replacement of the absolute monarchy by a constitutional one, and it proposed a series of reforms to save China. But just a year later, in 1898, the reformists suffered a crushing defeat, and in 1900 the Qing rulers were humiliated by eight foreign powers during the Yihetuan (or Boxer) upheavals. Chen's outlook on life and politics became more and more radical under the impact of these events. In 1904, in Anhui, he published *Suhua bao*, a newspaper written in vernacular Chinese. In 1908 he went to Shanghai, where he joined an underground terrorist group and learned how to make bombs. By now he had already left Kang and Liang way behind in his political views, and he was advocating the overthrow of the Qing by force.

Even before the fall of the Qing in 1911 Chen was arrested for his political activities in Anhui. After his release he was driven into exile in Japan. There he collaborated with Sun Yatsen, founder of the republican nationalist Guomindang and chief architect of the Qing's overthrow, but he never joined Sun's organisation. On his return to China during the 1911 Revolution he became political director of the revolutionary army in Anhui. But after the Nationalists compromised with Yuan Shikai, representative of the *ancien régime*, he was once again forced into exile in Japan, where he published a revolutionary newspaper. Returning to China in 1915, he founded the journal 'Youth' in Shanghai, renamed 'New Youth' the following year. 'New Youth' was to play a major role in the further unfolding of the Chinese Revolution. In 1917 'New Youth's' editorial board moved north to Beijing, where Chen was invited to become Dean of Letters at Beijing National University, China's highest and most progressive institution. Here were gathered many of China's best scholars, including Li Dazhao, who was to become a founder and early martyr of the Chinese Communist Party; Dr Hu Shi, the philosopher; Lu Xun, the essayist; Qian Xuantong, the historian; and Zhou Zuoren, the essayist. With their help and that of some students, 'New Youth' quickly gained in circulation and influence.

In any case, circumstances favoured its rapid growth. The war in Europe had temporarily loosened the West's economic grip on China, so that a national bourgeoisie was born, and with it a modern working class. At the same time, revolution was brewing in Russia, and in 1917 the Bolsheviks took power in a revolution that decisively influenced modern China's course. Lastly, many ideological and social movements sprang up throughout the world, and especially in Europe, at the end of the war. Thus encouraged, some Chinese intellectuals began to search more earnestly than ever for new solutions to the problems China had faced ever since it was dragged into the world's eddy by Western businessmen and soldiers. At the same time these social and political developments gave these intellectuals a ready-made audience of tens of thousands, and a firm social base on which to realise their ideals.

'New Youth' did not begin as a directly political publication.

In the early days it campaigned on two main fronts: against China's traditional ethics and social practices; and against classical Chinese, which was still used for most written communication. The campaign against traditional ethics was known as the New Thought Movement, and the campaign against classical Chinese was known as the Literary Revolution. On the first front 'New Youth', especially Chen Duxiu, took Confucius as the main target. Confucianism had dominated China for over two millenia, and was the ideological mainstay of the whole reactionary system. For Chen and his comrades, China's backwardness was due above all to her ossification under Confucian teaching, and they believed that there could be no social progress until the Chinese people were freed from the Confucian grip. The Literary Revolution was closely linked to this struggle against Confucianism. Classical Chinese, which was based on the spoken language of over a thousand years ago, differed radically from modern spoken Chinese. It was so hard to learn that mediocre scholars could not write a simple letter in it even after studying it for ten years. So until it was replaced by a written form based on modern spoken Chinese, mass illiteracy would remain and progressive intellectuals would never be able to awaken the people. This was not the first time that Chen had called for language reform. As early as 1904 he had published a newspaper with articles in the vernacular. But it was only now that the conditions for a literary revolution had fully ripened. Now, despite stiff opposition from the literati, daily speech finally won out, and living Chinese replaced dead Chinese as the official means of communication.

Yet Chen Duxiu's main contribution to the New Thought Movement and the Literary Revolution lay less in his constructive achievement than in his destructive energy: in his dauntless urge to discredit, criticise and destroy everything traditional. He was among the greatest iconoclasts in the history of human thought; and like all iconoclasts and pioneers, he worked not with a scalpel but with a bulldozer. For him the main thing was to pull down the dilapidated house of the past, and this he did to devastating effect. But for a long time he had only the vaguest idea of what sort of house to put in its place, except that it must be in the Western style. So during the first four years of 'New

Youth' Chen Duxiu should properly be called a Westerniser or a radical bourgeois democrat. He admired almost everything Western, especially great events and people from the past three centuries of European history; these he cited enthusiastically in his writings, comparing them with events and people from the Chinese past. Great names like Francis Bacon, Jean-Jacques Rousseau, Auguste Comte, Charles Darwin, Louis Pasteur, Victor Hugo, Emile Zola, Kant, Hegel, Goethe, Dickens and even Oscar Wilde he introduced indiscriminately as models for Chinese youth to admire and emulate. But he did not know these people well, nor did he have a sound grasp of Western thought. He mastered no European language, so all his new knowledge he acquired through Japanese translations; and his Japanese was not good either. The result was that all he learned from the West were a few broad concepts such as humanism, democracy, individualism and scientific method. Of these he singled out democracy and science as the two surgeons capable of saving China.

The October Revolution of 1917 had an enormous effect on Chen's thinking, but it was not until later that Chen definitively embraced marxism and concluded that China would never become modernised unless, like the Bolsheviks, it carried out an economic as well as a political revolution.

It was above all May Fourth that precipitated this change in Chen's thinking. On 4 May 1919 a student movement broke out in Beijing and spread to all China's big cities. This movement was in protest against the decision of the Paris Peace Conference to transfer German concessions in China to Japan, and against the Beijing Government for acting as Japan's tool. May Fourth was under the direct influence of Chen's 'New Youth' journal. It was 'New Youth's' first victory, but also its first big test. May Fourth quickly split the 'New Youth' leaders into two rival camps. For some time a process of differentiation had been going on among the journal's main supporters. Now, this process quickened. Chen Duxiu and Li Dazhao went further left and plunged into revolutionary work, while Hu Shi and others moved further right under the pretext of 'retreating to the study'.

As a leader of May Fourth and its chief inspirer, Chen was the main target for repression. In June he was seized and gaoled for three months. After his release he left Beijing University for good, and began a critical review of the doctrines he had earlier indiscriminately adopted. In September 1920 he declared himself a marxist.

Now that he had committed himself wholly to the revolution, he began to work towards the establishment of a Communist Party in China. In August 1920 he set up a Socialist Youth Corps in Shanghai. At the same time, Marxist Study Groups were organised in big cities throughout China. In July 1921 the CCP held its First National Congress in Shanghai. Chen was elected General Secretary, and the following year he represented the Party at the Fourth Congress of the Communist International (Comintern) in Moscow. He was re-elected leader at the next four party congresses, and led the party during the Revolution of 1925-27.

The Revolution of 1925-27 has been called a tragedy by some historians, and it certainly ended in tragic defeats. What was Chen's role in that tragedy? There are various answers to this question, which has been the subject of much heated controversy. The view of the Comintern and (until recently) of the CCP was than Chen was an opportunist and a bungler whose wrong policy led the revolution to defeat. According to this view the main if not the exclusive blame for the defeat was Chen Duxiu's. But not everyone agrees with this assessment. Some of Chen's fellow-revolutionaries and many scholars believe that Chen's mistake was to be too faithful to the directives of the Comintern, which was then controlled by Stalin and Bukharin, and that he was merely Stalin's scapegoat. My own experience of the events of 1925-27, and my later reflection on them, also led me to this position.

Chen Duxiu was dismissed as party leader at the August (1927) Emergency Conference of the Central Committee. He was succeeded by Qu Qiubai, who under Moscow's orders switched to an adventurist line culminating in the disastrous Guangzhou (Canton) Insurrection of December 1927. In retirement, Chen wrote several letters to the party warning against putschism and demanding a critical review of policy, but this merely widened the gap between him and the new leaders.

In late 1929 Chen could acquaint himself for the first time with the Russian Left Opposition's views on China through documents brought back to China by Communists who had studied in Moscow. Until then Chen had no true understanding of the differences between Trotsky and Stalin on the Chinese revolution. These documents opened up a new field of vision for him, and helped dispel doubts that had vexed him for years. He soon went over to the positions of the Left Opposition, and wrote to the CCP leaders demanding that the issues in the Chinese Revolution should be put up for discussion in the party and in the whole world movement. He was promptly expelled as a result, and in protest he wrote his famous *Open Letter to All Comrades* of 10 December 1929 and put his name to the statement *Our Political Views* signed by 81 veteran party members. Needless to say, all were expelled from the party. A few months later, in February 1930, Stalin tried to 'win Chen Duxiu back' by inviting him to Moscow. Chen refused, thus severing all ties with the party he had founded nine years earlier.

Chen then organised his followers into a Left Opposition and published the paper *Proletariat*. In May 1931 four Trotskyist groups merged to form the Chinese section of the International of Bolshevik-Leninists, of which Chen was elected General Secretary. But in October 1932 he was arrested and put before the Nanjing Military Tribunal, where he faced the death sentence. In court he behaved every inch like a revolutionary leader, and from the dock he denounced the Guomindang's regime of terror. His arrest and trial led to a nationwide campaign to free him. As a result he was spared the death penalty and given a thirteen-year gaol sentence instead.

Chen stayed in prison until shortly after the outbreak of the Sino-Japanese War in 1937, when he was freed along with other political prisoners. But he was still kept under strict watch, and this prevented him from doing revolutionary work. After a brief stay in Wuhan he was compelled to live in a small town near Chongqing in southwest China, where the Guomindang had its wartime capital. His health had worsened in prison, and on 27 May 1942 he died of heart sickness and phlebitis, aged sixty-four.

Chen spent his last years in great poverty, bad health and isolation. Nevertheless, the Guomindang and the CCP persecuted him to the end. In the summer of 1938 the CCP began a strident slander campaign against him. This campaign was directed by Wang Ming, who was Stalin's personal representative in China. Wang Ming accused Chen of 'collaborating with the Japanese imperialists'. At the same time the Guomindang prohibited Chen from resuming his literary activities. All he could do during those hard times was to think and to exchange opinions by letter with a few old friends. After his death these letters and a few articles from the years 1940-42 were compiled by one of his former pupils and published in Shanghai in 1948. In 1949 Dr Hu Shi, once an old friend of Chen's but later a staunch supporter of Chiang Kai-shek, reprinted this collection of writings in Taiwan, and wrote an introduction to it in which he welcomed Chen's ideas as those of a 'prodigal returned'. As for the CCP, they regarded Chen as a renegade, and even some Trotskyists thought the same, although for different reasons. So what was Chen's new position, and did it represent his final reconciliation with bourgeois thought?

The main themes of Chen's last letters and articles were as follows. First, no revolutions would break out during the war, and only if the Allies defeated the Axis would revolutionary crises happen. Socialists throughout the world were therefore duty-bound to support the democratic Allies against the fascist Axis. Second, there is no essential difference between bourgeois and proletarian democracy, but only a difference of degree. Proletarian democracy is therefore an extension rather than a negation of bourgeois democracy, and it is wrong to say that bourgeois democracy is historically superseded. Third, capitalism is the root of war, which only world revolution can end. Fourth, the struggle for national liberation is interlinked with proletarian revolution in the advanced countries, and the forces behind these two struggles make socialist revolution together. Fifth, the Soviet Union under Lenin was qualitatively different from the Soviet Union under Stalin. The former was socialist, the later was not. (Chen died before he could elaborate on what kind of regime the Soviet Union under Stalin had become.) Sixth, although Lenin's regime was not like Stalin's, Lenin was partly to blame for Stalin's crimes, since it was he who had counterposed proletarian dictatorship to democracy in general. Seventh, a true socialist revolution is one in which democracy, or more exactly democratic rights, are respected and extended.

Clearly Chen's thinking had changed greatly during the early war years, but his views, however muddled, still fell far short of a reconciliation with his old enemy, the bourgeoisie. Instead, they represented a return by Chen in his old age to the positions he had held as a young man. It is interesting to ask why this happened, especially since in my experience it is not uncommon for intellectuals in backward countries to revert in this way to the ideas of their youth.

China's isolation was broken down by guns and ships. 'Modernisation' stemmed not from gradual change based on evolutions within its own society, but from outside pressures. Development of this sort is inevitably by leaps and bounds, and is condensed and telescoped. In China the transition from democratic radicalism to the founding of a modern socialist movement took some twenty years. In Britain and France the same process took several centuries, and in Russia it took several scores of years.

Moreover, China's progress from democratic agitation to full-blown Communism took place in one and the same person: Chen Duxiu. Chen was China's Belinsky, Cherneshevsky, Plekhanov and Lenin rolled into one. True, he did not reach the stature of these great Russians, but he traversed the entire gamut of their thinking, from the first awakening of individualism to the struggle for socialist collectivism. Thus Chen embodies what Russian marxists referred to as combined development. However, combined development is both a privilege and a curse. It explains not only Chen's merits but also his defects. Chen rapidly and boldly assimilated an impressive lists of isms, but in none of them did he reach real depth. In his teens he became a 'left-wing Confucianist', in his twenties he was intoxicated by Western democracy, in his thirties he criticised Confucianism, and at 41 he became a marxist. Inevitably he retained elements of older ideologies among the new ones as he raced from one system to the next. And by the time that he embraced marxism, he had reached an age where new thinking rarely sinks deep into the soul. It is therefore understandable that in the last years of his life Chen returned in part to his intellectual first love, 'pure' democracy.

But there were of course other factors that disposed Chen to look favourably on democracy. Above all he was appalled by the degeneration of the Stalinist regime in the Soviet Union. It was the Moscow trials that initially led him to rethink the Leninist view of bourgeois democracy.

How, then, should one appraise Chen's life? Despite his political failures and his intellectual limitations, Chen was not only modern China's bravest thinker, but one of history's great revolutionaries. This is not only because of his leading role in the Chinese revolution, but also because of his personal indomitability. He did not hesitate to give up a brilliant career for the uncertain and hard life of a revolutionary. He heroically bore the loss of his family and his two sons (murdered by the Guomindang in 1927 and 1928). He stuck to his beliefs under the threat of imprisonment and death. And during the last years of his life, when he was gravely ill and desperately poor, he refused to accept money offered him by the Guomindang through one of his old friends. All this shows that Chen was a man of revolutionary mettle, and his memory remains that of a great revolutionary. Another appraisal of Chen is that he was 'an oppositionist for life to any established authority', and Chen himself liked this description of his career.

Gregor Benton

Writers and the Party:
The Ordeal of Wang Shiwei, Yanan, 1942

Wang Shiwei was never a big name in Chinese Communism, and nor — I suspect — would he ever have wanted to be. He was gifted as a translator and a writer of fiction, but he hardly shone as a theoretician, and spoke more to the heart than to the brain. The main value of his 1942 articles, published below, therefore lies less in their theoretical depth than in what they reveal of the mood and feelings of the only audible part of Yanan opinion still outside direct party control in early 1942: the writers and intellectuals. Wang's articles stirringly reflect the concerns of these people. For writing them, he would eventually be shot.

Wang Shiwei was only one of many city intellectuals who, as patriots and socialists, went by secret and dangerous paths to the Communist headquarters at Yanan after the outbreak of war with Japan in 1937. Many radical writers joined this migration, and their work soon began to appear in the Yanan press.

In early 1942, shortly after Mao had started his Rectification Campaign against bureaucratic tendencies in the party, some of these writers began to voice their own disquiet about life in Yanan. In particular they denounced the growth of a privileged elite, removed from the concerns of ordinary Chinese, in the comparative security of the capital of the Communist bases. Their criticisms evidently alarmed the authorities, who moved quickly to silence them. The woman writer Ding Ling attacked the lack of sexual equality in Yanan, the privileged position of the wives of some leaders, and the sexism of Yanan males; she was subsequently criticised as a 'narrow feminist'.[1] Xiao Jun, a talented Manchurian writer, denounced leading cadres for the high-handed way they treated people, and argued that the Communists should inject the spirit of religious fervour and idealism into their work. Other writers were also disturbed by what they saw as symptoms of moral degeneration among the party leaders. Wang Shiwei voiced his disgust over the selfishness of some leaders, the widening of income differentials, the suppression of free speech, and the growing alienation of young people from the party. The 1942 writers were united against the lack of 'true human feeling' in the party, and wanted a return to the revolutionary ideals of equality and solidarity, an end to authoritarian methods, and an end to the unnecessary elaboration of ranks and distinctions.

The writers also dealt in their essays with the role of literature in a revolutionary society. They argued that writing must be free of direct political control, and that one of the main functions of revolutionary writing should be to monitor tendencies towards bureaucracy and privilege in the revolutionary state. In support they cited arguments of Lu Xun, modern China's best-known writer and a sympathiser with the Communists, who had said that 'politics wants to preserve the status quo; and thus places itself in an opposite direction to literature as a symbol of discontent'.[2]

A second reason they believed literature should be free of politics was because it dealt intimately and inevitably with questions of human spirit, to which politics has no answers. Wang Shiwei described writing's task as to change people's 'hearts spirit, thinking, consciousness', and to remake the human soul, 'starting with ourselves and our own camp'. For the poet Ai Qing, who shared some of Wang's convictions, the writer is 'the recorder of emotions, the nerve or the eye of wisdom of a nation, i.e. in the sphere of emotions, impressions, thoughts, and mental action, the loyal soldier who protects the nation or class to which he belongs'.[3]

Clearly the writers were out to strengthen the revolution and not, as their critics claimed, to weaken it. They invariably stressed the moral superiority of Yanan, with all its shortcomings, over the Guomindang areas. Most had proud records of revolutionary work. Ding Ling, who had come to the Communist base back in 1936, had been a revolutionary ever since the mid-twenties, and had spent three years in prison after the execution of her husband, the Communist writer Hu Yepin, in 1931. Xiao Jun had fought in the Manchurian resistance to Japan before coming to Yanan.

Wang Shiwei, the most outspoken and consistent of the Yanan dissidents and the only one to die for his beliefs, is the least known of the Yanan group, although his essay 'Wild Lily' has been widely read by new generations of Chinese youth in recent years (see for example Yi Ming, pp. 39-44 above). Wang Shiwei was born in Kaifeng, Henan Province, in 1907, and enrolled at Beijing University in 1925, although he never graduated.[4] In 1926 he joined the underground Communist Party in Beijing at the behest of his fellow provincial Chen Qichang and his classmate Wang Fanxi, both later to become leaders of Chinese Trotskyism. His friends saw him as a man of strong emotion, quick to lose his temper and fired with a strong sense of justice.

In Beijing Wang Shiwei had his first taste of party criticism, in an episode that foreshadowed his later tormented relationship with the party establishment and reveals much of his stubborn and impulsive character. He had fallen unhappily in love with his fellow student and party member Li Fen, to whom 'Wild Lily' is dedicated. He wrote her an unending stream of love letters, although she always rejected his advances. The secretary of the party branch, who was said to be also infatuated with Li Fen, called a meeting to criticise Wang Shiwei's relentness suit of her. Only his friend Wang Fanxi spoke up in his defence, on the grounds that love is a private matter, and that the party had more important things to do than criticise people's personal lives during the grave political crisis in the capital after the execution of Communist leaders in early 1927.

Wang Shiwei began his writing career in Beijing, where he contributed articles and short stories to Hu Shi's 'Contemporary Review' and other journals. He continued to write throughout his life, and in 1930 published a collection of short stories called *Xiuxi* ('Rest'). By then he and his wife Liu Ying were living in extreme poverty in Shanghai. It was around this time that his closest friends were driven out of the party as Oppositionists, and soon he too became an Oppositionist of sorts. With their help he got work translating Hardy's *Return of the Native*, which solved his money problems for a while; and he also translated various political writings for them. But he passionately believed that social revolution was never so radical as the revolution in the soul, since unreformed human nature — the source, as he saw it, of Stalinism — would taint any future revolution that failed to deal with it. As a result, his Trotskyist friends considered him an emotional revolutionary rather than a hardened

Bolshevik. In late 1937, after sending his wife and baby daughter to safety in Hunan, he made his way to Yanan, where he worked for the Communists as a writer and translator.

1942 was a tough year for the Communist war effort in China. The base areas were in deep economic and military crisis as a result of the tightening Guomindang blockade to the south and intensified pressure from the Japanese army to the east. Territory and population were being lost. In this crisis the party desperately needed support, but it did not always go skilfully and tactfully about getting it. Many of its officials acted more like bureaucrats than like revolutionaries: they had fallen into set routines, they mostly put their own interests first, and they showed little concern for the welfare of ordinary people. This, then, was the background to Mao's Rectification Campaign, which singled out bureaucratism, dogmatism, sectarianism and a failure to cherish the masses as its main targets. In starting this campaign Mao was incidentally preparing the way for the political destruction of the 'right opportunist' tendency led by the CCP's main Stalinist, Wang Ming, and so for the further strengthening of Mao's position as party leader.

The dissident writers were at first heartened by Mao's attacks on bureaucracy, and they enthusiastically repeated his criticisms and added some of their own. As for Wang Shiwei, he saw the Rectification Campaign as a struggle between Mao's 'orthodox' group, which he supported, and the 'unorthodox' faction.[5] He may even have hoped that Mao would back his libertarian manifesto. He was to be rudely disillusioned.

At first the writers got widespread support, especially from young people in Yanan. The official press complained of resistance to party policies by groups with ultra-democratic and ultra-egalitarian ideas, and many spectators at Wang's later trial at first dissented from the official condemnation of him.[6] A party historian has written: 'Some people openly said that the struggle against Wang was a case of emptying the chamber pot, and that because of his mistakes everyone was pouring piss over his head. Many people were sympathetic to Wang's arguments and proposals.'[7]

The party leaders, shocked by the depth of feeling they had stirred up, were forced for a while to cease fire against the bureaucrats and self-servers in the party and to turn their guns instead against the writers. In May 1942, in his talks at the Yanan forums on art and literature, Mao went out of his way to rebut views like those of the writers on the role of literature as social criticism.[8] These talks were a main turning point in CCP cultural policy. Before them cultural policy could still be a matter for debate on the left in China; after them the party rigorously imposed its will on writers and artists.

The main theme of Mao's talks was the need to bring art and literature down to the horizons of the masses, and to subordinate art and literature to immediate political requirements. The writer's task was not, he said, to light up the dark side of life in the bases, but to reflect and extol its bright side.

Mao also summoned writers to develop a literature that was truly national in form and that could stir and enthuse the peasant imagination. But by subjecting literature to rigid control, he necessarily restricted the interplay of experimentation and choice that is at the root of literary innovation, and with the passage of time achieved the very opposite of what he intended.

The writers were hardly a tightly-knit group, and under party pressure their common stand soon collapsed. All but Wang Shiwei and Xiao Jun disavowed their earlier views, and Ding Ling was even prepared to announce Wang's expulsion from the Anti-Japanese Writers' Association.[9] During the next two years Ding Ling went through a long period of thought reform, during which she gave up creative writing and became a journalist. Others of the writers lost the urge to write altogether, fearful of further attacks from the ideological purists. The literary scene in Yanan now resembled more than ever that in the Soviet Union under Stalin. An all-powerful party machine alone decided what could be published, sold and read. The temporary license for criticism was withdrawn.

Wang Shiwei alone among the writers was put on a much publicised quasi-trial for his views. He was the scapegoat, first, because he was the least known of the writers, and therefore the least likely to attract public sympathy; second, because he took his criticisms of Yanan society further than the others; third, because of his past Trotskyist associations; and last, because he refused to eat his words.

It is said that in the early days of the anti-Japanese war Mao himself was prepared to welcome former Trotskyists to Yanan, but was overruled by Wang Ming, the newly returned Moscow emissary.[10] The failure of the Trotskyist factions to join wholeheartedly in the war of resistance to Japan did not make them popular, and the word Trotskyist soon became synonymous in the party with 'Japanese spy'. The charge of Trotskyism was therefore damaging, and must have played a big part in swinging opinion in Yanan against Wang Shiwei. Even so, many still spoke up in his defence.

Evidence of various sorts was offered to prove that Wang Shiwei had not given up his Trotskyist beliefs: he had described Stalin as boorish and unattractive; he had condemned the Moscow purges and the sentencing of Zinoviev; he had refused to brand the Russian Oppositionists as fascists, and continued to insist that the Chinese Trotskyist leaders Chen Qichang and Wang Fanxi were 'communists of humanity'; he had made a distinction between a political party of the workers and a peasant party with proletarian leaders; and he was allegedly negative about the wartime united front with the Guomindang.[11]

But 'Wild Lily' suggests that Wang's position on the united front was in fact quite orthodox. As for his other views, they were by no means only his. Mao himself is reported to have expressed views earlier that were similar to Wang's on the Moscow purges and the Trotskyists,[12] and Wang Ming and his supporters had made a similar assessment of the class nature of the CCP as late as 1941.

Wang Shiwei stuck to his views even though he was attacked and humiliated before an audience that at times numbered over a thousand. On the fifth day of his trial he asked to be allowed to resign from the party and 'go his own way', since he no longer felt able to 'reconcile himself with the party's utilitarianism'. On the seventh day he withdrew this request, 'made in an abnormal state of mind', after he had been 'touched by the love of comrades'.[13]

After his ordeal, Wang disappeared from public view for two years. He was later seen by visiting journalists sticking labels on match-boxes in a Yanan workshop.[14] According to a 1962 speech of Mao's, Wang was shot by security forces during the evacuation of Yanan, presumably in 1947, an action that Mao gave as an example of a wrongly ordered execution, though he approved of the other penal sanctions against Wang for daring to write articles attacking 'us'. Curiously, Wang was then remembered by Mao as a 'Guomindang agent'.[15]

It cannot be emphasised enough that the writers' dissatisfaction with some aspects of Yanan life did not amount to a rejection of the resistance to Japan, of which the Communist Party was the only effective organiser at the time, or of the basic social order that had emerged in the Red capital. Yanan had much going for it; and its bureaucratic tendencies were never so pronounced in the guerrilla zones outside Yanan, where the real war was being fought. Thus when the Communist authorities made it clear that the writers would have to choose between accepting the system, faults and all, or being shut out from the great national struggle, it is not surprising that most preferred to eat humble pie. However, after the immediate pressures for wartime solidarity were relieved, first Xiao Jun and then Ding Ling were in trouble again.

More positive assessments of Yanan than Wang's can be found in works of Gunther Stein and Harrison Forman, or, more recently, in Mark Selden's *The Yenan Way in Revolutionary China*. To those who visited it from Chongqing or Xian, Yanan's bracing upland climate was matched by a moral vigour that set it apart from the inescapable corruption of a moribund regime that by 1944 was scarcely capable of putting up effective resistance to the renewed Japanese offensives.

Even by the standards of the People's Republic, Yanan life had a degree of informality and conviviality that could not be recaptured when the Communist leaders moved into their quarters in the grounds of the Imperial Palace in Beijing. But in 1942 such a development would have seemed inconceivably remote. The issues then, when the war was nearly five years old and the initial excitement had long since worn off, were rather the difference between Yanan life and the writers' ideal of a revolutionary society.

Wang's 'Politicians, Artists' first appeared in the Yanan journal *Guyu*, vol. 1, no. 4, 17 February 1942. 'Wild Lily' first appeared in two parts in *Jiefang ribao* ('Liberation Daily'), 13 and 23 March 1942. It appeared in English translation in Gregor Benton, 'The Yenan Literary Opposition', *New Left Review*, no. 92, July-August 1975.

Notes

1. Ding Ling's essay and Xiao Jun's are translated in Gregor Benton, 'The Yenan Literary Opposition', *New Left Review*, no. 92, July-August 1975. They and other writers from this period are discussed in Merle Goldman, *Literary Dissent in Communist China*, Cambridge, Mass. 1967.
2. Quoted in Tsi-an Hsia, *The Gate of Darkness*, Seattle 1968, p. p. 253.
3. Quoted in D.W. Fokkema, *Literary Doctrine in China and Soviet Influence, 1956-1960*, The Hague 1965, p. 13.
4. The following biographical sketch of Wang Shiwei is based on the recollections of Wang Fanxi.
5. *Lun Wang Shiweide sixiang yishi* ('On Wang Shiwei's Ideology'), Ji-Lu-Yu Bookstore, no place given, 1944, pp. 21 and 61.
6. *ibid.* pp. 59-60.
7. Hu Hua, quoted in *Mingbao Yuekan* (Hongkong), February 1966, p.92.
8. There is an edited version of these talks in Mao Zedong, *Selected Works*, vol. 3. For the original published text see *Mao Zedong ji* (Tokyo), vol. 8.
9. Lin Yü-t'ang, *Vigil of a Nation*, London 1946, p. 238 fn.
10. Chang Kuo-t'ao's memoirs in *Mingbao Yuekan*, January 1941, pp. 90-92.
11. *Lun Wang Shiweide sixiang yishi*, pp. 61-69.
12. Chang Kuo-t'ao, *loc. cit.*
13. *Lun Wang Shiweide sixiang yishi*, pp. 62-64.
14. Lin Yü-t'ang, *Ni ming* ('Anonymous'), Taibei 1958, p. 134.
15. 'Talk at an Enlarged Working Conference Convened by the Central Committee', *Mao Zedong sixiang wansui* ('Long Live Mao Zedong Thought') 1969, p. 421. (Received into the officially published canon of Mao's writings in July 1978: *Peking Review*, 1978, 27, p. 21.

Wang Shiwei

Politicians, Artists

There are two sides to the revolution: changing the social system, and changing people. Politicians are the revolution's strategists and tacticians; they unite, organise and lead the revolution. Their main task is to transform the social system. Artists are the 'engineers of the soul', and their main task is to transform people's heart, spirit, thinking and consciousness.

The filth and darkness in people's souls are the product of an irrational social system, and the soul's fundamental transformation is impossible until the social system has been fundamentally transformed. In the process of transforming the social system the soul too is transformed... The tasks of the politician and the artist are complementary.

The politicians command the revolution's material forces; the artists arouse the revolution's spiritual forces. The politicians are generally cool, collected people, good at waging practical struggles to eliminate filth and darkness, and to bring about cleanliness and light. The artists are generally more emotional and more sensitive, good at exposing filth and darkness, and at pointing out cleanliness and light...

The politicians understand that during the revolution the people in their own camp will be less than perfect, and things will rarely be done ideally. They takes the broad view, making sure that the wheel of history advances and that the light wins. The artists, more passionate and more sensitive, long for people to be more lovable and things to be more splendid. When they write they take small things as their starting points: they hope to eliminate the darkness as far as they can so that the wheel of history can advance as fast as possible. As the practical transformers of the social system, the politicians take things more seriously; the artists as the soul's engineers, go even further in demanding perfection of people. In uniting, organising and leading the revolution and waging practical struggles, the politicians are superior. But the artists are better at plunging into the depths of the soul to change it — transforming our side in order to strengthen it, and transforming the enemies so as to undermine them.

The politicians and the artists each have their weak points. If the politicians are to attack the enemy successfully, establish links with allied forces, and strengthen our side, they must understand human nature and the ways of the world, be masters of tricks and devices, and be skilled in making and breaking alliances. Their weakness springs from these very strengths. When they use them for the revolutionary cause they become the most beautiful and exquisite 'revolutionary art', but unless they are truly great politicians they are bound to make use of them for their own fame, position and interest, thus harming the revolution. In this respect we must insist that cat's claws be used only for catching rats and not for seizing chickens. Here we must distinguish politicians from artists; and we must be ever on our guard against cats that are good not at catching rats but at taking chickens. The main weaknesses of most artists are pride, narrowness, isolation, inability to unite with others and mutual suspicion and exclusion. Here we must ask the engineers of the soul to start by making their own souls clean and bright. This is hard and painful, but it is the only way to greatness.

The Chinese revolution is especially hard. The difficulties of changing the social system are well known, but few realise that changing people's souls is even harder. 'The further east you go, the darker society becomes.' Old China is full of gore and pus, darkness and filth, all of which have inevitably stained the Chinese who grew up in it. Even we, the revolutionary fighters creating a new China, cannot escape this cruel fact. Only if we have the courage to look it in the face can we understand why we must be even more rigorous in our efforts to transform souls, so as to accelerate and win the struggle to change the social system.

Lu Xun was a fighter all his life, but anyone who understands him will know that at heart he was lonely. He struggled because he recognised the laws of social development and believed that the future was bound to be better than the present; he was lonely because he saw that even in the souls of his own comrades there was filth and darkness. He knew that the task of transforming old China could only be carried out by the sons and daughters of old China, despite their filth and darkness. But his great heart could not help yearning for his comrades to be more loveable.

The revolutionary camp exists in old China, and the revolution's fighters have grown up in old China, which means that our souls are inevitably stained. The present revolution requires that we ally not only with the peasants and the urban petty bourgeoisie, but with even more backward classes and strata, and that we make concessions to them, thus becoming contaminated with yet more filth and darkness. This makes the artist's task of transforming the soul even more important, difficult and urgent. To boldly expose and wash away all that is filthy and dark is as important as praising the light, if not more important. Exposing and cleansing is not merely negative, because when darkness is eliminated the light can shine even brighter. Some people think that revolutionary artists must 'direct their fire outside', and that if we expose our weaknesses we give the enemy easy targets. But this is a short-sighted view. Though our camp is now strong enough for us to have no fears about exposing our shortcomings, it is not yet fully consolidated; self-criticism is the best way of consolidating it. As for the maggots and traitors in anti-Communist secret service organs, they would concoct rumours and slanders even if we were flawless; they even hope that we will hush up our faults and shun those who might cure them, so that the darkness grows.

Some who think highly of themselves as politicians smile sarcastically when they speak of artists. Others who pride themselves on being artists shrug their shoulders when they mention politicians. But there is always some truth in objective reflections: each would do well to use the other as a mirror. They should not forget that they are both children of old China.

A truly great politician must have a soul great enough to move the souls of others and cleanse them; thus a great politician is a great artist. An artist who has a truly great soul is bound to have a part to play in uniting, organising and leading the forces of revolution; thus a great artist is also a great politician.

Finally I would like to appeal warmly to artist comrades: be even more effective in transforming the soul, and aim in the first place at ourselves and our own camp. In China transforming the soul will have an even greater effect on transforming society. It will determine not only how soon but even whether the revolution suceeds.

Wang Shiwei

Wild Lily

While I was walking alone along the river bank, I saw a comrade wearing a pair of old-style padded cotton shoes. I immediately fell to thinking of Comrade Li Fen, who also wore such shoes. Li Fen, my dearest and very first friend. As usual my blood began to race. Li Fen was a student in 1926 on the preparatory course in literature at Beijing University. In the same year she joined the party. In the spring of 1928 she sacrificed her life in her home district of Baoqing in Hunan Province. Her own uncle tied her up and sent her to the local garrison — a good illustration of the barbarity of old China. Before going to her death, she put on all her three sets of underclothes and sewed them tightly together at the top and the bottom. This was because the troops in Baoqing often incited riff-raff to debauch the corpses of the young women Communists they had shot — yet another example of the brutality, the evil, the filth and the darkness of the old society. When I got news of her death, I was consumed with feelings of deep love and hatred. Whenever I think of her, I have a vision of her pure, sacred martyrdom, with her three layers of underclothes sewn tightly together, tied up and sent by her very own uncle to meet her death with dignity. (It seems rather out of place to talk of such things in tranquil Yanan, against the warbled background of a Yutangjun and the swirling steps of the golden lotus dance; but the whole atmosphere in Yanan does not seem particularly appropriate to the conditions of the day — close your eyes and think for a moment of our dear comrades dying every minute in a sea of carnage.)

In the interest of the nation, I will not reckon up old scores of class hatred. We are genuinely selfless. With all our might we are dragging the representatives of old China along the road with us towards the light. But in the process the filth and dirt is rubbing off on us, spreading its diseases.

On scores of occasions I have drawn strength from the memory of Li Fen — vital and militant strength. Thinking back on her on this occasion, I was moved to write a *zawen* under the title 'Wild Lily'. This name has a two-fold significance. First, the wild lily is the most beautiful of the wild flowers in the hills and countryside around Yanan, and is therefore a fitting dedication to her memory. Secondly, although its bulbs are similar to those of other lilies, they are said to be slightly bitter to the taste, and of greater medicinal value, but I myself am not sure of this.

What is lacking in our lives?

Recently young people here in Yanan seem to have lost some of their enthusiasm, and to have become inwardly ill at ease.

Why is this? What is lacking in our lives? Some would answer that it is because we are badly nourished and short of vitamins. Others that is because the ratio of men to women is 18:1 and many young men are unable to find girlfriends. Or because life in Yanan is dreary and lacks amusements.

There is some truth in all these answers. It is true that there is need for better food, for partners of the opposite sex and for more interest in life. That is only natural. But one must also recognise that young people here in Yanan came with a spirit of sacrifice to make revolution, and not for food, sex and an enjoyable life. I cannot agree with those who say that their lack of enthusiasm, their inward disquiet even, are a result of our inability to resolve these problems. So what is lacking in our lives? Perhaps the following conversation holds some clues.

During the New Year holiday I was walking home in the dark one evening from a friend's place. Ahead of me were two women comrades talking in animated whispers. We were some way apart so I quietly moved closer to hear what they were saying.

'He keeps on talking about other people's petty-bourgeois egalitarianism; but the truth is that he thinks he is something special. He always looks after his own interests. As for the comrades underneath him, he doesn't care whether they're sick or well, he doesn't even care if they die, he hardly gives a damn!'

'Crows are black wherever they are. Even Comrade XXX acts like that.'

'You're right! All this bullshit about loving your own class. They don't even show ordinary human sympathy! You often see people pretending to smile and be friendly, but it's all on the surface, it doesn't mean anything. And if you offend them, they glare at you, pull their rank and start lecturing you.'

'It's not only the big shots who act that way, the small fry are just the same. Our section leader XXX crawls when he's talking to his superiors, but he behaves very arrogantly towards us. Often comrades have been ill and he hasn't even dropped in to see how they are. But when an eagle stole one of his chickens, you should have seen the fuss he made! After that, every time he saw an eagle he'd start screaming and throwing clods of earth at it — the self-seeking bastard!'

There was a long silence. In one way, I admired the comrade's sharp tongue. But I also suddenly felt depressed.

'It's sad that so many comrades are falling ill. Nobody wants people like that to visit them when they fall ill, they just make you feel worse. Their tone of voice, their whole attitude — they don't make you feel they care about you.'

'Right. They don't care about others, and others don't care about them. If they did mass work, they'd be bound to fail.'

They carried on their conversation in animated whispers. At this point our ways parted, and I heard no more of what they had to say. In many ways their views were one-sided and exaggerated. Perhaps the picture they drew does not apply widely; but there is no denying that it is useful as a mirror...

Running into 'Running into difficulties'

On 'Youth Page' no. 12 of this paper ['Liberation Daily', the paper in which Wang Shiwei's article first appeared], I read an article titled 'Running into difficulties' which aroused my interest. Here are two passages from that article.

'Recently a middle-aged friend arrived from the Guomindang rear. When he saw that young people in Yanan were incapable of putting up with anything and were constantly grumbling he raised his voice: "What's all this about? We people in the outside world have run into countless difficulties and suffered constant ill-treatment..."'

'He was right. Life in Yanan may anger or offend you. But in the eyes of someone who has run up against countless difficulties and who has experienced the hardships of life, they are mere trifles. But it is an entirely different matter in the case of immature young people, especially those of student origin. Their parents and teachers coddle them into adulthood, whispering to them about life with love and warmth and teaching them to imitate pure and beautiful emotions. The ugliness and bleakness of their present situation is entirely new to them, and it is not surprising that as soon as they come up against difficulty they begin to bawl and to feel upset.'

I have no idea what sort of person this author's 'middle-aged friend' is, but in my view his sort of philosophy, which is based on the principle of being contented with one's lot, is positively harmful. Young people should be treasured for their purity, their perceptiveness, their ardour, their courage, and their energy. They experience the darkness before others experience it, they see the filth before others see it; what others do not wish or dare to say, they say. Because of this they are more critical, but this is by no means 'grumbling'. What they say is not always well-balanced, but it is by no means 'bawling'. We should enquire into problems that give rise to 'grumbling', 'bawling' and 'disquiet', and set about removing their causes in a rational way. (Yes, rational! It is completely untrue that young people are always engaged in 'thoughtless clamour'.) To say that Yanan is superior to the 'outside world', to tell young people not to 'grumble', to describe Yanan's dark side as some 'slight disappointment' will solve no problems. Yes, Yanan is superior to the 'outside world', but it should and can be better still.

Of course young people are often hot-headed and impatient — an observation that appears to be the main theme of 'Running into difficulties'. But if all young people were to be mature before their time, how desolate this world would be! In reality, young people in Yanan have already seen a great deal of the world — after all, the grumbling conversation between the two women comrades that I quoted earlier was held in whispers in the dark. So far from resenting 'grumbling' of this sort, we should use it as a mirror in which to inspect ourselves. To say that youth 'of student origin' are 'coddled into adulthood, whispered to about life with love and warmth and taught to imitate pure and beautiful emotions' is very subjectivist. Even though most Yanan youth come from 'a student background', are 'inexperienced' and have not 'seen more than enough of life's hardships', most arrived in Yanan after a whole series of struggles and it is not true to say that they experienced nothing but 'love and warmth'; on the contrary, it was precisely because they knew all about 'hatred and cold' that they joined the revolutionary camp in the first place. From what the author of 'Running into difficulties' says, all the young people in Yanan were brought up pampered, and only 'grumble' because they miss their candied fruit. But it was because of 'evil and coldness' that they came to Yanan in search of 'beauty and warmth', that they identified the 'evil and coldness' here in Yanan and insisted on 'grumbling' about it in the hope of alerting people's attention and reducing it to a minimum.

In the winter of 1938 our party carried out a large-scale investigation of our work and summoned comrades to 'unfold a lively criticism' and to 'give full vent to their criticisms, no matter whether they were right or wrong'. I hope we have another such investigation, and listen to the 'grumbles' of the youth.

'Inevitability', 'the heavens won't fall in' and 'small things'

'Our camp exists amidst the darkness of the old society, and therefore there is inevitably darkness in it too.' Of course, that's 'marxism'! But that is only one-sided marxism. There is an even more important side which the 'masters of subjectivist factionalism' have forgotten, i.e. the need, after having recognised the inevitability of such darkness, through Bolshevik activism to prevent its emergence, to reduce its growth, and to give full play to the ability of consciousness to transform objective reality. Given present conditions, to clean out all traces of darkness from our camp is impossible. But to destroy as much of it as we can is not only possible, but necessary. The 'great masters', however, have not only failed to emphasise this point, but have scarcely even mentioned it. All they do is point out that is is 'inevitable' and then doze off to sleep. They use 'inevitability' as an excuse for self-indulgence. In their dreams they tell themselves: 'Comrade, you are a product of the old society, and there is a tiny spot of darkness in your soul. But that is inevitable, no need to get embarrassed about it.'

After the 'theory' of 'inevitability' comes the 'national form theory' known as 'the heavens won't fall in'. Yes, it is impossible for the heavens to fall in. But what of our work and our cause? Will they suffer as a result? The 'great masters' have given little or no thought to this problem. If this 'inevitability' is 'inevitably' allowed to pursue its course, then the heavens — the heavens of our revolutionary cause — will 'inevitably' fall in. I suggest we should not be so complacent.

The so-called 'small things' theory is linked with this. A criticises B. B tells A he shouldn't waste his time on 'small things'. Some 'great masters' even say: 'Damn it! It's bad enough with the women comrades, now the men are spending all their time on trivia too!' It is true that there is probably no danger in Yanan of such big problems as treason against the party or the nation. But each individual through the small things he does in the course of his everyday life, either helps the light or helps the darkness. And the 'small things' in the lives of 'great men' are even more capable of calling forth warmth or desolation.

Egalitarianism and the system of ranks

According to what I heard, one comrade wrote an article with a similar title for his departmental wall newspaper, and as a result was criticised and attacked by his department 'head' and driven half-mad. I hope this story is untrue. But since there have been genuine cases of madness even among the 'little devils' [orphan children who acted as personal assistants to the Communist cadres], I fear there may be some madness among adults. Even though the state of my nerves is not as 'healthy' as some people's, I still have enough life in me not to go mad under any circumstances. I therefore intend to follow in the footsteps of that comrade and discuss the question of equality and the ranking system.

Communism is not the same as egalitarianism, and we are not at present at the stage of Communist revolution. There is no need for me to write an eight-legged essay on that question, since there is no cook crazy enough to want to live in the same style as one of the 'heads'. (I don't dare write 'kitchen operative', since it sounds like a caricature; but whenever I speak to cooks I always address them in the warmest possible way as 'comrade kitchen-operatives' — what a pitiful example of warmth!) The question of a system of ranks is rather more difficult.

Those who say that a system of ranks is reasonable use

roughly the following arguments: (1) they base themselves on the principle of 'from each according to their ability, to each according to their worth', which means that those with more responsibilities should consume more; (2) in the near future the three-thirds government [the 'tripartite system' under which the Communists nominally shared power with the 'petit bourgeoisie and the enlightened gentry' in the areas under their control] intends to carry out a new salary system, and naturally there will be pay differentials; and (3) the Soviet Union also has a system of ranks.

In my opinion all these arguments are open to debate. As for (1), we are still in the midst of the revolution, with all its hardships and difficulties; all of us, despite fatigue, are labouring to surmount the present crisis, and many comrades have ruined their precious health. Because of this it does not yet seem the right time for anyone, no matter who, to start talking about 'to each according to their worth'. On the contrary, all the more reason why those with greater responsibilities should show themselves willing to share weal and woe with the rank and file. (This is a national virtue that should be encouraged.) In so doing, they would win the profound love of the lower ranks. Only then would it be possible to create iron-like unity. It goes without saying that it is not only reasonable but necessary that those with big responsibilities who need special treatment for their health should get such treatment. The same goes for those with positions of medium responsibility. As for (2), the pay system of the three-thirds government should also avoid excessive differentials; it is right that non-party officials should get slightly better treatment, but those officials who are party members should uphold our excellent traditions of frugal struggle so that we are in a position to mobilise even more non-party people to join us and co-operate with us. As for (3), excuse my rudeness, but I would beg those 'great masters' who can't open their mouths without talking about 'Ancient Greece' to hold their tongues.

I am not an egalitarian, but to divide clothing into three and food into five grades is neither necessary nor rational, especially with regard to clothes. (I myself am graded as 'cadres' clothes and private kitchen', so this is not just a case of sour grapes.) All such problems should be resolved on the basis of need and reason. At present there is no noodle soup for sick comrades to eat and young students only get two meals of thin congee a day (when they're asked whether they have had enough to eat, party members are expected to lead the rest in a chorus of 'Yes, we're full'). Relatively healthy 'big shots' get far more than they need to eat and drink, with the result that their subordinates look upon them as a race apart, and not only do not love them, but even... This makes me most uneasy. But perhaps it is a 'petty bourgeois emotion' to always be talking about 'love' and 'warmth'? I await your verdict.

Marie Holzman

Love and Marriage in People's China

Marie Holzman lived in China between 1975 and 1981, and knew leading members of the democratic movement. Her account of attitudes towards marriage among young Chinese is based on personal observation and on what her Chinese friends told her. During the ten years of the Cultural Revolution foreign visitors to China reported optimistically on progress towards women's liberation there, and for a time many Western feminists looked on China as a society where a new type of woman was being born. Now this is no longer so. Writers like Holzman, Claudette Broyelle and others who know China well have shown that the past still weighs heavily on China's women, and that after the disappointments of the Cultural Revolution old attitudes are still strongly entrenched.

Marie Holzman's book *Avec les Chinois* was published by Flammarion in 1981. This article was translated into English by Kenneth Barr.

Each month newspapers like 'China Youth' carry numerous letters about love-problems. We publish two such letters below. During the ten years of the Cultural Revolution love was a taboo subject, but now it is once again discussed freely in books, newspapers and films. For some young people, relations between men and women in China, burdened with what the Chinese call 'two thousand years of feudalism', are not developing fast enough. Traditions, prejudices and restrictions are equally cramping for young people in love: either the parents object to a marriage for reason of status, or the party interferes. The party strongly recommends — one might say orders — young people not to marry before their twenty-fifth birthday. Ideally the combined age of both partners should not exceed 52, for example 25 plus 27. But if the man is, say thirty, the rule is relaxed, and his bride-to-be may be as young as 23. The rule for men is relaxed for social reasons, e.g. in the case of orphans and only children, since it is generally accepted that a bachelor is not capable of doing his own cooking and housekeeping.

Once they reach the age of 25 young women enter the so-called marriage-market. A friend of the family, usually an older married woman, will agree to look for a suitable partner. In the case of Xiao Huang (Xiao means little and is placed before the surname instead of comrade or Miss), a nice girl living in my neighbourhood, the 'search' took two years, during which time she was introduced to no less than 17 young men. She met most of them after work, in the company of one or two girlfriends. The young men also came with friends, and together the group would go out walking in the park. The chaperones knew one another already and quickly arranged for the young couple to have some time alone together. But Xiao Huang was a very demanding young lady and seldom agreed to meet her suitor a second time. She always had a different reason: he's stupid, he's ugly, he's smaller than I am... One day a young actor was introduced to her. He was tall, handsome and charming. Xiao Huang was very impressed and talked about no one else but him, but then, after three months, she began to ask questions. In respectable circles in China actors have a bad name. Respectable Chinese believe that actors have loose morals, that they are too free with one another when on tour, and that they are unfaithful to their partners. And so Xiao Huang got one of her girlfriends, who knew the actor's uncle, to make a few discrete enquiries. The uncle, not knowing that he was talking to a friend of Xiao Huang's, told her that his nephew had already had many girlfriends. That was enough to put Xiao Huang off him, because at 27 she was still a virgin and she wasn't interested in having a husband who was not. Shortly after, a soldier was introduced to her. The soldier was not handsome, but his social status was similar to her own and he seemed to be serious. Because she was afraid of becoming an old spinster and above all wanted children, she agreed to marry him, to the great delight of her parents and go-betweens.

Arranged marriages like Xiao Huang's are still more common, even in Beijing, than marriages of love.

Women take their revenge in a strange way. Today it is the men who have to shower their fiancées with presents if they want to win them over. In traditional China families used to exchange pieces of silk, jewellery and other valuable presents on the occasion of a marriage. Today only the man gives presents, and in general the groom's family takes responsibility for the wedding reception. These receptions are vigorously attacked by the party, which would prefer to use the money banked in the form of family savings than wasted on festivities. In Beijing, wedding receptions are kept on a fairly modest scale, but elsewhere setting up a new home calls for a proper celebration. Because Chinese flats are nearly always very small, receptions are held in restaurants; here a hundred or more guests can eat and drink for hours on end. Parents of limited means can easily spend more than 500 yuan on such a reception and parents with higher salaries spend even more.

If the suitor is to satisfy his loved one, he has to go to still more trouble. These young ladies have become so greedy that there are numerous jokes about them, some in the form of poems. In translation these folk verses lose much of their humour, but the following poem gives an idea of what Chinese girls think is the ideal husband.

> One complete set of home furnishings including two
>   armchairs,
> Two parents to look after the babies,
> Three objects that turn, (a watch, a bicycle and a sewing
>   machine), plus a television,
> Four clothed seasons (clothes for the four seasons),
> Five pairs of leather shoes — and someone to clean them,
> A gift of six months' wages,
> Seven times ten yuan a month (at least!),
> Eight hundred sentences (a good talker),
> Nine: he drinks neither wine nor tea, and does not smoke
>   [nine and wine are pronounced the same in Chinese],
> Ten divided by ten: I'm happy, and if not I'll lay about
>   me.

Many a young man has come unstuck on the astonishing materialism of these Chinese women. Poorer men who are unable to satisfy their girlfriends' expensive tastes see them married off to men with no brains but with well-filled wallets. Moralising stories are printed in the newspapers to remind young women about sound values like honesty and diligence, and to dissuade them from frivolity. But these stories quite often have a strong humorous streak, as the following example from 'Beijing Daily' of 9 July 1979 shows:

Xiao Wang had dusted all the furniture that he needed for his marriage and had arranged everything according to his fiancée Xiao Li's instructions. He had virtually run himself into the ground buying things: a cupboard, a chest-of-drawers, a desk with five compartments, folding chairs, collapsible stools, a round table, a square table, armchairs, and so many other bits and pieces that at first sight there was no room to swing a cat. But when Xiao Li came to inspect the room she suddenly discovered an empty corner behind the door and said: 'But there's nothing in this corner here! Now what do we have to fill it up?' Xiao Wang replied spiritedly: 'Alright then, let's keep it as somewhere to put our love.' Xiao Li roared with laughter: 'Oh you', she said, 'love is an affair of the heart, it isn't something material. How could love occupy a space?'

Sex before marriage can get you labelled a deliquent or even sent to a rehabilitation centre for punishment. There are ten such centres near Beijing. They take in offenders aged from 13 to 18. Many girls are sent there by their parents, angry that their daughters should have given in to their boyfriends' advances. In the rehabilitation centres these girls are kept under stricter control than at ordinary schools and are not allowed home. Young boys from richer families protect their virginity more for practical than for moral reasons. As Li Meng told me:

I don't have a girlfriend because it's too risky. If I were to go to bed with a girl and then go off her, it's only natural that I would want to stop seeing her. But if she wanted to get her own back on me she could go around telling everyone that I'd raped her, and that might get me thrown in prison.

This does indeed seem to be one way in which Chinese girls protect their virginity. Once it becomes known that a girl has had a lover, it is hard for her to find a good husband. But there are also cases in which the girl's father, wanting to put an end to a relationship of which he does not approve, will accuse her boyfriend of having taken her virginity. Pinned to the door of the court-house you can see ridiculous statements like: Comrade X is sentenced to five years' goal for raping Comrade X thirty times over a period of six months.

Nowadays Chinese women work outside the home and the old maxim that 'the man works while the woman stays at home' no longer holds. But even though Chinese women are supposed 'to support half of heaven on their shoulders', most of them still do lowly work and it is my impression that they are not treated equally. In a textile factory that I visited in 1979, 80 per cent of the workers were women but 11 of the 15 members of the revolutionary committee were men. We were told that women still had a long way to go before they freed themselves from centuries of feudal culture and that at the moment their cultural level was not high enough for them to hold positions of responsibility. Now one characteristic of my Chinese girlfriends that has always troubled me has been their lack of fighting spirit. It is almost as if Chinese women don't experience sexual inequality in the same way as western women do; this makes it all the more difficult for a woman whose head is full of feminist slogans to come to grips with Chinese femininity. I'll limit myself to reporting a conversation that I had in July 1979 with my girlfriend Xiao Han, whose views I believe were not unlike those of many other girls I knew.

Xiao Han, 'Last week our school held a competition to select the best students for a language course organised by the United Nations. 20 boys and 5 girls were to be selected.'

Me, 'Why? Are boys better at languages?'

Xiao Han, 'No, but the idea is that those who follow this course will get important positions abroad, and it's more practical to send a man than a woman.'

Me, 'Don't you think that in a competition the best people should be selected irrespective of their sex?'

Xiao Han, 'Yes, of course.'

Me, 'Do women always have to contend with this sort of discrimination when they look for work?'

Xiao Han, 'Yes, for example factory managers prefer to hire men.'

Me, 'Is that because they're stronger?'

Xiao Han, 'No, it doesn't have anything to do with strength. Factory managers prefer not to hire women because once women are married they have to do all sorts of domestic work, which means that they're absent more often than men. It's usually OK for them to arrive late if they have small or sick children and leave early to do the shopping and prepare dinner.'

Me, 'But I thought that the men also helped with the house-keeping?'

Xiao Han, 'When they are newly married, it's true that they help with the housekeeping, and also when they retire, but as a rule the man has a more important job than the woman, so he is away from home more often and gradually leaves more and more of the house-keeping to his wife. But it's not only his work that keeps him away from home: in restaurants only one person in ten is a woman, and in the parks you never see women playing cards or chess with the men. Even the onlookers are all men. On the riverbanks, all the anglers are men. That's because women don't have time to do nice things.'

Me, 'Do you think that's normal?'

Xiao Han, 'I don't know, I've never thought about that question.'

Beating women is so common that no one even talks about it. Most of the Chinese men I knew admitted to beating their wives. True, they didn't do it often, only when they reach the end of their tether. A nice lad of 24 with big soft eyes once confided in me: 'I'm very sad, my girlfriend has walked out on me. We'd already known each other for 6 months and I hadn't even hit her once.' That makes me suspect the worst! Before the revolution China was known all over the world for its tea houses where rich men went to relax in the company of beautiful women. Prostitution was then a normal part of social life, and while the prostitutes were not respected, at least they were not reviled. In the course of this century their position declined rapidly and in place of the prostitutes came the bar-girls. Misery drove thousands of women into prostitution and many became addicted to opium. The new government was not prepared to accept this. Prostitution was for the Communists one of China's worst evils and they energetically went to work to rid her of it. For a long time they believed that they had succeeded and Chinese cadres proudly told foreign tourists: 'Prostitution does not exist here.'

But in November 1978 the Japanese film *Nostalgia*, whose heroine is a prostitute, appeared on Chinese screens. Now, in

China nothing happens by chance, and so it seemed to me from the showing of this film that prostitution must still be a problem for the Chinese leaders. But none of my friends would confirm my hunch.

I talked about it with Xiao Han, the least prudish of my girlfriends, and she assured me, with an air of injured virtue, that prostitution no longer existed in China.

A few months later a number of young women were sent down to the countryside for having sold their charms, and Xiao Han told me that since the Cultural Revolution there had been a serious revival of prostitution in the countryside and in the towns. I asked her how long she has known this.

'I always knew it,' she replied surprised.

'So in November you were just telling me nonsense?'

'......'

'Can I believe you this time?'

'Sure, you know I would never lie to you,' she replied.

Letters from young people to the Chinese press

Four years ago when I was working in a factory, I got to know a boy, Xiao Wang. We liked each other a lot and shared the same ideals. Thanks to his help I was accepted into university last year, and together we decided to work hard, each in our own field. Because I was afraid that my parents would disapprove of my relationship with Xiao Wang, I didn't talk about it with them, but recently they found out what's going on.

Both my parents are party members from an academic background, and they are opposed to our marriage because Xiao Wang's parents are workers. They confronted me with this choice: either I break with them, or I break with Xiao Wang. Surely its wrong to deny one's feelings and to throw out one's morals just because someone doesn't do the same work or have the same social status? Am I somehow worth more just because I go to university? But I would also find it difficult to break with my parents. They have done such a lot for me, and they only have me, how could I cause them pain now that they're old? Which path must I choose?

Zhang Jing
Nanjing, 31 July 1979.

I am a young peasant and teach at the school run by our production brigade. Five years ago I got to know a girl who was sent to work in the countryside from the city. Her name was Yang Yanying. Later, Yanying was chosen as a brigade teacher. We have consistently helped each other and truly love one another. When my parents heard of this they told me that I must end the relationship. They said that a girl from the city who is the daughter of a party member can't marry a poor peasant, because rich and poor don't mix. I said that we live in a new society where marriage is free and where there is no difference between town and country that could come between two people who are truly in love.

Finally I convinced them. I thought Yanying's parents would certainly approve, since they are high officials. I was wrong. When her parents learnt of our plans they flew into a rage. They thought it was degrading that the daughter of a party member should marry a peasant. In January Yanying was transferred to the city of Luoyang where she now works in a factory. Her parents now oppress her even more and have beaten her. She is having a hard time both physically and emotionally. Freedom to marry is guaranteed by law, so I don't understand why young people who were born into a new society cannot marry freely. Is it true that love is not possible between city folk and country folk?

You Zhuanyun
Henan, 5 July 1979.

Anita Rind

To be Feminist in Beijing

Feminism is nothing new in China. In the early years of the twentieth century women's organisations, mainly Christian, agitated for female equality, especially in education. When the movement against imperialism arose, feminism soon became linked to broader social issues, and many radical women joined the Communist Party after its founding in 1921. But these Communist women put their main emphasis on class and developed no systematic critique of women's oppression as a sex; those few who did try to do so (like Ding Ling in 1942) were criticised as 'narrow feminists' and silenced. Since the founding of the People's Republic in 1949 women's position has improved beyond recognition, but the voice of feminism as such has not been heard. Although separate organisations were set up to represent women's interests, these organisations were set up under party control and largely followed the party line on women's questions. Rarely have they criticised the many fundamental disadvantages that women still suffer — despite the progress — in the home, the school, the factory, the farm, the army and the party. This is why the wall-poster that Anita Rind discusses in her article is so interesting and potentially important. After years of stifling regimentation under the 'gang of four', when personal introspection was considered 'bourgeois' and 'impure', educated youth in China have started asking basic questions about their personal identity and belief. At the same time Western ideas have become popular in the universities. It is not surprising that 'bourgeois' feminism, which centrally considers questions of identity, should have begun to find support there.

This article was translated into English by Murray Smith.

How can one be a feminist in People's China? The different Constitutions worked out since 1949 have made women the equals of men. There has been huge progress, but this progress has often been only in theory, since Chinese women, who form more than half the population, still have a long way to go before they can truly be considered as 'half of heaven' in their country. However, one voice, that of a woman student at Beijing University, has dared to speak out in an effort to break free from the traditions of thousand of years that the party, in line with its political objectives, deplores; and from a persistent 'male chauvinism' that official speeches rarely mention.

By deciding, with the help of two or three companions, to set up a Chinese Women's Study Association at Beijing University, this woman student has laid what is perhaps the first stone of feminism in People's China. The undertaking should be neither ignored nor forgotten, even if its future remains precarious. This young woman needed courage to do what she did under a regime in which the party has an ideological monopoly. She also had to confront, practically alone, difficulties similar to those with which Western feminists are regularly faced.

The Chinese Women's Study Association was presented to the public by its organiser on 18 December 1980 in one of the University buildings.[1] About 200 students, both men and women (including some French, Japanese and Americans), had responded to the personal invitations issued by the founder and her friends.

At the time the climate in the university seemed to favour this initiative: elections had taken place six days earlier, [see above, pp. 88-97] and these were preceded by a period of relatively free discussion. In these elections the university's 8,000 students chose two of their number to represent them in the people's congress of Haidian district, to which the University belongs. Among the eighteen candidates was one woman. It was this woman who was later to become the organiser of the Society.

Her campaign slogan was 'Oriental Beauty'. A surprising theme for a feminist, you might say, but one that well expresses Chinese women's need to define themselves as such, to find their own identity, and thus to discover their role in Chinese society.

At the start of the campaign, the woman candidate put up a wall-poster developing this idea. The poster was almost immediately torn down. She then put up others, which almost all met the same fate. Directly or indirectly, she was taken to task in counter-posters, including many by women students. All of them attacked or criticised her choice of election theme, on the grounds that it was not a 'political programme'. It was decided to stage a debate. The room where the debate was held was packed with people, and the debate was stormy. The candidate was booed and lost some ground, but for all that she refused to admit that she was beaten. In the days that followed, she put up a new wall-poster under the title 'Women are human beings too'.[2] This text deserves quoting at length. It is written in a repetitive style, and uses romantic symbols and much rhetoric. But above all it was a cry of protest, and clearly it distils years of bitter experience.

'Yet another poster! My thinking is like the sections of a sliced snake that one wants to piece together again. I have difficulty in structuring it. Gaiety and life have abandoned me. My tears flow without end. I want to shout very loudly: women are human beings too!

'From the platform in this big hall, it was not the people who were booing me that I saw, but sincere human beings. My nerves were very on edge, but I did my best to reply. At the end of the meeting, people approached me and surrounded me — people who were full of compassion.

'I hate my own feelings of weakness, and the fact that I am not brilliant. I hate being a woman. It seems that everywhere being a woman generates impurity.

'A woman? Women too are human beings. Women too are citizens. I am one of those young people who has suffered from the inequalities of this society. Like my male student comrades, I lived a carefree childhood and an ardent and blind youth, during which I scorned hardship and overflowed with courage. Like the whole nation, I suffered ten years of difficulties (during the Cultural Revolution). Like the rest of the youth of the seventies, I had to interrupt my studies and to waste eight years of my life in the countryside.

'Along with others, I too went to honour the memory of Prime Minister Zhou Enlai and was treated as a counter-revolutionary as a result.[3] The evil forces in China did not forgive me for my youth. They treated me violently because I am a woman.

'Perhaps it is only today that I truly understand the objective causes of these difficulties and this violence, or at least some of them: I am a woman. You should not reject my energies and my struggle solely because I am a woman! Why can't women too carry within them thoughts and passions, just like other human beings?

'Are courage and the spirit of self-sacrifice the prerogative of the male sex? Why can't I, in these democratic elections, stand up and bring you my tears?

'Women are human beings too. Why should their specific attributes, their interests, their development as a sex and many other aspects of their womanhood not be important questions? Don't the interests of women mingle with the ocean of the interests of the people? Should not women's rights form part of democratic rights? Why do people only find fault with me when the question of women is raised? Some people can't stand reading my posters. In that case, in the name of the honour of Beijing University, and in the name of democracy, perhaps I should not have the right to express myself?

'But that would mean that we can discuss in complete equality great affairs of state, but we cannot approach the woman question in scientific fashion.

'The male candidates are not particularly good-looking. Why should you demand that women candidates are? Why do people always immediately associate the woman question with the idea of sex? As part of the right of human beings to fulfil themselves, women too should be allowed to freely develop their own personalities.

'Women are not machines for making children. They are human beings, and as such they must fight for their rights, their interests and their fulfilment. Why can people not accept this idea? Cannot women's point of view widen and reinforce the overall understanding of things?

'Women too are human beings. Why should I be weaker than men? And even if I am, I want to be responsible for it, to be responsible for myself. I hope that women citizens, future women candidates, are more fortunate, stronger and more perfect than I am. I hope that through struggle we women acquire the right to be human beings and the right to take up responsibilities and the honours that flow from them.

'Or perhaps the problem of women is really of no importance? It is to you, as human beings, that I put this question.'

On 12 December, the day of the election at the University, the author of this manifesto got 700 of roughly 6,000 votes cast. Tenacious, refusing to let herself be discouraged, she then decided to set up a body that would allow for discussion and reflection on the condition of women in China. About 70 students, men and women, agreed to join with her in working out the statutes of the future society.

Its statement of aims said, 'Women are a concrete expression of the human race. The study of women as human beings is an important part of the study of the human race.' The Society's objectives include 'improving Chinese women's awareness of themselves and women's personal development, putting an end to women's self-censorship, and calling on society as a whole to alter the context of their lives'. To achieve these objectives, the accent is placed exclusively on study, analysis of documents, and the exchange of ideas in the spirit of the Hundred Flowers. This prudence is understandable. The very setting up of such a group is already an act of insane foolhardiness in People's China.

In any case, it is a breath of fresh air in the face of the continual outpourings of the official propaganda machine, in a society whose collective mentality is still rigid and conventional where women are concerned. It is also an exemplary initiative, insofar as it goes beyond the simple demand for equality with men and touches on a fundamental problem: the search for, and recognition of, the identity of women in a given society.

Is this burst of energy doomed to an early death? The original plan was that all the Society's members (their number is not known) would meet every six months to take stock of the work and research done. The first of these general meetings should in principle have been held around 18 June 1981. But in the meantime the climate at the university has changed, so people are keeping their heads down and hoping that a new thaw will soon come.

Appendix: Women Students and the Future

Several 'wildcat' opinion polls were conducted during the election campaign at Beijing University. One of them sounded out the views of some 120 women students. The results (which were displayed on a wall-poster) throw revealing light on the feelings and ideas that young Chinese women intellectuals today have about their lives. The poll investigated (a) certain aspects of university life and (b) personal relations.

To the question 'Why are you at university?' a small majority replied that they considered it an indispensable passage into professional life, while only a third spoke of the chance of 'acquiring knowledge'. The rest did not exactly know what they were doing at university.

'What do you think about your professional future?' Only forty-three (or less than half) were confident that they would find a good job. About fifty were content to hope for the best, while at least ten had 'neither confidence nor hope'.

'What do you think of the idea of a woman being elected as representative for the university?' None rejected the idea, but only forty-one positively favoured it, while the rest were indifferent.

'What is your attitude towards political activity in the faculty?' Only a dozen or so actively participated, while others were merely 'interested', without taking part. Only two women students admitted to having 'no interest'.

'How do you envisage your relations with men?' All felt concerned by the problem, but the majority (sixty-one) said that they were only moderately interested in the company of men, although they were 'not opposed to it'. Some twenty said that they were 'very interested'. Seventeen confided that they 'are not in the habit', eleven that 'they don't really want to', four that 'they like the idea of having relations with men but feel embarrassed', and six that they 'viewed the idea with repugnance'. The majority said that being a woman was not a problem in their relations with men. But several were 'strongly aware' of their sex without making clear whether they felt that to be a woman was an advantage or a disadvantage. Finally, six women students said they would like to be able to 'take the initiative more', in other words to move away from traditional ideas and, say, ask a male colleague out.

And their love life? The majority said they would prefer to remain alone if they could not find the ideal companion. Some twenty thought that they would find a boyfriend while they were students and 'have a stable relationship with him'. Some ten thought that 'you shouldn't talk about love but just prepare yourself for it' and two thought that 'you have to stay single to develop your career'.

None of them was ready to obey their partner unconditionally, even though some twenty admitted that living with someone would mean constraints and restrictions on their personal life and about the same number hoped to have a husband stronger than they. Only a few (nine) wanted to devote themselves to their partner and a similar number said they were prepared 'to sacrifice their professional life'. Less than thirty thought that a man and a woman should share power equally, but many more thought that each should have his or her own profession.

A majority (sixty-two) said that they wanted to 'become learned', and a few more wanted the opportunity to 'develop interests in a wide range of subjects'. In addition, many other aspirations were mentioned, some of them quite surprising: to perfect patience, to be intelligent and clearsighted, to improve relations and contacts with others, to be an accomplished wife and excellent mother (twenty-five of the students interviewed), to be elegant, fearless (fifteen), competent (thirty-seven), generous (fifty-three), honest, firm and energetic (forty-one) and tender (thirty-three). Finally, three of them were not afraid to be seen as 'weak and delicate'.

Notes:

1. It is only recently that it has been possible to assemble information and documents about the Chinese Women's Study Association. Unfortunately the present political climate prevented me from meeting the Society's founder.

2. Although the great mass of students were very reticent about her campaign, the four main male candidates gave her their support after the publication of this wall-poster. The candidate who was eventually elected was present at the first meeting of the Society.

3. The reference is to the demonstrations of 5 April 1976 in Tiananmen Square in Beijing, organised in memory of the former Prime Minister Zhou Enlai, who had died three months earlier. Harshly repressed (there were several dozen dead) and characterised at first as counter-revolutionary, the incident is today judged to have been 'entirely revolutionary'.

Julien Blaine and Anna Gipouloux

The Stars: A New Art Movement in China

The avantgarde group of artists and painters known as Xingxing ('The Stars') maintained close links with political dissidents. Ms Li Shuang, aged 24, was a member of Xingxing, although she herself was considered apolitical. In July 1981 the Chinese foreign ministry is said to have given her and the French diplomat Emmanuel Bellefroid, a China expert, permission to marry. Li then moved into Bellefroid's flat in the foreigners' compound in Beijing. Suddenly, in September, she was seized by plainclothes police near the compound gate. At first no reason was given for her arrest. The French ambassador protested on her behalf, but she was held incommunicado. Then, in November, the Chinese authorities announced that Li Shuang had been sentenced to two years' re-education through labour on a charge of delinquency. At the same time Bellefroid was accused of giving dissidents money and of carrying messages for them abroad, but the Prime Minister Zhao Ziyang said that there was no connection between the Bellefroid case and that of Li Shuang. Li's father, a professor of architecture, and her mother, a professor of English, were sent to re-education camps during the Cultural Revolution. Li's grandfather, a former businessman, was said to have been beaten to death by Red Guards in 1966.

Julien Blaine, a poet, has published a special issue of the French review *Doc(k)s* (which he directs) about the avantgarde in China.

This article first published in the French newspaper *Libération*, 21 September 1981, was translated into English by H.F. Ashworth.

October 1980. Autumn in Beijing. From above the Gate of Heavenly Peace, the last great portrait of Mao, in its loneliness, overlooks the huge Tiananmen Square at the end of which rises the marble of his mausoleum. The founding fathers, Marx and Engels, and their two heirs, Lenin and Stalin, have disappeared, surreptitiously whisked away at dead of night by Japanese cranes... On the west side of the world's most famous square, at the beginning of September, the People's Assembly met. To the north, all the gold of the imperial tiles rushes in petrified waves against Coal Hill.

To the east of the hill is the Museum of Fine Arts. Here twenty-three young artists are defying conventions and the bureaucracy to stage an extremely successful exhibition. They have had little publicity, save for a small notice in 'People's Daily' which they paid for themselves. The Xingxing exhibition, the second of that name, began on 20 August 1980. In one room on the third floor of the museum were more than a hundred works: oil paintings, gouaches, watercolours, sculptures, and wood-engravings. Ten days later it had already attracted 50,000 visitors. The news was passed along the backstreets with such speed that the paintings soon disappeared from sight in a room packed tighter than a tin of sardines. The museum had to agree, whether it liked it or not, to open a second room. The crowd kept growing: 7000 people on the first Sunday, 9000 on the second. Eventually the exhibition was extended for a few days.

Something very special had happened. Usually the people of Beijing are not so keen to frequent such places. One intellectual confessed to me that he never went to the museum because the exhibitions were not interesting, even though they were usually of contemporary works. So who are these artists (all of them between twenty and thirty years old) who draw these huge crowds of intellectuals and young people? Essentially they are a group of friends. Originally there were two of them, a painter, Huang Rui, and an engraver, Ma Desheng. The group, which was closely associated with the unofficial literary review *Jintian* ('Today'), quickly swelled. In September 1979, having tried in vain to find a suitable room, they organised a wildcat exhibition along the railings of the very museum that this year is officially showing their work. This wildcat exhibition was banned and there was a police crackdown. The Stars had made their debut... A few days later, on 1 October (the thirtieth anniversary of liberation) these young artists and the young democrats of 'Beijing Spring' gathered in the streets to demand freedom of speech and creativity. In the photographs that were published throughout the press a man on crutches stood in the front row of the demonstration: Ma Desheng. Ma Desheng is one of the most remarkable people I have ever met and ever will meet, even if I live to be a thousand. You would have to see him to believe him: the way he dances to rock music on his wooden crutches; the way he understands in a flash what I want to say and to know; and the way he exudes sheer life in all directions. Ma Desheng is an engraver, and for that there is a reason. He used to work during the daytime and to return home at nightfall. He wanted to be a painter and use oil-colours, but by the time he got back to his tiny room it was so dark that he could no longer make out the colours. And so he became an engraver in black and white.

In November the authorities allocated these rebel artists a pavilion in Beijing's Beihai Park. If their success was instant, it is because they do not separate creativity in all its forms from everyday life, which in turn is due to their political commitment. Ma Desheng put it like this: 'Either the regime changes, or we'll all end up in gaol.' The visitors to the exhibition share this conviction. In the Golden Book of 1980 — a series of school exercise books which accumulate daily — are comments like 'I want the Stars to shine more brilliantly than the sun' (the sun being Mao), and 'When I saw Xingxing I had the feeling that I was at Democracy Wall, and I was very happy'.

In 1979 *Jintian* openly supported the exhibition. This year *Jintian* is again present, although rather more discreetly, and doubles as a catalogue for the show. The young writers whose work is published in it have written poems to illustrate some of the pictures. The political convictions that underlie much of this avant-garde art are also evident in some of the exhibits, for example Wang Keping's sculpture 'Idol', about which most people comment only in whispers. 'Idol' is of red wood, worked into a portrait: an impenetrable face with the familiar heavy, hanging features and thick lips; to one side the veiled gaze of Buddha; to the other, the wide-open eye of a leader, with a starred cap for good measure. No one is deceived, but no one risks saying the obvious. For it would not do to recognise Mao in this stiff Buddha.

Like all the other exhibitors, Wang Keping is an amateur; he earns his living as a television playwright and his sculpting is only a side-line. But it is often said in China that these sideline activities are more important than the mainline ones. The wood that he uses is retrieved from the Beijing saw-mills, so that he has little choice of materials. Nevertheless he gets a lot out of them and has clearly found his own style. His works are strong, very personal and scandalous in their insistent eroticism. Many people say that they cannot understand them. They refuse to see his work and to admit that they have seen it. This happens so often that Wang Keping has made up a dialogue which he has posted at the entrance to the exhibition as a wall-poster. In it he states his artistic convictions. Beauty is an end in itself. All that the artist has to say is contained in the work, and only the work, under the onlooker's gaze, creates meaning. The artist's intention is only one of the many parts of its meaning. And to conclude he says: 'You don't have to ask the artist to explain; he is no more enlightened than you.' Things that for a westerner no longer pose problems are a revolution in China, where for years young people have had hagiographies thrust down their throats in which young girls always have nice red cheeks, the flags flap in the winds of Maoism and the leaders gaze steadfastly towards a radiant future. It is hardly surprising that the lewd bodies and the splendid phalluses of Wang Keping make the good souls of official orthodoxy blush and stammer.

Bao Pao is another sculptor who exhibits with the Stars. He works in stone, and is a professional. Beautiful, sober sculptures with pure lines. He is over forty, but has never been able to exhibit before because he is accused of 'Westernism'. He is said to be too like Henry Moore...

Works of art are expected not only to have a clear meaning, but to be constructive. The artist is happy because socialism is good. But the paintings of the Stars do not overflow with joy. How could they, when all these young people have for one reason or another suffered under the regime? They belong to the generation that was sacrificed to the Cultural Revolution. Too young to share its enthusiasms, they knew only its tragedies and lies. They are like 'Those Tired of the Garden of Illusions' that their friend Yan Li paints — dismembered puppets lying limply under an abundant and complex forest of signs, to which a splendid mixture of blues lends a dream's magic.

Yan Li, at twenty-six, is one of the most promising young talents of this exhibition. A worker in a machine-tool factory, he has been painting for three years and is distancing himself little by little from the influences in his first paintings, for example Matisse and Dali. Laughing, he recounts his many difficulties. Paint is far too dear, and he cannot buy good quality colours. One tube costs five yuan — about £1.50 — and he only earns forty yuan a month. The same goes for canvas, for which he substitutes cotton smeared with glue; and for wood, which he has to find where he can. Even so, he still spends half his wages on paint. He also lacks space. Accommodation is particularly hard to get in Beijing, and you have to have two children before you can get even two rooms. In such circumstances it is absurd to think of getting a workshop. But there is no sadness in the keen face and beautiful eyes of this young painter, who is also a poet. Yes, he would very much like to change his job and to have more time to give to his art, but that's impossible, so it's not worth worrying about.

Another exemplary story is that of Li Shuang. This young woman, one of three women in the group, is twenty-three years old. She paints theatre scenery for 38 yuan a month.

She has a beautiful face, delicate and vigorous, and a lovely smile, but her works are poignantly sad. Her self-portrait shows the straight, stiff body of a faceless woman, her legs bonded tightly together. In another picture, which explodes with reds and has the title 'The Child and the Altar', Li Shuang displays memories of her childhood; we see a dog and a faceless child, which she says is herself. There are wood-engravings in which the themes of solitude, abandonment and despair dominate. Li Shuang has a 'bad class origin'. Her father, a professor of architecture, studied in Hong Kong, and her mother is from a family of capitalists. Her father, who was purged as a 'rightist' in 1957, has just been rehabilitated. Li Shuang spent her childhood and youth being pushed aside, mistrusted, insulted, having stones thrown at her by other children, and being afraid. How can she be expected to paint that joyful 'socialism' that makes for a good painting in official eyes? And what about Ma Desheng, whose physical handicap meant that he was not allowed to go to university?

The Stars are not about to reject their origins and their choice of society, but it is clear that they have found their main inspiration through art. The works exhibited in 1979 in Beihai Park justified themselves by the shock they created. The oil-paintings — a scandal in themselves — the ink drawings and the engravings remained realist, even conventional, and what was most noticeable was the abundance of female nudes. This year, the scandal is that of the art itself. Few nudes, but abstract paintings in search of form, space and colour. For example, a series by Huang Rui: work of blues, whites and pinks, which got the title 'The Four Seasons' when his friends pointed out that it was 'as though the weather is different in each one'.

We can also admire three hyper-realist canvasses by a young soldier, Mao Lizi. For one of them, Mao has chosen three cigarette ends, two matches and some footprints. Can you imagine anything more absurd and in worse taste than to paint such prosaic reality? An almost surrealist collage of cut paper, in pop-art style, signed by Qu Leilei, staggers a public that, in foreign art, prefers the uninspired French paintings of the Third Republic to unknown contemporary works, which arc usually dismissed as bourgeois and decadent. This urge to present themselves above all as creators and artists is once again most evident in the sculpture of Wang Keping, who has deliberately suppressed the titles of twenty-seven of his twenty-nine works.

In the Golden Book someone has written: 'You shouldn't be too abstract. You should be more careful, and take the masses into consideration.' Another says more bluntly: 'If you want to understand this, go to a lunatic asylum.' But the break with tradition is not absolute. Many of these artists painted on rice paper at first, and one painter of impressive talent, Bo Yun, still does so. He uses Chinese ink mixed with Prussian blue, thus creating dark poetic landscapes. His presence in the Stars group shows that they are keen to integrate the gains of the past while creating the art of the future in this country of ancient traditions. Does not Qu Leilei represent China as a sleeping lion, surrounded by pictoral forms that in some cases hark back to drawings on neolithic pottery?

Most of the painters consider oil-paint, which is more versatile, permitting errors and corrections, to be better suited to self-expression. The self, says their manifesto, is 'the only virgin territory still to be conquered'. They have opened a breach in conformism, but the door is for the moment only slightly ajar, like Ma Desheng's engraving where a small female stands, half-hidden, between the two halves of a heavy nailed door like those in the Imperial Palace. Will the doors open, or will they close again? Everyone will have their own opinion.

They work in offices, workshops or factories. A few are convalescing after a long illness, which allows them to paint more and see each other more often. Artists, engravers, painters, sculptors, they meet each other, read aloud the poems of their friends from *Jintian*, talk together and dance.

Now their review is banned and their exhibitions are endangered, but they still stick together. They know the narrow limits to their precarious freedom, but they still seek out one another's company. They diffuse life from every pore. They dream, but they have no illusions.

Well sheltered in my Western Europe, I remember their courage. To look at them, a small tribe lost in an immense land and an infinite people, one might imagine that they lived in complete security and happiness. But since 14 September, when I received Emmanuel's letter, I have become insomniac.

Meng Ke and Huang Rui and Ma Desheng and Li Shuang, and Xiao Chen and Bei Dao and Maman and Ling Ping and Chao Yan and Ta Chun and Xiao Pu and Gang Zhu and all the others...

They changed me, they made me believe in happiness, in serenity, in security... I became a splendid pretext for meetings, for feasts, for drinking and for reading poems...

You would hardly believe that these artists had a day at the factory or the workshop behind them, when we met each other at nightfall in their homes. They spoke about their banned journal, but the future lies before them and it could all soon begin again.

It is important to understand the wild energy that enabled them to create or recreate the history of art in five years. Cut off from their ancestral roots by the Cultural Revolution, they looked to the West and in a few months reinvented everything: fauvism, cubism, impressionism, surrealism, Dada, expressionism, pop-art and hyper-realism. And through this reconstruction, which will doubtless be repeatedly criticised, banned and suppressed, they are on the way to finding an identity. This identity is for the future, truly for the future, whatever may happen.

They made the first attempt at renewal during the seventies, and they will have their first successes in the eighties... Imagine thirty cyclists who, at nightfall, return to Beijing after having staged the first ever international poetry reading at Yuan Ming

Yuan. Imagine them as they yell out their poems, standing amid the ruins of a palace, or in the centre of the Circular Garden of Light. Imagine them in one of the last of the old traditional houses of Beijing, dancing to rock music on a cassette which they got from God knows where.

And remember too that there will always be someone who wants to shut them up.

Søren Clausen

A Boat-trip down the Yangzi

Søren Clausen, a Danish sinologist, wrote this article on returning from China in 1979, when the democratic movement was still tolerated. It shows vividly how the intellectual climate had changed since the last stages of the Mao era, and the openness with which problems and ideas were approached. It was translated from the Norwegian by Hugh Rodwell.

If you are in Chongqing in Western China and are heading for Wuhan in Central China, there is really only one sensible way to travel — by river-boat. Chongqing (China's temporary capital during the Second World War) and the huge industrial city of Wuhan are linked by the Yangzi Jiang, the Big River as it is called in Chinese, the Son of the Sea. On this stretch of the river trips downstream are rapid. The 1250 miles are covered in two-and-a-half days or perhaps slightly more, depending on the current. Upstream, heading west, the trip takes at least twice as long. The strength of the current is due to the descent of the giant river from the mountains of eastern Sichuan to the Hubei lowlands.

The current is especially powerful in the famous Yangzi Gorge. This gorge is one of China's most impressive natural spectacles. The ferry route from Chongqing, closed for many years because of the violent repercussions of the Cultural Revolution in Sichuan province, has recently been opened to foreigners. Persistent factional fighting made towns in the province unsafe for several years, but now the door is ajar.

The ferry is known as Number 48 — it is also called The East is Red, but then so is every other ferry in China. I have just been down to look at the engine whose vibrations shake the whole ship and set my teacup dancing. Around the engine-room, in the unbearable heat and noise, are the sleeping quarters of the fifth class: two large rooms with closely packed bunks. The ferry is a floating class society with five decks and five classes, a confusion of companion-ways and corridors. Each class has its own toilets, bathrooms, observation areas, dining rooms and so on. It is a miniature replica of Chinese society: at the bottom, around the machine room, live the peasants; they spit on the floor, and heaps of cabbages lie around in the corners. Above is a deck for young workers and petty officials, families with children; here, people spit where possible into buckets provided for the purpose, and eat sweets. In the third class are comfortably off people with good manners — they don't stand and gape when they see a foreigner. They live in cabins with eight bunks and one wash-basin. Reading is their favourite pastime.

Next we come to my own class. Cabins for two people in the bow of the ferry, with hot and cold water, an observation saloon and a promenade deck. I am the only foreigner aboard — and the authorities don't allow foreigners to travel in a class cheaper than this. All the rest are intellectuals, professors and journalists, one or two senior officials and a couple of officers. In this class etiquette holds sway. You don't ask a fellow-passenger 'What's your name?', but: 'Your honourable surname?' In the observation saloon, with its beautiful furniture, the conversation is about art and history. And then there is the first class. At the top, on the sun deck. Entry is forbidden, so I don't know if there is anybody there.

Everywhere on the ship loudspeakers watch over our safety and welfare. Every other minute the radio programme is interrupted by an exhortation. 'Those comrades disembarking at the next port should be getting ready now. Mind you don't stumble as you leave the ship!' 'Those comrades who have not yet had lunch should go to the dining room at once as it will be closing shortly.' 'Don't waste food. If you can't manage all your rice, then ask the staff for a smaller helping next time. Remember that if everyone in China saved one grain of rice a day, that would make 15,000 tons of rice a year!' 'Don't entrust your luggage to people you don't know. The class struggle is extremely complex!'

The loudspeakers decide when you should go to bed and when you have to get up and wash. They fuss after you the whole time, like an anxious mother. They are at their most relentless in the morning, and they can't be turned off: 'Workers — Peasants — Soldiers — Passengers! It's time to get up! It's six o'clock! Let us work together to make the great plan of the Four Modernisations a success before the end of the century!'

On the first day I spend a lot of time at the third class rail-

ings enjoying the scenery. The ferry forges heavily and pro-
saically through a classical Chinese landscape painting with
sheer crags, wooded mountain sides and pagodas half-hidden in
the mists. Just above my head the loudspeaker is blaring. (In my
own class it is quickly turned down if someone switches on the
music programme.) It is a programme about the recently dead
Prime Minister Zhou Enlai. A group of small children swear
eternal loyalty to Zhou Enlai in shrill chorus: 'Beloved grandfather Zhou, rest secure, we shall ever preserve your memory
and proceed along the trial you have blazed, holding high the
banner of Mao Zedong Thought and carrying out the Four
Modernisations...' Between choruses the children are tearfully
urged on by a school mistress. Then the chorus starts up again at
a Disney-like tempo and pitch.

As we chug along in this way, I start reflecting on the tears
that Zhou Enlai's death has produced. With my own eyes I had
seen my fellow students at Beijing University weep tears so big
you could actually hear them splashing as the news of his death
came over the radio in January 1976. I also took part in a
remembrance meeting for Zhou at a factory: 3000 weeping people
packed tightly together in a small canteen. In later months these
acts of remembrance for Zhou grew into tumultous mass
demonstrations, culminating in the famous Qing Ming demonstrations in Beijing's Tiananmen Square in April 1976.

These demonstrations marked the beginning of a political
movement. The movement was directed partly against Maoism
and its spokespersons, and partly against an undemocratic city
government that ruled more through the secret police than
through the revolutionary committees. At the time the protests
were crushed and hundred of people were imprisoned and
beaten, but two-and-a-half years later, in November 1978, they
were released as heroes and champions of freedom. This was the
signal for a new wave of demonstrations and wall-posters in Beijing and Shanghai, with demands for freedom and democracy.
This movement still admires Zhou Enlai and sees him as its rally-
ing point.

And so Zhou Enlai has come to play an important political
role after his death, even a revolutionary one. But there is also
an element of emotional masturbation about the worship of

Zhou Enlai. You weep with others and in so doing become a new person.

The children finish off with a tearful list of political slogans. Their tiny voices break with the effort as we sail sedately through the swirling eddies. A ferry painted in cheerful colours with five decks and five classes, and gabbling loudspeakers blaring out political slogans into a classical landscape painting which is imperturbably sublime in its antiquity. I begin to muse on what the children's slogans must sound like out there — in the painting. Incomprehensible small cries, meaningless signals from New China to Old.

In the evening the ferry docks at Wanxian, the last stop before the gorge. We make fast for a few hours. The water level is too low and the channel too narrow for the helmsman to risk the passage through the gorge in the darkness of the night. Most of the passengers stream ashore and race up endless flights of steps cut into the mountain, up to Wanxian and the orange market.

Here you can buy the famous Wanxian mandarins, big and juicy, renowned throughout China as the best! In a few seconds the place is transformed into an impenetrable human swarm. Nearest the stall people are climbing on the backs of those already being served. The lean-to is swaying under the pressure. A queer business, this panic, for there are easily enough oranges to go round. I see to it that I get a full basket, and then climb down to the boat again, helped by two eager locals. Their only business this evening seems to be to make sure that their foreign guest returns post-haste to the boat after buying the oranges.

Back on board I get a visit from the cook in the forecastle. He puts in an enormous amount of work, 18 hours a day. When he isn't in the kitchen preparing delicious meals for the second-class dining room, or in the firing room fetching fresh boiled water for the passengers, he is in the observation saloon where he officiates as a guide for the Chinese passengers. He has a tale for every crag and outcrop that we pass. It is wonderful to listen to him. Once we have got through the formalities of inquiring about brothers and sisters and so on, he gives me a little speech about his philosophy of life. He explains that there is an 'up' and a 'down' in every society. There are intellectuals and there are ordinary working people. But we are all of us important! He is from peasant stock himself, but that doesn't make any difference now, does it? That kind of work has got to be done too! Then he urges me to go to bed early — the loudspeaker repeats the entreaty a minute later — and retires.

When I turn out of bed next morning the scenery jolts me awake like a slap in the face. The broad river has become a narrow ribbon of raging whirlpools, shut in on both sides by sheer mountain walls. These are the ravines so splendidly described by Han Suyin in *The Crippled Tree*. In the old days they became the grave of many a sailor, and they are still not without danger. Not so long ago the boats on this stretch of the river were hauled upstream by long chains of men up on the land. Now it can be navigated with the help of a powerful engine. The ferry dances away on the raging current. The helmsman swings from side to side to steer clear of the rocks that leap into our path. I tear around the ship taking photos, to everybody's great amusement. I have already became notorious on board. (As I walk around the different decks I can hear people saying to each other: 'That bloke's from Denmark! He understands Chinese!')

I take a seat in the observation saloon, ready for the day's conversation. It's easy enough, and much simpler than it was a couple of years ago. A lot of Chinese are very interested in making contact with foreigners, and they make a great effort to understand our world. You just sit down with a book and before two minutes are up someone comes over to you and asks you what book it is. This is just a pretext to get talking. I discuss the problem of the criteria of objective truth with a professor of philosophy from Shandong. He had travelled thousands of miles to take part in a conference in Chengdu (the provincial capital of Sichuan) on this subject. He confided to me that in reality truth does not have a class character — quite contradicting what many people have believed in China until just recently.

And I discuss Keynes, Yugoslav market socialism and current reforms in Chinése pricing policies with an editor from the Theoretical Department of the 'People's Daily' in Beijing. He gave a lecture at the same conference as the philosopher, and he is to give a new lecture in Wuhan. He has real status, a secretary is constantly at his side and etiquette creates problems.

We both find it hard to come up with the appropriate grimace for the occasion. At the same time each of us is curious to learn something of the other. I'm not the only one curious to know about the editor. The following day, on Sunday morning, my fellow passengers in the second class arrange a 'study meeting' where everyone will have the chance to put questions to the editor. He gives rapid, confident answers to a number of extremely general questions on economic theory. 'How does the law of value operate under socialism?' they ask, and 'Will the class struggle intensify under socialism, or will it gradually die away?' The editor is relaxed, he urges us to view these questions undogmatically.

After the 'study meeting' I am granted a personal interview. The editor tells me of his impressions of a recent trip to Rumania and Yugoslavia. He thinks that the rate of investment in Rumania is higher than it need be — it is getting on for a third of the GNP — and lop-sided in its concentration on heavy industry. This means that ordinary people's living standards rise very slowly. In the editor's view, the Yugoslav rate of 20 per cent is more suitable. On the whole there is a lot to be learnt from Yugoslavia, says the editor. But we mustn't forget to distinguish between Yugoslavia's good and bad sides. 'They also have "market socialism" and a significant degree of unemployment, you see', he points out. (Yugoslavia was really 'in' during my few months in China, and the debate on how much can be learnt from the Yugoslavs is one of the big current issues there. The crucial point in the present wave of economic reform is precisely how far you can profitably go in giving production units economic independence.)

Our editor belongs to the 'orthodox' school in the economic controversy. He is unable to accept the theory that the law of value is the fundamental law of socialism. This theory has been propounded most notably by the recently rehabilitated veteran economist Sun Yefang (who was criticised by the Maoist wing as long ago as 1962). The editor's view, which accords with Stalin's, is that the law of value is historically bound up with commodity production and will gradually die out with it. But at the same time he enthusiastically advocates fully exploiting economic mechanisms based on the law of value. This is how he describes the main thrust of economic reform: the system of depreciation is to be made more business-like, so that the sums written off bear a reasonable relationship to the capital invested; the enterprises are to accumulate more capital of their own which they will be able to deploy independently; part of the profit is to be distributed as a bonus to the hardest working workers; the banks and interest rates are to play a more significant part in economic life.

All this implies rather fundamental change in economic life and economic theory. New concepts are enthusiastically adopted, while familiar theses glide away into the shadows of doubt. This becomes especially clear when I ask the editor if the Soviet Union really is a capitalist country — and what kind of capitalism? 'This is also something we are speculating about at the moment!' he answers with a big smile. 'We used to view this question too simplistically.' (After the schism between China and the Soviet Union at the start of the sixties the Chinese characterised the ruling class in the Soviet Union as a 'monopoly bourgeoisie', but at no time have they made a proper economic analysis of the Soviet form of 'capitalism'.)

My conversation with the eminent comrade from the 'People's Daily' is interrupted by our peerless cook, who leads us down to the observation deck in the third class. The food is hoisted up from the kitchen below. Marvellous dishes in luxurious abundance. We eat quickly while the spectators outside press their noses flat against the windows. They follow my movements impassively and with the closest attention. The most persistent ones — the cook chases the throng away at regular intervals — seem to think that they may just possibly, given sufficiently detailed study for a long enough period, come to understand the incredible phenomenon, a foreigner. But at the same time they are the most embarrassed. When I talk to them they smile vacantly and understand nothing.

In that sense China is like it always was. But the real change has taken place among the passengers in the second class, those who are educated, the leaders. They speak their minds so freely that it can give you a physical shock if you have known the intellectual climate in Beijing in the last stages of the Mao era. Above all they ask questions, about everything, because it's modern to have solid, first-hand information about foreign countries.

I have long, almost confidential conversations with a charming white-haired lady, a mathematician from Beijing. She questions me closely about Denmark and myself. When the trip is nearing its end and it's time to pack, she says: 'You know a little about China; tell me what you think are our most serious faults or failings.' It is natural for me to criticise the educational reforms. I speak of the mistaken use of examinations based purely on books, the terrible pressures of studying at a place of higher education (and the waste of so much good potential, since the textbooks are often of low quality); favouritism towards children from an intellectual background; and so on. She starts to tell me how the examination system has spread down to the elementary school and increased the pressures on the students there, and how the curriculum has been changed. Singing, music, art and similar subjects have been cut to make way for maths and physics and foreign languages. Bookishness has increased tremendously. Soon the children won't be allowed to play any more! She herself has a daughter at school, and not too long ago she went to a parents' meeting and criticised the low priority given to creative subjects. But she got no understanding for her views from the teachers, whose only wish was to do their best to speed up the Four Modernisations. 'The worst thing is that you don't promote development by producing impractical book-worms — once you're in a job what you really need is imagination and flexibility.'

She has put her finger on one of the most obvious contradictions in China's current economic programme, the 'modernisation plan' of the Deng Xiaoping era. This problem isn't new. The radical militancy of the Red Guards in the first stages of the Cultural Revolution and the violent attacks on school authorities and teachers sprang from an oppressive school system. And in the course of collecting fuel for the rocket of modernisation, methods are being used that may soon change the rocket's course. This goes not just for education, but for the entire policy of economic and social development. No one knows what social forces will be set in motion by the present wave of reform. But if the democratic movement is suppressed, the party will become ever more debilitated and will have problems justifying its monopoly of power. Then the party itself might become a hindrance to development. My fellow passengers in the second class will have to make full use of their newly won freedom of speech, and more besides. But above all development will depend on what happens in the lower classes...